Christian Müller

Holzleimbau
Laminated Timber Construction

Birkhäuser – Publishers for Architecture
Basel · Berlin · Boston

Wir danken den folgenden Unternehmen und Institutionen, die diese
Publikation finanziell unterstützt haben.
We would like to thank the following companies and
institutions who kindly sponsored this publication.
Wolfgang Ritter Stiftung, Bremen
PHB Burgbernheimer Holzbau, Burgbernheim
Poppensieker & Derix, Westerkappeln
Paul Stephan, Gaildorf
Sigrid und Heinz Ohnesorge, Bergisch Gladbach

Übersetzung ins Englische/Translation into English:
Gerd Söffker, Philip Thrift, Hannover
Gestaltung/Layout and cover design:
Christiane Hemmerich, Tübingen

A CIP catalogue record for this book is available from the Library of
Congress, Washington D.C., USA

Die Deutsche Bibliothek - CIP Einheitsaufnahme

Müller, Christian: Holzleimbau = Laminated timber Construction / Christian
Müller. [Übers. ins Engl.: Gerd Söffker ; Philip Thrift]. - Basel ; Berlin ; Boston :
Birkhäuser, 2000
 ISBN 3-7643-6267-7

© 2000 Birkhäuser – Publishers for Architecture,
P.O. Box 133, CH-4010 Basel, Switzerland

Printed on acid-free paper produced
from chlorine-free pulp
Printed in Germany
ISBN 3-7643-6267-7
ISBN 0-8176-6267-7
9 8 7 6 5 4 3 2 1

Inhaltsverzeichnis
Contents

Dank
Acknowledgements

Dr.-Ing. Christian Müller
Sophie-Charlotten-Straße 37
D-14059 Berlin
e-mail: christianmueller@sireconnect.de

Wolfgang Ritter Stiftung
Braut Eichen 16a
D-28757 Bremen

PHB Burgbernheimer Holzbau GmbH & Co. KG
Rothenburger Straße 46
D-91593 Burgbernheim
Tel. 09843 98120
Fax 09843 981250

PHB Redekiner Holzbau GmbH & Co. KG
Industriegebiet
D-39319 Redekin
Tel. 039341 9710
Fax 039341 97150

PHB Prümer Holzbau
Kuckel GmbH & Co. KG
Prümtalstraße 23
D-54595 Prüm
Tel. 06551 95060
Fax 06551 4640

Poppensieker & Derix GmbH & Co. KG
Industriestraße 24
D-49492 Westerkappeln
Tel. 05456 93030
Fax 05456 930330

Paul Stephan GmbH + Co. KG
Holzleimbau - Ingenieurbüro
Gartenstraße 40
D-74405 Gaildorf
Tel. 07971 2580
Fax 07971 258370

Sigrid und Heinz Ohnesorge
Nußbaumer Garten 12
D-51467 Bergisch Gladbach

Auch wenn die Idee zu einem Buch schnell geboren ist, so bedurfte die Realisierung doch vieler glücklicher Umstände und tatkräftiger Unterstützung. Der erste Schritt bis zur Dissertation gelang unter kritischer und anregender Begleitung meines Doktorvaters Prof. Dr.-Ing. habil. Oskar Büttner in Weimar, dem Ort des Wirkens Otto Hetzers. Sigrid Ohnesorge, die Urenkelin Otto Hetzers, und ihr Mann Heinz bewahrten über Jahre die verbliebenen Originalphotographien der Otto Hetzer AG und machten so eine umfangreiche Dokumentation dieses Zeitabschnittes möglich. Das Archiv der Firma Nemaho in Doettinchem, das ich freundlicherweise nutzen konnte, ermöglichte eine weitergehende Darstellung vieler Bauwerke seit 1921 bis in unsere Zeit.

Der technische Sprung über den Atlantik wird im Archiv der Firma Sentinel Structures in Peshtigo, Wisconsin, nachvollziehbar, welches mir bei unserer Amerikareise durch Andreas Rhude zugänglich gemacht wurde. Gemeinsam suchten wir die ersten Holzleimbauten der dreißiger Jahre in Amerika auf und waren sehr beeindruckt von der dortigen Entwicklung der Technologie. Bei all den Reisen war meine Frau Nicola ausdauernde und tatkräftige Unterstützung.

Ohne die Sponsoren hätte das Buch nicht in der vorliegenden Form erscheinen können, weshalb Ihnen hiermit ganz besonders gedankt sei.

Ein Teil der Gebäudephotographien entstand durch den Einsatz von Susann Fricke, welche viele Stunden vor Ort und im Labor die Gebäude ins rechte Licht rückte. Auch Christoph Messow sei hier für seine Mithilfe vor Redaktionsschluß gedankt. Die Lektorin Ria Stein vom Birkhäuser Verlag verhalf dem Buch zu einer gut gewichteten Abrundung des Themas. Den letzten gestalterischen Schliff vollbrachte Christiane Hemmerich, die dem Fachbuch zu einer optisch ansprechenden Erscheinung verhalf.

Mit herzlichem Dank an die Sponsoren:

Wolfgang Ritter Stiftung
Firma PHB
Firma Poppensieker
Firma Stephan
Sigrid und Heinz Ohnesorge

Even though the idea for a book is quickly conceived, putting that idea into practice requires a series of fortunate circumstances and energetic support. The first step, the completion of the thesis, was carried out with the discerning and thought-provoking help of my doctoral supervisor, Prof. Dr.-Ing. habil. Oskar Büttner, in Weimar – where Otto Hetzer was based. Sigrid Ohnesorge, great-granddaughter of Otto Hetzer, and her husband, Heinz, looked after the remaining original photographs of Otto Hetzer AG for many years and hence rendered possible a comprehensive record of that period. The archives of the Nemaho company in Doettinchem, which were kindly made available to me, enabled a detailed presentation of many structures from 1921 to the present day.

The transatlantic crossing in technical terms became comprehensible through the archive material of Sentinel Structures of Peshtigo, Wisconsin, which was made accessible to me by Andreas Rhude during our American journey. Together, we searched for the first American laminated wood structures of the 1930s and were highly impressed by the technological developments that had been realized there. During all my travels my wife, Nicola, was a dedicated and vigorous support.

Without my sponsors this book could not have been published in its present form; therefore, a very special vote of thanks is due to those who have made this book possible.

I am indebted to the work of Susann Fricke, whose many hours in the field and in the darkroom resulted in many of the excellent photographs of buildings. Thanks also go to Christoph Messow for his invaluable assistance prior to publication. At Birkhäuser, Ria Stein ensured that this subject was given a professional, balanced presentation. And the final creative polish was provided by Christiane Hemmerich, who gave the book its visually engaging design.

My very special thanks to the sponsors:

The Wolfgang Ritter Foundation
PHB Burgbernheimer Holzbau GmbH
Poppensieker & Derix GmbH
Stephan GmbH
Sigrid and Heinz Ohnesorge

Vorwort
Preface

Ziel dieses Buches ist die umfassende Darstellung der Entwicklung des Holzleimbaus von seinen Anfängen bis heute. Die Idee zu diesem Buch entstand bei den Recherchen anläßlich meiner Dissertation zu diesem Thema, wobei sich beeindruckendes Bildmaterial ansammelte.

Für den Bauinteressierten, ob Fachmann oder Laie, stellen die Gebäude oft nur Einzelbauwerke dar, deren Gesamtzusammenhang in der Entwicklung nicht erkennbar wird. Das vorliegende Buch soll einen Überblick über die Vielfalt der Bauwerke und Tragwerksformen anhand von ausgewählten Beispielen geben. Für den Architekten oder Bauingenieur ergibt sich damit eine Grundlage für die eigene planerische Arbeit.

Dokumentiert werden die Bauwerke mit historischen und zeitgenössischen Photographien, welche teils auch das Alter und die Veränderung der Gebäude zeigen. Um eine ausreichende Abstraktion alter und neuer Gebäude zu erreichen, werden die meisten Photographien schwarz-weiß abgebildet.

The aim of this book is to provide a comprehensive account of the development of laminated wood construction, from its beginnings to the present day. The idea for the book grew as I carried out research for my thesis on this subject and as the visual quality of the material became apparent.

For those with an interest in buildings and construction, whether layman or professional, the buildings themselves are often only individual structures whose place within the overall development is not readily identifiable. It is the intention of this book to provide a review of the diversity of buildings and structural forms by means of selected examples. Architects and engineers will therefore be given a basis for their own creative work.

The buildings are portrayed by means of both historical and new photographs, some of which depict the age of a structure and the changes it has undergone. In order to achieve a convenient common ground between old and new buildings, most photographs are reproduced in black-and-white.

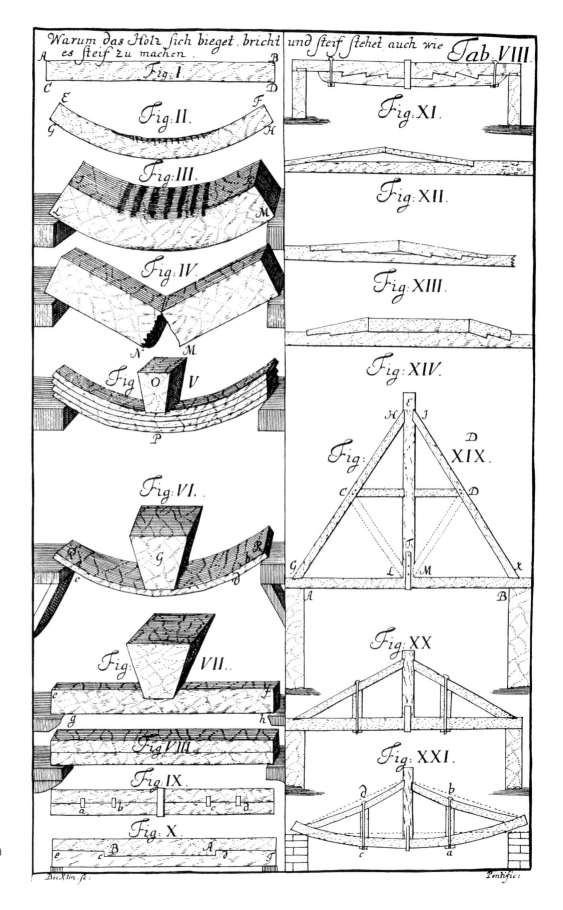

„Warum das Holz sich bieget, bricht und steif stehet, auch wie es steif zu machen ist", 1726.
"Why timber bends, breaks and remains stiff, and how it can be made rigid", 1726.

Vorläufer des Holzleimbaus
The forerunners of glued laminated timber

Die Entwicklung der hölzernen Tragwerke hängt unmittelbar mit dem Verständnis des Tragverhaltens einer Konstruktion – seiner Statik – und der Kenntnis von der Festigkeit des Materials zusammen. Je größer die zu überbrückenden Spannweiten waren, um so wichtiger wurde die Optimierung des Tragverhaltens.

Da erst am Ende des 18. Jahrhunderts Eisen als Baumaterial in ausreichender Menge zur Verfügung stand, wurden bis dahin alle Konstruktionen hauptsächlich in Holz, Lehm oder Stein ausgeführt. Materialgerecht eingesetzt eignet sich Stein nur in vorwiegend druckbeanspruchten Tragwerken wie zum Beispiel Wänden und Bogenkonstruktionen. Holz dagegen trägt sowohl auf Druck als auch auf Zug und Biegung und bot daher Verwendung für sehr unterschiedliche Tragwerke.

Das einfachste Tragwerk – der Balken – als rein biegebeanspruchtes Bauteil, reichte über lange Zeit aus und konnte den größeren Spannweiten und Lasten durch Reduzierung der Abstände zwischen den Balken oder Vergrößerung der Querschnitte angepaßt werden. Die konstruktive Verbindung zweier Hölzer zu einem gemeinsam wirkenden Querschnitt stellt dabei einen ersten Entwicklungsschritt zur Optimierung des Tragverhaltens bei gleichzeitiger Minimierung des Materialeinsatzes dar. Bei schubfester Verbindung kann damit eine vierfache Tragfähigkeit gegenüber den einzelnen Querschnitten erreicht werden.[1]

Nachdem derartige Maßnahmen nicht ausreichten, griff man zu Hänge-, Spreng- und Hängesprengwerken, welche ihre Lasten hauptsächlich über Normalkräfte wesentlich effizienter abtragen konnten. Seit ihrer Verwendung stellten die Holzverbindungen und ihre Festigkeiten den Hauptschwachpunkt dar. Die große Nachgiebigkeit bei Schwinden und die Einwirkung durch Feuchtigkeit führten oft zu Schäden.

Diese Tragwerke wurden bis ins 18. Jahrhundert aufgrund von überlieferten handwerklichen Erfahrungen und Versuchen immer weiterentwickelt, wie wir sie

The development of timber structures is directly related to the understanding of the loadbearing, i.e. structural, behaviour of a construction and the knowledge of the strengths of the materials. The greater the distance to be spanned, the more important it was to optimize the structural behaviour.

As it was not until the end of the 18th century that iron became available in sufficient quantities to be used as a building material, up to then all structures had been erected using mainly timber, clay and stone. In terms of material properties, stone is only suitable for structures loaded principally in compression, e.g. walls, arches. Timber, on the other hand, can accommodate both tension and compression, and so it offered scope for a wide diversity of structures.

The simple solid timber beam or floor joist, as an element subjected purely to bending, was for a long time perfectly adequate and could be adapted to cater for longer spans and greater loads by reducing the spacing between beams/joists or by enlarging the cross-section. The physical connection of two pieces of timber to form a composite section represents the first step on the way to optimizing the loadbearing behaviour while at the same time minimizing the consumption of material. In a shear-resistant connection, this results in a four-fold increase in the loadbearing capacity, compared to the individual cross-sections.[1]

As such measures became inadequate, builders resorted to slung or arched framing or combinations of the two, all of which could carry the loads imposed on them primarily by way of axial forces and hence much more efficiently. Since then, it has been the joints and their strengths which have represented the main weak points. Movement caused by shrinkage and ingress of moisture frequently led to damage.

These structures continued to be developed into the 18th century through the practical experiences

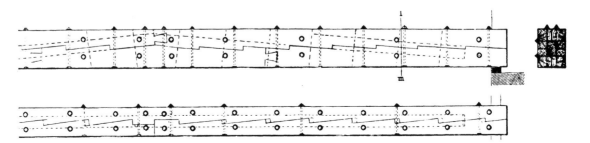

Zusammengesetzter Balken im Rathaus von Amsterdam.
Composite (indented) beam in Amsterdam City Hall.

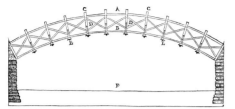

Andrea Palladio, Brücke über die Cismone, 1570.
Andrea Palladio, bridge over the River Cismone, 1570.

zum Beispiel 1726 in dem Buch über den Brückenbau von Jacob Leupold (1647-1727) systematisch dargestellt finden.[2] Neben diesen Tragwerken gab es aber schon sehr früh die ersten hölzernen Bogenkonstruktionen wie zum Beispiel die Brücke über die Cismone von Andrea Palladio, die er 1570 in seinen *Vier Büchern zur Architektur* veröffentlichte.[3] Darin entwickelt er aus dem geraden Fachwerkträger eine Bogenbrücke mit doppelten diagonalen und vertikalen Hängepfosten. Das günstige Bogentragverhalten über Druckkräfte wird durch diese biegesteife Ausbildung auch für Biegebeanspruchung aus einseitigen Lasten ausgebildet.[4]

Rechnerisch erfaßbar wurden all diese Tragwerke erst mit Entwicklung der Baustatik im 19. Jahrhundert, wobei Louis Marie Henri Navier (1785-1836) auf der Grundlage der Arbeiten von Coulomb, Bernoulli und Euler zum Begründer der Baustatik wurde.[5]

Bereits 1561 machte der französische Architekt Philibert de l'Orme (1515-1577) in seinem Buch *Nouvelles Inventions pour bien bastir et à petits fraiz* die Erfindung eines hölzernen bogenförmigen Bohlenbinders bekannt. Dieser setzte sich aus senkrecht stehenden, 1,3 m langen Bohlen zusammen, welche an den Enden radial abgesägt waren und zwei- oder dreilagig mit Holznägeln bei versetzten Stößen verbunden wurden. Bei Bedarf wurden die Längsseiten der Bohlen

of carpenters handed down over the years and through tests, as is carefully illustrated in, for example, Jacob Leupold's (1647-1727) book on bridge-building (1726).[2] Besides these structures, however, there had been early experiments with timber arches; for example, the bridge over the River Cismone by Andrea Palladio, which he described in his book *Quattro libri dell'architettura* (1570).[3] From a straight girder, Palladio developed an arch bridge with crossing diagonals and hangers perpendicular to top and bottom chords. This rigid form of the advantageous arch behaviour (via compressive forces) also made it suitable for asymmetric loads causing bending.[4]

These structures were only able to be analysed mathematically with the dawn of structural analysis in the 19th century. Louis Marie Henri Navier (1785-1836) continued the work of Coulomb, Bernoulli and Euler to become the father of modern-day structural engineering.[5]

As early as 1561, the French architect Philibert de l'Orme (1515-1577) announced the invention of a sort of composite timber member in his book *Nouvelles Inventions pour bien bastir et à petits fraiz*. This was composed of two or three planks on edge, 1.3 m long, the ends of which were sawn off radially, joined together with wooden pegs at staggered joints.

Philibert de l'Orme, Bohlenbogen-binderkonstruktion, 1561.
Selbstbildnis des Philibert de l'Orme.
Philibert de l'Orme, composite timber arch, 1561, and self-portrait.

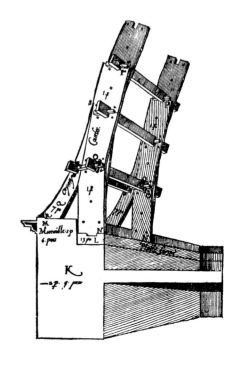

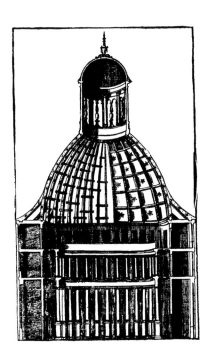

Philibert de l'Orme, Entwurf zum Wiederaufbau des Nonnenklosters, Paris, 1561.
Philibert de l'Orme, Entwurf einer Basilika.
Philibert de l'Orme, design for the rebuilding of a convent, Paris, 1561.
Philibert de l'Orme, design for a basilica.

bogenförmig zugeschnitten. Die einzelnen Bohlenbinder standen im Abstand von etwa einem Meter und wurden durch verkeilte Querriegel gegen seitliches Ausknicken gehalten.

Neben dem Vorteil einer stützenfreien Überspannung von Räumen berichtet de l'Orme auch von dem wesentlich geringeren Materialverbrauch gegenüber herkömmlichen Dachkonstruktionen, welcher zum Beispiel bei dem Neuaufbau des Daches des Schlosses Limours nur ein Viertel betragen habe. Über die Verwendung bei Dachstühlen und Scheunen mit bis zu 15 m Spannweite hinaus entwarf er eine Basilika mit einer Spannweite von 48,75 m.

Für den Wiederaufbau des Nonnenklosters am Montmartre in Paris entwarf er einen Kuppelbau mit etwa 60 m Spannweite, welcher 200 Jahre später Vorbild zur Überdachung der Getreidehalle in Paris werden sollte, deren Kuppel durch Bohlenbinder radial überspannt wurde.[6] Auch Brücken mit Spannweiten von 200 bis 400 m meinte Philibert de l'Orme damit bauen zu können.[7]

Nach einigen kleineren Bauwerken unter Verwendung von Bohlenbindern gelang der große Durchbruch 1783 bei dem Wettbewerb zur Überdachung der Getreidehalle (Halle au blé) in Paris. Hier konkurrierten die Architekten Legrand und Molinos mit ihrer hölzernen Kuppel nach dem de l'Orme'schen Prinzip gegen den Entwurf einer steinernen Kuppel von Le Camus de Mézières, J.-D. Antoine und Rondolet und die gußeiserne Kuppel von Bélanger.

Die Kuppel bestand aus de l'Orme'schen Bindern mit einer Spannweite von 41 m. Das Besondere dieser

The longitudinal sides of the planks were cut to an arch shape as required. These individual arches were positioned about 1 m apart and lateral buckling was prevented by transverse rails held in place by wedges.

Besides the advantage of an uninterrupted span, de l'Orme reported that his system required considerably less material than conventional roof constructions (the new roof to Château Limours was said to use only one-quarter the amount of material originally used). His roof trusses and barns employed spans of up to 15 m, but he even designed a basilica with a span of 48.75 m.

De l'Orme designed a dome with approx. 60 m span for the rebuilding of the convent at Montmartre in Paris. Two hundred years later this served as the model for roofing over a grain store in Paris, whose dome was carried by composite ribs spanning radially.[6] He believed that bridges with spans of 200-400 m would also be feasible.[7]

After a few smaller structures making use of composite beams, the great breakthrough came in 1783 with the competition for the roof over the Halle au blé (grain store) in Paris. The contenders were: Legrand and Molinos with their timber dome based on de l'Orme's principles, the stone dome of Le Camus de Mézières, J.-D. Antoine and Rondolet, and Bélanger's cast iron dome.

The dome comprised de l'Orme ribs spanning 41 m. The special feature of this dome was its 24 window strips arranged radially. These were not only supported on the dome but in fact interrupted the

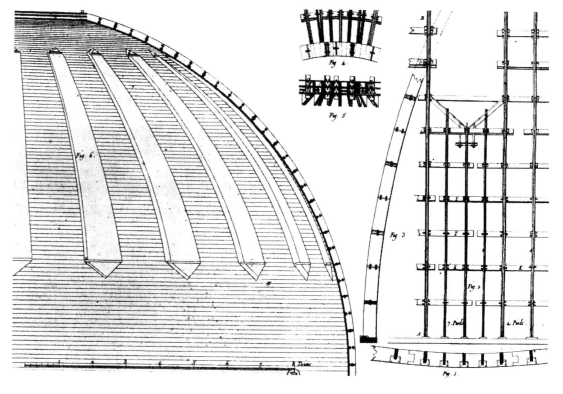

Legrand und Molinos, Halle au blé, Paris, 1783, Außenansicht, Konstruktion der Holzkuppel, Schnitt.
Legrand and Molinos, Halle au blé (grain store), Paris, 1783, view, details of timber dome, section.

David Gilly, Entwurf einer Basilika nach Philibert de l'Orme, 1797.
Design for a basilica after Philibert de l'Orme by David Gilly.

Kuppel waren ihre 24 radial verlaufenden Fensterbänder, welche nicht nur auf der Kuppel auflagen, sondern die radiale Tragwirkung der Kuppel sogar durchtrennten. So wirkten die zusammengefaßten Bohlenbinder statisch als einzelne Bögen, deren horizontale Auflagerkraft nur durch die unteren Ringe aufgenommen wurde. Die Kuppel brannte 1802 ab und wurde durch eine gußeiserne Kuppel von Bélanger ersetzt.

Der Bau dieser Bohlenbinder-Kuppel im Jahr 1783 führte zu einer Reihe nachfolgender Projekte auch in Deutschland.[8] Bereits 1787-1789 baute Carl Gotthard Langhans für die Königliche Tierarzeneischule in Berlin eine hölzerne Kuppel mit 16 m Spannweite. David Gilly (1748-1808) wird zum großen Verfechter dieser Bauweise in Preußen und beschreibt 1797 in seiner Schrift *Ueber Erfindung, Construction und Vortheile der Bohlendächer...* die bis dahin entstandenen Bauwerke.[9]

Angeregt durch diese Bauten entwarf 1802 der Hofbauinspektor Heinrich Gentz aus Berlin auf Betreiben Goethes das Lauchstädter Theater unter Verwendung zweilagiger Bohlenbinder mit 16,5 m Spannweite.[10] Die halbkreisförmigen Zweigelenkbinder standen im Abstand von 3 m. Dieses heute noch erhaltene Bauwerk zeigte auch deutlich die Mängel der de l'Orme'schen

radial loadbearing effect of the dome. So the coupled composite ribs acted structurally as separate arches whose horizontal thrust at the base could only be resisted by ring beams. The dome burned down in 1802 and was replaced by Bélanger's cast iron design.

The building of this dome with composite ribs in 1783 led to a series of follow-up projects, in Germany as well.[8] Soon after, in 1787-1789, Carl Gotthard Langhans designed a timber dome with 16 m span for the Royal Veterinary School in Berlin. David Gilly (1748-1808) became the greatest advocate of this form of construction in Prussia and described the structures built up to that time in his work *Ueber Erfindung, Construction und Vortheile der Bohlendächer...* (1797).[9]

Inspired by these constructions, in 1802 the Inspector of the Royal Buildings, Heinrich Gentz from Berlin, designed the Bad Lauchstädt theatre, employing two-part composite members with 16.5 m span.[10] The semicircular two-pin ribs were placed at 3 m centres. This building still stands today and illustrates very clearly the shortcomings of de l'Orme's system. The weakness of the ribs in bending and the horizon-

Bauweise. Die Biegeweichheit des Binders und die horizontalen Auflagerkräfte führten schon in den ersten Jahrzehnten zu starken Verformungen der Widerlager und einem Durchhängen der Binder.[11] Ebenso verzichtete Gentz auf eine Ausbildung von Querriegeln, wodurch die Stabilisierung gegen Biegedrillknicken (Kippen) sehr verschlechtert wurde. Dies machte zuerst eine Verstärkung durch Strebepfeiler und dann 1906 die Erneuerung der Widerlager und die Verstärkung des Bogens auf drei Lagen erforderlich.[12]

Die Nachteile dieser Bauweise liegen in der zeitaufwendigen und verschnittreichen Herstellung der Bretter und ihrer zur Hälfte geschwächten Biegesteifigkeit an den Stößen, welche sich bei ständiger Biegebeanspruchung besonders bemerkbar machen. Damit mußte jede Abweichung des Bogens von der idealen Stützlinie unter Eigengewicht zu starken Verformungen führen.

Die seinerzeit größte Kuppel in Deutschland mit einer Spannweite von 33,5 m entwarf Georg Moller 1822-1827 in Darmstadt für die Ludwigskirche. Im Ge-

tal thrust at the springing led to severe deformations of the supports and sagging of the ribs during the first decades.[11] Gentz also neglected to include transverse rails, an omission which considerably reduced the ability to resist torsional-flexural buckling. This made it necessary to strengthen the construction with buttresses and then in 1906 to renew the supports and increase the ribs to three members each.[12]

The disadvantages of this form of construction are the time-consuming production of the planks with their many cuts and the 50% reduction in bending strength at the splices, a weakness which manifests itself particularly in cases of constant bending stresses. Hence, every deviation of the arch from the ideal line of pressure under dead loads was predestined to lead to severe deformations.

The, at the time, largest dome in Germany (span 33.5 m) was designed by Georg Moller for the Ludwigskirche in Darmstadt (1822-1827). In contrast to the Halle au blé, he arranged single and double radial ring beams of oak to accommodate the hoop tension

Carl Gotthard Langhans, Anatomiegebäude der Königlichen Tierarzeneischule, Berlin, 1787-1789, Schnitt, Grundriß.
Carl Gotthard Langhans, Anatomy College of the Royal Veterinary School, Berlin, elevation, plan.

Rechts **Heinrich Gentz, Theater Bad Lauchstädt, 1802, Zustand nach der Erneuerung 1906: Ansichten, Längs- und Querschnitte, Grundrisse in Logenhöhe (links) und Parterrehöhe (rechts).**
Right Heinrich Gentz, Bad Lauchstädt theatre, built in 1802, condition after refurbishment in 1906: elevations, sections, plan on boxes level (left), plan on stalls level (right).

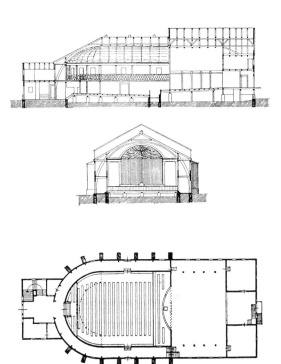

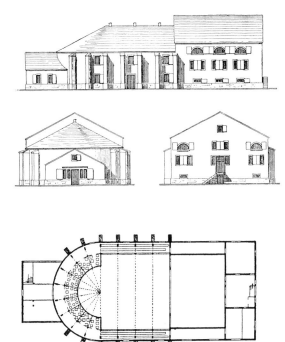

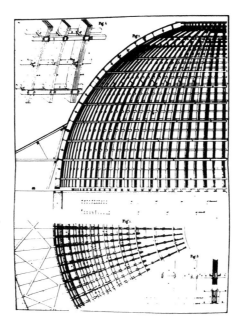

Rechts **Georg Moller, Ludwigskirche, Darmstadt, 1822-1827, Ansicht und Kuppelkonstruktion.**[14]
Right Georg Moller, Ludwigskirche, Darmstadt, 1822-1827, elevation, details of dome.[14]

Unten **Zollinger-Bauweise, 1904, Knotenpunkt. Zollinger-Dach im Bauzustand.**
Below node point of Zollinger system, 1904. Zollinger roof under construction.

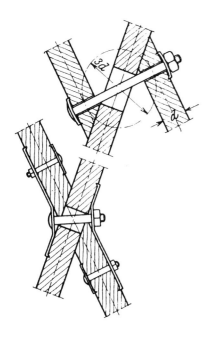

gensatz zu der Halle au blé ordnete er einfache und doppelte radiale Ringbalken aus Eichenholz zur Aufnahme der Ringdruck- und Zugkräfte an, wodurch ein räumliches Tragverhalten ermöglicht wurde. Die Ludwigskirche wurde Ende des Zweiten Weltkriegs ein Opfer der Brandbomben.[13]

Der de l'Orme'sche Bohlenbinder fand dann um 1904 seine Übertragung ins Räumliche durch die Weiterentwicklung des Merseburger Stadtbaurates Fritz Zollinger (1880-1945), welcher die zweilagigen Bohlenbinder zu einem rautenförmigen, gekrümmten Flächentragwerk aufspreizte. Die einzelnen Brettlamellen paßten sich mit ihrer Oberkante der Krümmung an. An den geschmiegten Stößen, an denen jeweils eine Lamelle durchgeht, werden sie mit einem Bolzen verschraubt.[15] Aufgrund der räumlichen Kraftzerlegung wäre hier ein biegesteifer Anschluß erforderlich, welcher aber nicht erreicht wird und daher bei großen Spannweiten zu starken Verformungen führt.[16]

Neben dem senkrecht stehenden, vielfach gestoßenen Bohlenbinder sind die ersten horizontal liegenden unverleimten Brettschichtträger seit der Brücke über die Limmat bei Wettingen in der Schweiz nachweisbar. Der Zimmermeister Hans Ulrich Grubenmann (1709-1783) errichtete diese Brücke 1764-1766 zusammen mit seinem Sohn. Die zwei parallelen siebenlagigen Bogenträger, zwischen denen die Fahrbahn teils aufgeständert, teils abgehängt verläuft, hatten eine Spannweite von 61 m. In Fahrbahn- und Deckenebene befanden sich die starken Aussteifungsverbände. Das Besondere dieser Brücke waren die kraftschlüssig miteinander verzahnten und verbolzten Balken, welche so als

and compression, thus enabling a three-dimensional loadbearing behaviour. The Ludwigskirche was destroyed by incendiary bombs in the closing stages of World War II.[13]

Around 1904 the de l'Orme composite member was transformed into a three-dimensional frame through the work of Fritz Zollinger (1880-1945), City Building Surveyor in Merseburg near Leipzig. He opened out the two-part ribs to form a diamond-shaped, curved, plate-like structure. The top edges of the individual planks followed the curve of the roof. At each mitred joint, where one plank passes through, the planks were connected with bolts.[15] Owing to the three-dimensional distribution of forces, a rigid connection is necessary; however, this is not achieved, which results in severe deflections over long spans.[16]

Besides the vertical, multiple-spliced composite members, the bridge over the River Limmat near Wettingen, Switzerland, illustrates the first use of horizontal non-glued composite sections. Master-carpenter Hans Ulrich Grubenmann (1709-1783) erected this bridge in 1764-1766 together with his son. The two parallel seven-part arches, with a through-deck partly supported, partly suspended, spanned 61 m. Strong bracing was located at deck level. The special feature of this bridge was the interlocking, pinned beams which, forming a compound element, lent the bridge great stiffness. It was burned down on 17 June 1799 at the command of the French General Massena.[17]

In North America Theodore Burr built a 60-m-span bridge over the River Delaware (1804-1806). This con-

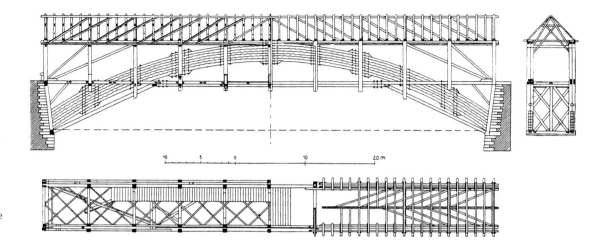

Rechts **Hans Ulrich Grubenmann, Brücke bei Wettingen, 1764-1766, Längs-, Querschnitt und Grundriß.**
Unten **Theodore Burr, Brücke bei Trenton, New Jersey, 1806.**
Right Hans Ulrich Grubenmann, bridge near Wettingen, Switzerland, 1764-1766, sections and plan.
Below Theodore Burr, bridge over the River Delaware near Trenton, USA, 1806.

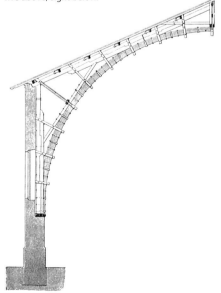

Emy, Bogendach, 1828: oben fünf, unten acht gebogene Bretter 4,5 x 13 cm.
Emy, arch roof, curved planks 45 x 130 mm, five above, eight below.

gemeinsamer Träger dem Bogen eine hohe Steifigkeit gaben. Die Brücke ging am 17. Juni 1799 auf Befehl des französischen Generals Massena in Flammen auf.[17]

In Nordamerika baute Theodore Burr 1804-1806 eine Brücke mit einer Spannweite von 60 m über den Delaware, welche aus zwei Brettlamellen-Bögen mit abgehängter versteifter Fahrbahn bestand.[18]

Bekannt wurde diese Bauweise erst 1828 als Emy'-scher Bohlenbinder durch die Veröffentlichung des französischen „Genie-Offiziers" (technischer Offizier) Emy, *Description d'un nouveau system d'arcs*.

Die flach aufeinander liegenden Bohlen ließen sich leicht biegen und ersparten den aufwendigen, verlust-reichen Zuschnitt einzelner bogenförmiger Bretter. Die Verbindung der einzelnen Lagen erfolgte mit Hilfe von Spannbolzen und -zangen, die zu einer erhöhten Rei-bung und damit Kraftübertragung zwischen den Bohlen führen sollten. Da die Verbindung nicht als voll-kommen kraftschlüssig anzusehen ist, kommt es bei Biegebeanspruchungen zu einer gegenseitigen Ver-schiebung der Lamellen. Dies und die ebenfalls gerin-ge Steifigkeit der Emy'schen Bohlenbinder führte bei wechselnden Belastungen je nach Spannweite zu star-ken Verformungen. Um die Steifigkeit bei großen Spannweiten zu erhöhen, schlug er 1841 einen zwei-bzw. dreigeteilten Bogen vor, welcher sich am Auflager aufspreizt und zusätzlich ausgesteift ist. Hierdurch kann eine gewisse Einspannung erzielt werden, was zu einer Reduzierung der Verformungen führt.[19] Diese Konstruk-tion schlug er zum Beispiel für die Überdachung von Großhallen bis zu 100 m Spannweite vor.

sisted of two composite arches with suspended, stiff-ened deck.[18]

This form of construction was first designated as the Emy composite system through the publication of *Description d'un nouveau system d'arcs* in 1828 by the French engineering officer Emy.

The flat planks were easily bent and so the time-consuming, high-wastage cutting of individual curved planks was avoided. The separate layers were connected with the help of clamping bolts and col-lars, which were intended to increase the friction be-tween the laminations and hence lead to a transfer of forces between the layers. As the connection is not a proper interlock, bending stresses cause the lami-nations to be displaced with respect to each other. This and the likewise low stiffness of the Emy com-posite members led, depending on the span, to severe deflections under changing load patterns. In order to improve the stiffness for long spans, in 1841 Emy proposed a two- or three-segment arch which was splayed out at the supports and provided with additional bracing. This leads to a certain degree of restraint which in turn results in lower deflections.[19] He proposed using this form of construction for the roofs of large halls with spans of up to 100 m.

Paul Joseph Ardant published a detailed scientif-ic study of arch structures in 1847.[20] In loading tests on circular de l'Orme and Emy arches, he compared the ensuing support reactions and the deflections of the structures under various loading cases right up to failure.[21]

Eine ausführliche wissenschaftliche Untersuchung von Bogentragwerken veröffentlichte Paul Joseph Ardant 1847.[20] In Belastungsversuchen kreisförmiger Bögen nach de l´Orme´scher und Emy´scher Bauweise verglich er unter verschiedenen Lastfällen die entstehenden Auflagerkräfte und die Verformungen des Tragwerkes bis zum Bruch.[21]

Die Versuchsvorrichtung zeigt einen aus 5 Nadelholz-Brettlamellen (15 x 2,7 cm) hergestellten Bogen von 12,12 m äußerem Durchmesser. Die Lamellen wurden durch 13 eiserne Bänder und durch 24 Schraubenbolzen zusammengehalten. Die Stöße sind so angebracht worden, daß sie immer durch volles Holz der darüber und darunter befindlichen Lamelle gedeckt werden. Die Kurve m-m gibt die unbelastete Bogenform vor Beginn, die Kurve n-n eine Stunde nach Belastungsbeginn und die Kurve r-r im Bruchzustand wieder. Da die kreisförmige Bogenform nicht der idealen Stützlinie für Gleichstreckenlasten oder Einzellasten entspricht, kam es zu starken Biegebeanspruchungen, welche dann zum Versagen führten. Durch die elastische Verbindung der einzelnen Bogensegmente

The test rig consisted of an arch with 12.12 m outside diameter made from five laminations (150 x 27 mm) of coniferous wood. The laminations were joined together by 13 iron straps and 24 bolts. The joints were arranged in such a way that they were always covered by the solid timber of the lamination above and below. Curve m-m represents the shape of the arch prior to loading, curve n-n the shape one hour after applying the first loads, and curve r-r the shape at failure. As the circular arch form does not correspond to the ideal line of pressure for uniformly distributed linear loads or point loads, severe bending stresses were induced which led to collapse. The bending strength was further reduced by the elasticity of the connections between the individual segments of the arch.[22] Therefore, Ardant proposed stiffening the Emy arch with a truss of straight, solid timber sections, thereby improving the stiffness, particularly at the ends.

The hall for the 4th German Choirs Festival, which took place in Vienna in 1890, employed a combination of de l'Orme and Emy systems, with semicircular

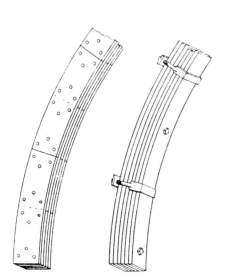

Emy, Entwurf einer Bogenbrücke, 1828.
Emy, design for an arch bridge, 1828.

Bogen nach de l'Orme und Emy im Vergleich: links (de l'Orme) ebene, hochkant gestellte und aufeinander genagelte Lamellen, rechts (Emy) flachgelegte und verbolzte.
Comparison of de l'Orme and Emy arches: left, de l'Orme version comprising flat planks on edge and nailed together; right, Emy version comprising planks laid flat and pinned together.

Emy, Entwürfe von Großhallen, 1828.
Emy, designs for large halls, 1828.

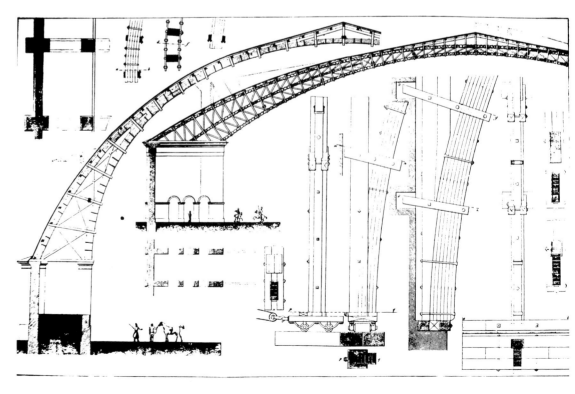

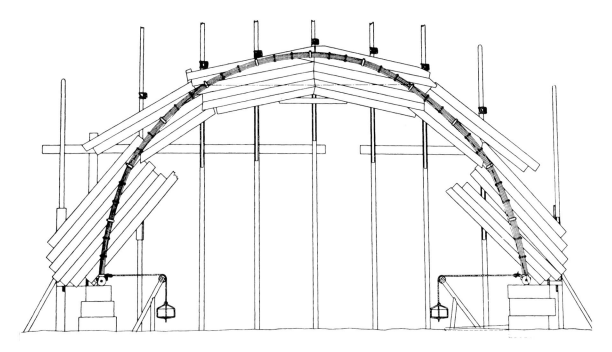

Paul Joseph Ardant, Aufriß einer Versuchs-vorrichtung, 1847.
Paul Joseph Ardant, test rig, 1847.

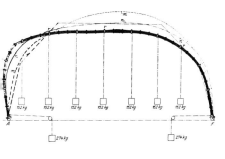

Ardant, Versuch mit gleichförmig verteilten Gewichten.
Ardant, test with evenly spaced loads.

Ardant, verbessertes biegesteifes Spreng-werksdach anstelle eines Bogens, 1847.
Ardant, improved strut frame roof instead of an arch, 1847.

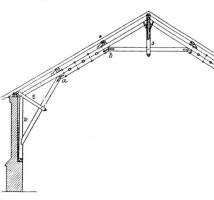

wurde die Biegesteifigkeit zusätzlich geschwächt.[22] Daher schlug Ardant vor, den Emy´schen Bogen durch ein aufgesatteltes Fachwerk aus geraden Vollholzquerschnitten zu versteifen, wodurch besonders in den Ecken eine erhöhte Steifigkeit erzielt werde.

Eine Kombination aus de l´Orme'scher und Emy'scher Bauweise stellt die Festhalle für das vierte deutsche Sängerbundfest 1890 in Wien dar. Die halbkreisförmigen Binder spannten über 56 m, wobei sie durch die seitlichen Galerien zusätzlich ausgesteift wurden. Der zusammengesetzte Rechteckquerschnitt bestand aus gebogenen Bohlen als Ober- und Untergurt und drei senkrecht bogenförmig zugeschnittenen Bohlen im Stegbereich mit 26 cm Breite und 51,5 cm Höhe.[23]

Die Weiterentwicklung zu den verleimten Brettschichtholzkonstruktionen erfolgte aber nicht direkt, sondern nahm den Weg über den einfachen Einfeldträger.

Nach den zimmermannsmäßigen, konstruktiv ausgebildeten, zusammengesetzten Trägern entwickelte Georg Ludwig Friedrich Laves 1842 einen der Momentenlinie angepaßten Träger. Er schnitt einen Balken der Länge nach auf, spreizte ihn auseinander und fixierte diesen Abstand mit eingeklemmten Hölzern. Durch den größeren Abstand zwischen Ober- und Untergurt verringerten sich unter Biegebeanspruchung die Spannungen. Da im geschlitzten Bereich keine Schubspannungen zwischen den Querschnittsteilen übertragen werden konnten, mußten die Auflagerpunkte hierfür

ribs spanning in excess of 56 m. Side galleries provided additional stiffening. The composite rectangular section (260 mm wide x 515 mm deep) consisted of curved planks for the top and bottom flanges and three vertical planks cut to a curved shape forming the web.[23]

However, the further developments which finally led to glued laminated construction did not follow on directly from this but instead took a detour via the simple single-span beam.

After the carpentry-based constructions of composite beams, Georg Ludwig Friedrich Laves developed a beam in 1842 which corresponded to the bending moment diagram. He sliced a beam lengthwise, forced it apart and held it in this position by means of pieces of timber clamped between. The increased distance between top and bottom chords reduced the bending stresses. As no shear stresses could be transferred across the longitudinal slit, the supports had to be designed to accommodate such stresses. So yielding of the supports represents the weakness of this beam design.[24]

The Stephan composite member was first made public in 1902. This represented a further development of the de l'Orme design, employing composite-section bracing diagonals to improve the stiffness of top and bottom chords. An example of this form of construction dating from 1906 can still be seen at Copenhagen station. Despite being favoured for a

Festhalle für das vierte deutsche Sängerbundfest in Wien, 1890, Ansicht, Längsschnitt, Querschnitt.
Hall for the 4th German Choirs Festival, Vienna, 1890, general view and sections.

ausgebildet werden. Diese stellten bei eintretender Nachgiebigkeit sogleich den Schwachpunkt des Trägers dar.[24]

Der Stephan'sche Bohlenbinder wurde 1902 erstmals veröffentlicht. Er stellte eine Weiterentwicklung des de l'Orme'schen Bohlenbinders dar, welcher zur Erzielung größerer Steifigkeit in Ober- und Untergurte mit aussteifenden Diagonalen aus Brettlamellen zusammengesetzt wurde. Ein noch erhaltenes Beispiel dieser Bauweise ist die Bahnhofshalle in Kopenhagen von 1906. Trotz einer großen Anzahl an ausgeführten Bauwerken konnte der Stephan'sche Bohlenbinder den Durchbruch des Holzleimbaus nicht verhindern. Die Hauptursache lag in seiner aufwendigen Herstellung und der großen Anzahl an Knotenpunkten.

Zusammenfassend ist das Problem aller Tragwerksentwicklungen im Holzbau bis zu diesem Zeitpunkt in den nachgiebigen oder gering belastbaren Verbindungsmitteln zu sehen. Im Bereich des Stahlbaus waren diese Probleme relativ gut und sicher durch Nieten zu beherrschen, bis sich die Schweißverbindungen durchsetzten.

Bereits 1809 schlug Carl Friedrich Wiebeking in seinen *Beyträgen zur Brückenbaukunde* das Verleimen stark gekrümmter Bauhölzer vor:[25] „Solche Verbindung der kleinen Bretter zu einem ganzen Baustücke, deren

great number of structures, the Stephan system could not prevent the triumph of glued laminated construction. The main reason for its demise was the elaborate production and the large number of nodes.

To summarize, the problem of all structural developments in timber construction up to that time was the inadequate strength of the means of connection. In structural steelwork such problems could be relatively easily and safely mastered by using rivets, until they were replaced by welding.

As early as 1809 Carl Friedrich Wiebeking, in his *Beyträgen zur Brückenbaukunde*, proposed gluing highly curved timber for building purposes:[25] "I cannot recommend strongly enough the joining of small planks – with staggered joints of course – to form whole elements for the construction of arch bridges and for stairs, in fact at all places where one requires highly curved building timber. The individual planks can be curved in a jig, even to form winders; hence they can be ingeniously combined to form arch bridges and stair stringers."[26]

The first structure built using glued laminated timber is generally acknowledged to be the assembly hall of King Edward College in Southampton (1860). But this remained a one-off construction without any known, direct successor.[27]

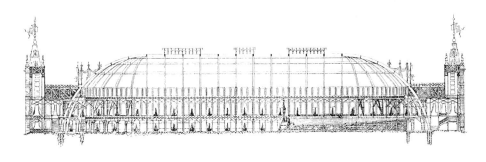

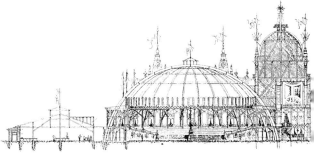

Ludwig Laves, Träger, 1842, hier für 10 m Spannweite.
Laves, beam, 1842, example for a 10 m span.

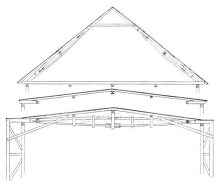

Anwendungsbeispiele des Laves'schen Trägers als Dreigelenkrahmen (oben) und Biegeträger (unten).
Examples of applications of a Laves beam as three-pin arch (top), and beam in bending (bottom).

Stossfuge abwechseln müssen, kann ich nicht genug beym Bau der Bogenbrücken und bey Treppen, kurz überall, wo man stark gekrümmte Bauhölzer nöthig hat empfehlen. Die einzelnen Bretter lassen sich nämlich nach der Lehre, selbst in Windungen krümmen; folglich ist eine Zusammensetzung davon zu Bogenbrücken und Treppenträgern sehr geschickt."[26]

Als erste verleimte Brettschichtholz-Konstruktion gilt die Versammlungshalle des King Edward College in Southampton von 1860, welche als singuläres Bauwerk ohne bekannte direkte Nachfolger blieb.[27]

Die Suche nach einem geeigneten Verbindungsmittel war damit der Ausgangspunkt der Entwicklungen Otto Hetzers in Weimar, welcher den Holzleimbau zwar nicht erfand, ihn jedoch zur Anwendungsreife entwickelte.

The search for a suitable means of connection formed the starting point for Otto Hetzer's work in Weimar. Although he did not invent glued laminated timber, he certainly refined the technique to make it suitable for practical applications.

Versammlungshalle des King Edward College in Southampton, 1860.
Assembly hall of King Edward College, Southampton, 1860.

Otto Hetzer und die Entstehung des Holzleimbaus
Otto Hetzer and the birth of laminated timber engineering

Karl Friedrich Otto Hetzer wurde am 11. Februar 1846 in Kleinobringen bei Weimar geboren. Seine Lehrzeit als Zimmermann verbrachte er von 1860-1863 in Apolda. Nach dem Deutsch-Französischen Krieg gründete er 1872 ein Dampfsägewerk und Zimmereigeschäft an der Kohlstraße in Weimar. Der wirtschaftliche Aufschwung der Stadt Weimar in der sogenannten Gründerzeit führte zur raschen Expansion des Betriebes, der 1883 in „Weimarische Bau- und Parkettfußbodenfabrik" umbenannt wurde. 1891 wurde Otto Hetzer zum Großherzoglichen Hofzimmermeister ernannt.

Aufgrund der beengten innerstädtischen Lage wurde das Unternehmen 1895 an die Ettersburger Straße verlegt. Das neue Grundstück besaß mit fast 26.000 m² ausreichend Platz für einen Gleisanschluß, ein Maschinenhaus, eine Schneidemühle, eine Parkettfabrik, einen Lagerplatz und eine Werksvilla.[28] Die Villa enthielt im Erdgeschoß die Geschäftszimmer und diente im Obergeschoß als Wohnung des Leiters.[29]

Die Leistungsfähigkeit der neuen Parkettfabrik wurde 1899 mit 150.000 m²/Jahr angegeben. Wie groß dimensioniert diese Fabrik war, ist daran zu erkennen, daß um 1900 erst 60.000 m² produziert wurden.[30] Zur Kapitalaufstockung wurde der Betrieb am 28. Januar

Karl Friedrich Otto Hetzer was born on 11 February 1846 in Kleinobringen near Weimar. From 1860-1863 he served an apprenticeship as a carpenter in Apolda and, following the Franco-Prussian war, he set up a steam sawmill and carpentry business in 1872 in premises on Kohlstrasse in Weimar. The economic boom years of the Second German Reich were felt in Weimar too and led to a rapid expansion of his business, which was renamed „Weimarische Bau- und Parkettfußbodenfabrik" (Weimar Building and Parquet Flooring Works) in 1883. The year 1891 saw Otto Hetzer appointed to the post of Carpenter to the Grand Ducal Court. The confined site in the inner city forced the company to move to Ettersburger Strasse in 1895, where a new site of nearly 26 000 m² provided adequate space for a direct railway link, a boiler house, a sawmill, a parquet flooring works, a warehouse and an impressive house.[28] The ground floor of the house served as offices, while the first floor was the home of the manager.[29]

The capacity of the new parquet flooring works was rated at 150 000 m² per year in 1899. The huge size of this factory becomes clear when we consider that around 1900 production had only reached

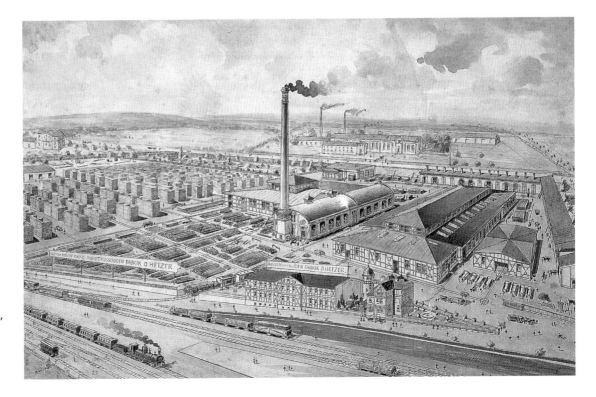

Ansicht des Firmengeländes der Otto Hetzer AG, Weimar, 1921.
View of Otto Hetzer AG works, Weimar, 1921.

Bildnis Otto Hetzer.
Portrait Otto Hetzer.

1901 in die Aktiengesellschaft Otto Hetzer Holzpflege und Holzbearbeitung AG umgewandelt: Allerdings blieb die Expansion des Geschäftes hinter den Erwartungen zurück. Zu Spitzenzeiten 1917 wurden bis zu 300 Arbeiter beschäftigt.

Die Erprobung der ersten Holzleimbinder und gebogenen Sparrendächer erfolgte erst nach 1900 auf dem neuen Werksgelände. Wahrscheinlich trug der Sohn Otto Hetzer jun. (geb. 1. Dezember 1876) maßgeblich zu der Entwicklung bei. Nach seinem Architekturstudium von 1897 bis 1901 an der Technischen Hochschule Berlin-Charlottenburg trat er 1901 in die Firma ein. Nach eigener Aussage bemühte er sich „... besonders um die Durchbildung und Einführung der Hetzer'schen freitragenden Holzdachbinder-Konstruktionen und um den Verkauf von Lizenzen und Patenten im In- und Ausland."[31]

In der Zeit von 1891 bis 1910 ließ sich Otto Hetzer fünf Neuentwicklungen patentieren. Nach Jahren der Arbeit mit Holzleim-Konstruktionen hatte Otto Hetzer den technischen Durchbruch auf der Weltausstellung in Brüssel 1910 erleben können. Die dort erstellte Ausstellungshalle der Deutschen Reichsbahn besaß eine Spannweite von 43 m, welche erst in den dreißi-

60000 m2.[30] An injection of cash was provided when the company was floated on the stock market from 28 January 1901 as Otto Hetzer Holzpflege und Holzbearbeitung AG. However, expansion remained short of expectations. Yet at peak periods (1917) the company employed up to 300 workers.

Tests on the first glulam beams and curved couple roofs were carried out after 1900 at the new plant. It was probably Hetzer's son, Otto Hetzer jun. (born on 1 December 1876), who was the main driving force behind these developments. He first joined the company in 1901 after studying architecture at the Berlin-Charlottenburg Technical Academy. According to his own statement he was particularly involved in "... the improvement and introduction of Hetzer clear-span timber roof structures and the sale of licences and patents at home and abroad."[31]

In the period from 1891 to 1910 Otto Hetzer was granted patents for five new developments. Following years of work with glued laminated constructions, Otto Hetzer was able to enjoy the technical breakthrough at the Brussels World Exposition of 1910. The German railway operator of that time erected an exhibition hall with a span of 43 m, a record

Otto Hetzer, Patent Nr. 63018, Fußboden, 1892.
Otto Hetzer, patent No. 63018, Floor, 1892.

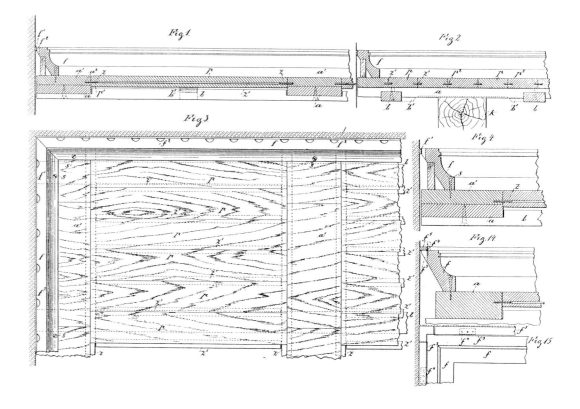

ger Jahren übertroffen wurde. Diese Halle wurde von dem Münchener Ingenieur Kügler und der Firma Steinbeis und Cons. aus Rosenheim errichtet.

Otto Hetzer sen. und jun. schieden auf Grund von persönlichen Differenzen mit dem Aufsichtsrat der Hetzer AG bereits 1910 aus dem Betrieb aus, und Otto Hetzer sen. verstarb im darauffolgenden Jahr.

Der von Otto Hetzer aufgebaute Betrieb bestand noch bis zu seinem Konkurs 1927 weiter und wurde im Februar 1934 an den Holzimporteur Häussler in Wismar verkauft. Ein Teil der Maschinen wurde von der Firma Nemaho in Holland übernommen.[32] Bis heute sind auf dem ehemaligen Werksgelände noch die Werksvilla, die ehemalige Leimerei und die Abbundhalle erhalten geblieben.

Patente Otto Hetzers

Hetzers Patente, die er 1891-1910 erwarb, stellen Probleme und Entwicklungen des Holzleimbaus anschaulich dar. Das erste Patent – DRP No. 63018 – beschreibt die Konstruktion eines unterlüfteten Dielenfußbodens, welcher bei Bedarf im Falle von Schwinden in den vorhandenen Richtleisten nachträglich zusammengeschoben werden konnte.[33]

Schon das zweite Patent von 1900 – DRP No. 125895 – stellt einen zusammengesetzten, kastenförmigen Holzträger dar, welcher dem Momentenverlauf parabelförmig angepaßt wurde. Die einzelnen Querschnittsteile wie Obergurte, Untergurte und Stege wurden durch ein nicht näher benanntes Klebemittel kraftschlüssig miteinander verleimt. Die beiden grundlegenden Probleme bezüglich der belastungsabhängigen Querschnittsoptimierung und der Wahl des Verbindungsmittels wurden hier erstmals gelöst. Die Verleimung mehrerer Einzelquerschnitte stellt ebenso ein wirksames Mittel zur Verhinderung des Verdrehens und Reißens dünnwandiger Holzquerschnitte dar.

Die rege Bautätigkeit um die Jahrhundertwende führte bei 6 m weit spannenden Balken für die üblichen Holzdecken zu einer Verknappung und Verteuerung großer Querschnitte.[34] Das DRP No. 163144 des Verbundträgers vom 10. Mai 1903 reagiert auf diesen Mangel. Otto Hetzer beschreibt hier die Herstellung eines Balkens großen Querschnitts aus einem der Länge nach parabelförmig zersägten Querschnitt, in dessen Fuge ein Brett unter Druck eingeleimt wird.

Zur Vorwegnahme bleibender Durchbiegungen unter Eigengewicht wird eine Verleimung mit gegensätz-

span which was not exceeded until the 1930s. The hall was the work of the Munich-based engineer Kügler and the Steinbeis & Cons. company from Rosenheim.

But 1910 also saw Otto Hetzer sen. and jun. depart from Hetzer AG as a result of disagreements with the Supervisory Board. Otto Hetzer sen. died the following year.

The company that Otto Hetzer had founded continued until it was declared bankrupt in 1927 and sold to the timber importer Häussler in Wismar in February 1934. Some of the machinery was taken over by the Dutch firm Nemaho.[32] The house, the former glue shop and the assembly shop still remain standing today on the site of the former factory.

Patents of Otto Hetzer

The patents which Otto Hetzer acquired in the years 1891-1910 clearly reflect the problems and developments in glued laminated timber construction. The first patent – DRP No. 63018 – describes the construction of a ventilated floor of wooden floorboards which, if required, could be subsequently pushed together in the guide fillets to compensate for any shrinkage.[33]

The second patent dating from 1900 – DRP No. 125895 – already shows a composite, box-shaped timber beam which reflected the distribution of bending moments through its parabola-like form. The separate flanges and webs were glued together such that forces could be transferred by an adhesive substance that was not described in detail. The two fundamental problems with regard to optimizing the cross-section depending on the load and the method of connection were solved here for the first time. The bonding of several separate pieces also represents an effective means of preventing twisting and cracking of thin timber sections.

The building boom around 1900 led to shortages of the larger sizes of timber and, consequently, price rises for the 6 m spans common for the wooden floors of that period.[34] Patent DRP No. 163144 (10 May 1903) for a composite beam was a response to these problems. In this patent Otto Hetzer describes the production of a beam with a large cross-section from one section sawn lengthwise to form a parabola and its complement, the joint between which was filled with a plank glued into place under pressure.

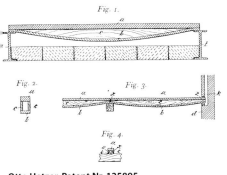

**Otto Hetzer, Patent Nr. 125895,
zusammengesetzter Holzbalken, 1900.**
Otto Hetzer, patent No. 125895, 1900,
composite timber beam.

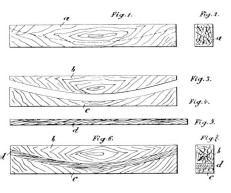

**Otto Hetzer, Patent Nr. 163144,
parabolisch zusammengesetzter Balken, 1903.**
Otto Hetzer, patent No. 163144, 1903,
composite beam sawn lengthwise to form parabola
and complement.

licher Vorverformung möglich. In einem Vortrag vor dem Berliner Architektenverein am 4. März 1907 berichtet der Regierungs- und Baurat Adams von Versuchen des Königlichen Materialprüfungsamtes in Berlin-Lichterfelde vom Juni 1904, die eine wesentlich höhere Belastbarkeit verleimter Träger gegenüber analogen Vollholzquerschnitten ergaben. Bei dem untersuchten Träger wurde ein 39 mm starkes Kiefernbrett in einen parabolisch aufgetrennten Fichtenholzbalken eingeleimt. Hierbei wurden Druck- und Zugspannungen von 380 bis 600 kg/cm² und Schubspannungen von 9 bis 25,5 kg/cm² gemessen. Die Durchbiegungen des verleimten Trägers betrugen dabei nur ein Drittel des Vollholzträgers.

Der Hetzer-Balken versagte trotz wesentlich höherer Zugfestigkeit des Fichtenholzes zuerst an der Unterseite durch Einreißen der Holzfasern. Daraus schließt Adams, daß die nennenswerte Erhöhung der Tragfähigkeit vor allem von der Hetzer'schen Holzbehandlung herrühren muß. Bei diesem Verfahren werden die Proteinstoffe des Holzes ausgelaugt und anschließend das Holz getränkt, was zu einer Härtung führt (das Mittel der Tränkung ist nicht bekannt).[35]

Vergleichswerte der mechanisch-technischen Versuchsanstalt der Technischen Hochschule in München von 1907 ergaben in einem Versuch die vierfachen Festigkeiten von Buchenholz, das nach Hetzer'scher Art gepflegt und getränkt wurde,[36] gegenüber unbehandeltem Buchenholz. Adams forderte daher genauere Untersuchungen zur Wirkung der Holzfestigkeiten und deren Anordnung im Querschnitt. Auch die Frage, ob das parabelförmige Brett besser als Druckbogen oder als „Zugseil" entsprechend den Spannungstrajektorien trägt, sei zu untersuchen. Die Versuche des Königlichen Materialprüfungsamtes konnten aber in jedem Fall die höhere Festigkeit der Leimfuge gegenüber den sie umgebenden Holzfasern durch Zugversuche rechtwinklig zur Fuge nachweisen.

1924 allerdings berichtet der Kontrollingenieur des Schweizer Eisenbahndepartements, Fritz Hübner, von Vergleichsversuchen zwischen Vollholz- und Brettschichtholzträgern, welche bei Holz des gleichen Baumes zu exakt denselben Festigkeiten führte, was im Gegensatz zu den Aussagen Adams steht.[37] Die heutige Auffassung ist, daß die Verwendung von verleimtem Brettschichtholz zu einer Homogenisierung des Materials und damit zu geringeren Streuungen führt, was eine höhere Belastbarkeit erlaubt.

Precambering to counter deflection caused by self-weight was also possible. In a lecture given at the Berlin Architectural Association on 4 March 1907 the City Surveyor, Adams, reported on tests by the Royal Materials Testing Office in Berlin-Lichterfelde from June 1904 in which glued beams achieved a considerably higher loadbearing capacity compared to similar solid timber sections. In the beam under test a 39-mm-thick pine plank was glued to a spruce beam sawn lengthwise to form a parabola and its complement. Tensile and compressive stresses of 380-600 kg/cm² and shear stresses of 9-25.5 kg/cm² were measured. The deflection of the glued beam was only one-third that of the solid section.

However, the Hetzer beam failed despite the much higher tensile strength of the spruce, initially on the underside through tearing of the wood fibres. Adams concluded from this that the notable increase in loadbearing capacity must stem, above all, from the way in which Hetzer treated the wood. The method involved leaching out the proteins from the wood and subsequently impregnating it, which led to a hardening of the wood (the impregnation substance is not known).[35]

A test carried out in 1907 by the Mechanical-Technical Test Centre at Munich Technical University resulted in beech which had been treated and impregnated using the Hetzer method[36] reaching a strength four times that of the untreated wood. Therefore, Adams called for more precise investigations into the effect of timber strengths and their positioning within the cross-section. He also posed the question of whether the parabolic plank worked better as a compressive arch or as a tensile catenary, following the stress trajectories. Tensile tests at right-angles to the joint carried out by the Royal Materials Testing Office proved in every case that the strength of the glue joint was higher than that of the surrounding wood fibres.

But in 1924 Fritz Hübner, a senior engineer employed by Swiss Railways, reported on tests comparing solid and laminated sections in which exactly the same strengths were obtained for timber from the same tree, i.e. the opposite of what Adams believed.[37] The current opinion maintains that the use of glued laminated timber leads to a homogenization of the material and hence to less scatter, which in turn permits a higher loadbearing capacity.

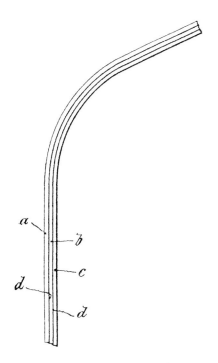

Oben **Otto Hetzer, Patent Nr. 197773, gebogenes Holzbauteil für vereinigte Dachpfosten und Sparren, 1906.**
Unten **Otto Hetzer, Patent Nr. 225687, Fachwerkträger aus Holz, 1907.**
Above Otto Hetzer, patent DRP No. 197773, curved timber member for combined roof posts and rafters, 1906.
Below Otto Hetzer, patent DRP No. 225687, timber truss, 1907.

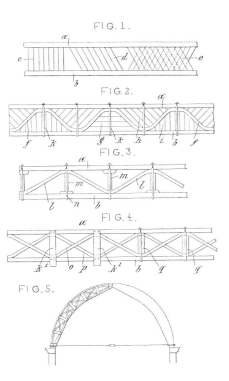

Insgesamt muß man feststellen, daß die Art der Sägeschnittführung trotz geringen Verschnittes je nach Länge relativ aufwendig in der Herstellung ist. Der Übergang zum Brettschichtträger mit mehreren Schichten ließ den parabelförmig verleimten Träger wieder in Vergessenheit geraten.

Im Jahr 1906 erwarb Otto Hetzer das Patent DRP No. 197773 für gebogene, verleimte Brettschichtträger aus zwei und mehr Lamellen, die auch unter Feuchtigkeit unlöslich miteinander verbunden sind. Damit ist Hetzer die Weiterentwicklung des Emy'schen Bohlenbinders gelungen, welche es ermöglichte, das Tragwerk der idealen Stützlinie weitestgehend anzupassen und stützenfrei große Räume zu überspannen und zugleich eine größtmögliche Biegesteifigkeit zu erzielen.

Ihre Verwendung wird für gebogene Sparrendächer empfohlen. Obwohl hier nicht ausdrücklich die Verwendung von Lamellen verschiedener Festigkeiten erwähnt wird, ermöglicht dieser Träger eine weitere Querschnittsoptimierung. So beschreibt Urban[38] die entsprechend ihrer Belastung angepaßte Verwendung des härteren Kernholzes am Rande und des weicheren Splintholzes im mittleren Bereich. Diese Vorstellung widerspricht allerdings heutigen Erkenntnissen, welche die Festigkeit mehr von der Größe der Jahresringe abhängig macht und nicht von der Unterscheidung in Kern- und Splintholz.

Abgeschlossen wird die Reihe der Hetzer'schen Patente mit dem DRP No. 225687 vom 21. September 1907 für einen Fachwerkträger aus Holz, bei dem die Diagonalen aus einem zickzackförmigen Holzstab bestehen. Besonders bei der Konstruktion von Bogentragwerken größerer Spannweite stellt die geringere Steifigkeit der Vollholzquerschnitte immer ein Problem dar, was bei wechselnden Lasten zu hoher Biegebeanspruchung und damit zu unerwünschter Schwingungsanfälligkeit führt.

Ziel war es daher, Teile der Stegkonstruktion in Richtung der Hauptspannungstrajektorien als Druck- oder Zugstreben auszubilden. Eine hohe Schubbeanspruchung der Vollholzquerschnitte parallel zur Holzfaser und zur Leimfuge konnte dadurch umgangen werden. Allerdings scheint dieser Fachwerkträger nicht zur praktischen Anwendung gelangt zu sein.

Zur Verbreitung dieser Patente in anderen europäischen Ländern wie der Schweiz, Holland, Schweden und Italien wurden Lizenzen vergeben.[39] Als maßgebende Wegbereiter des Holzleimbaus sind daher

In the end it must be admitted that just the one saw-cut along the length was still a relatively expensive production technique. And the transition to the laminated timber beam with several laminations brought about the demise of parabolic glued beams.

In 1906 Otto Hetzer was granted patent DRP No. 197773 for curved, glued laminated beams consisting of two and more laminations which are permanently joined together, even remaining connected when subjected to moisture. Thus Hetzer had taken the Emy composite member to its logical conclusion, enabling the structure to be closely matched to the ideal line of pressure, spanning large areas without intermediate columns and at the same time obtaining the highest possible bending strength.

It was recommended for curved couple roofs. Although the use of laminations with various strengths is not expressly mentioned here, this beam rendered possible a further optimization of the cross-section. Urban[38] proposed using the harder heartwood at the edges and the softer sapwood in the middle to match the stresses. However, this notion contradicts modern thinking, which says that the strength is more dependent on the size of the annual rings and not the distinction between heartwood and sapwood.

Hetzer's series of patents was concluded with DRP No. 225687 dated 21 September 1907. This dealt with a timber truss in which the diagonals consisted of zigzag-shaped members. The low stiffness of solid timber sections is always a problem when constructing arch structures with larger spans. With alternating loads this leads to high bending stresses and hence to a vulnerability to vibrations.

Therefore, the aim was to construct parts of the web as struts or ties in the direction of the main stress trajectories. This avoided the problem of high shear stress parallel to the grain and the glue joint in solid timber sections. However, this timber truss does not seem to have been used for any practical applications.

Licences were granted in order to market these patents in other European countries such as Switzerland, the Netherlands, Sweden, and Italy[39] Therefore, it should not be forgotten that, besides Otto Hetzer, the decisive pioneers of glued laminated timber are the engineers Terner and Chopard in Zürich, the Töreboda Limträ company in Sweden and

neben Otto Hetzer das Ingenieurbüro Terner und Chopard in Zürich, die Firma Töreboda Limträ in Schweden und die Firma Nemaho in Doetinchem, Holland, zu nennen.[40] Ab 1934 verwendete in den Vereinigten Staaten die Firma Unit Structures in Peshtigo, Wisconsin, die von Hetzer entwickelte Technologie.[41]

Die Entwicklung in der Schweiz

In der Schweiz verbreitete sich der Holzleimbau besonders durch das Wirken des Ingenieurbüros Terner und Chopard in Zürich, welches die Hetzer-Patente 1909 nach eigenen Versuchen erwarb.

Bernhard Terner wurde am 19. Juli 1875 in Dorohoy (Rumänien) geboren. Von 1897 bis 1902 studierte er an der ETH in Zürich. Im Jahr 1909 gründete Bernhard Terner mit seinem ehemaligen Assistenten beim Bau der Wendelsteinbahn, Charles Chopard, das Ingenieurbüro Terner & Chopard in Zürich. Charles Chopard wurde am 30. August 1879 in Moutier im Berner Jura geboren und absolvierte ebenfalls in Zürich sein Studium.

Neben Stahlbetonbauten stellte der Holzleimbau einen Schwerpunkt ihrer Arbeiten dar. Es entstand eine Vielzahl an Gebäuden und Hallen, wie zum Beispiel die Reithalle in St. Moritz, die Kuppeln der Universität Zürich und diverse Ausstellungs- und Veranstaltungshallen. Die Zusammenarbeit der Ingenieure Terner und Chopard endete 1933. Charles Chopard leitete das Büro bis zu seinem Tod am 16. November 1954.[42]

Bernhard Terners berufliche Tätigkeit verlagerte sich ab 1935 zusammen mit seinem Sohn Leopold nach Israel, wo sie die Firma B. & L. Terner, Ingenieure, Haifa gründeten. Am 23. September 1960 verstarb Bernhard Terner in Zürich.[43]

Die Entwicklung in Skandinavien

In Dänemark baute die in Kopenhagen ansässige Firma H. J. Kornerup-Koch seit 1914 Holzleimkonstruktionen in Lizenz. 1929 entstand in Kopenhagen eine Straßenbrücke in dieser Bauweise.[44]

Die Verbreitung in Norwegen und Schweden erfolgte mit Übernahme der Patentrechte durch den Ingenieur Guttorm N. Brekke (1885-1980), der diese für 60.000 Norwegische Kronen erwarb. Am 2. März 1918 wurde die Firma „A/S Trækonstruktioner" gegründet, welche eine Fabrik in Mysen in der Nähe von Kristiana in Norwegen aufbaute,[45] die bis 1924 Holzleimträger produzierte. Anstoß für diese Entwicklung war der Stahlmangel während des Ersten Weltkriegs.

the Nemaho company in Doetinchem, Netherlands.[40] From 1934 onwards the Unit Structures company in Peshtigo, Wisconsin, USA, also employed the technology developed by Hetzer.[41]

Developments in Switzerland

Engineering consultants Terner & Chopard in Zürich were particularly involved in making glulam popular in Switzerland. They purchased the Hetzer patents in 1909 following a number of their own trials.

Bernhard Terner was born on 19 July 1875 in Dorohoy, Romania. From 1897 to 1902 he studied at the ETH in Zürich and in 1909 founded the consultancy Terner & Chopard in Zürich together with Charles Chopard, his former assistant on the building of the Wendelstein railway. Charles Chopard was born on 30 August 1879 in Moutier in the Berner Jura and had also studied in Zürich.

Reinforced concrete and glued laminated timber represented two important aspects of their work. They were involved in many projects, e.g. the riding arena at St Moritz, the domes of Zürich university and various halls for exhibitions and other events. The collaboration between Terner and Chopard ended in 1933. But Charles Chopard continued to manage the practice until his death on 16 November 1954.[42]

Bernhard Terner's career took him to Israel in 1935, where together with his son, Leopold, he founded B. & L. Terner, Consulting Engineers, in Haifa. Bernhard Terner died in Zürich on 23 September 1960.[43]

Developments in Scandinavia

In Denmark the Copenhagen-based company H. J. Kornerup-Koch had been building glulam structures under licence since 1914. In 1929 a road bridge in Copenhagen was constructed using this method.[44]

This form of construction was spread throughout Norway and Sweden by the engineer Guttorm N. Brekke (1885-1980), who purchased the patent rights for the sum of NKr 60 000. A/S Trækonstruktioner was founded on 2 March 1918 and a factory was erected in Mysen near Kristiana, Norway;[45] glulam beams were fabricated here until 1924. The impetus for these developments was the shortage of steel during World War I.

Anzeige der Firma Kornerup-Koch, Kopenhagen.
Advertisement for Kornerup-Koch, Copenhagen.

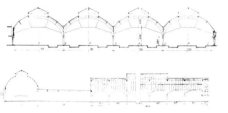

Bahnhof, Malmö. Quer- und Längsschnitt.
Malmö station, sections.

Bereits 1919 gründete Brekke ebenfalls die „AG Trägkonstruktion" in Töreboda, Schweden. Aufgrund ihrer zentralen Lage lieferte die Firma sowohl nach Norwegen als auch nach Schweden.

In Malmö entstanden 1922 zum Beispiel vier Bahnsteighallen, die mittels einer Querbahnsteighalle aus kreisförmigen Holzleimbindern verbunden waren. 1925 entstand der Zentralbahnhof in Stockholm in gleicher Bauweise.[46]

Die Entwicklung in Holland

Bereits 1920 entstand bei dem Bau einer Fabrikhalle für Elektromotoren in Doetinchem der erste Kontakt zwischen der Otto Hetzer AG und dem Holzhändler G.J. Horsting. Diese Verbindung führte zur Gründung der Firma Nederlandsche Maatschappij voor Houtconstructies (Nemaho). Zum Aufbau des Betriebes wechselten die Mitarbeiter Ebert, Koch und Schmidt aus Weimar zur Firma Nemaho.[47] In den ersten Jahren war die Verbindung noch so eng, daß zum Beispiel 1922 die Binder der Ausstellungshalle für die R.A.I. in Amsterdam in Weimar hergestellt wurden.

In den dreißiger Jahren exportierte die Firma Nemaho große Hallen nach Surinam, den Antillen und Kolumbien, einen Flugzeughangar nach Curaçao und eine Kunstdüngerfabrik nach Durban in Südafrika.

Die Entwicklung in Nordamerika

Seit 1920 wurde die europäische Entwicklung des Holzleimbaus in Nordamerika bekannt und untersucht. So sandte das U.S. Department of Agriculture Forest Products Laboratory (USDAFPL) in Madison, Wisconsin einen Beobachter in die Schweiz, um sich ein eigenes Urteil über diese Bauweise zu verschaffen. Obwohl der Bericht M. Knights zu einem positiven Ergebnis kam, entschloß man sich, die Entwicklung des Holzleimbaus nicht weiter zu verfolgen.[48]

So wurde die Entwicklung erst 1934 durch Max Hanisch sen. vorangetrieben. Max Hanisch wurde am 14. Mai 1882 in Vangrin, Pommern geboren und studierte Architektur und Bauingenieurwesen an der königlichen Baugewerksschule in Deutsch-Krone und Strelitz, Mecklenburg. Bereits 1906 lernte er die Hetzer'sche Bauweise in Weimar kennen. Im Jahr 1923 wanderte er in die USA aus.

Die erste Verwendung von Holzleimbindern geschah 1934 beim Bau der Aula des Gymnasiums in Peshtigo, Wisconsin. Die Produktion erfolgte in Zusam-

Brekke also founded AG Trägkonstruktion in 1919 in Töreboda, Sweden. Owing to its central location, the company supplied materials for projects in Norway as well as Sweden.

The four trainsheds in Malmö (1922), linked by a concourse with a roof supported on circular glulam arches, and Stockholm central station (1925), which employed a similar construction, are just two examples.[46]

Developments in the Netherlands

The first contact between Otto Hetzer AG and the timber importer G. J. Horsting had been back in 1920 during the construction of a factory for electric motors in Doetinchem. This connection led to the founding of Nederlandsche Maatschappij voor Houtconstructies (Nemaho). To assist in establishing the company, three employees (Ebert, Koch and Schmidt) from Weimar were seconded to Nemaho.[47] In the early years the contact was still so close that, for example, in 1922 the beams for the exhibition hall for the R.A.I. in Amsterdam were manufactured in Weimar.

In the 1930s Nemaho exported large halls to Suriname, the Antilles and Colombia, an aircraft hangar to Curaçao and a fertilizer factory to Durban, South Africa.

Developments in North America

The European developments in glued laminated timber had been known and investigated in North America since 1920. The US Department of Agriculture Forest Products Laboratory (USDAFPL) in Madison, Wisconsin, sent an observer to Switzerland in order to gain first-hand experience of this form of construction. Although M. Knight's report reached a positive conclusion, a decision was made to abandon any further experiments with glued laminated timber.[48]

So it was not until 1934 that developments got underway again with the work of Max Hanisch sen. Max Hanisch was born on 14 May 1882 in Vangrin, Pomerania, and studied architecture and structural engineering at the Royal School of Building in Deutsch-Krone and Strelitz, Mecklenburg. His first experience of the Hetzer technique was in 1906 in Weimar. He emigrated to the USA in 1923.

The first use of glulam beams was in 1934 for a school assembly hall in Peshtigo, Wisconsin. Product-

menarbeit mit der Thompson Boat Manufacturing Company in Peshtigo. Durch die Herstellung von Holzleimbauten konnten die saisonalen Schwankungen im Bootsbau wirtschaftlich ausgeglichen werden. Aus dieser Zusammenarbeit entstand der erste Holzleimbaubetrieb in Nordamerika, die Unit Structures Inc., welche von Peter Thompson und Max Hanisch geleitet wurde.[49]

Die für die Prüfung von Bauvorhaben verantwortliche Wisconsin Industrial Commission forderte aufgrund der geringen Erfahrungen mit verleimten Bauteilen die Verwendung zusätzlicher mechanischer Verbindungsmittel wie Schrauben und Metallbügel. Dies veranlaßte die Unit Structures zu genaueren Untersuchungen, welche sie durch die USDAFPL vornehmen ließ. Die von der Unit Structures hergestellten Binder wurden in einer Probehalle verwendet und längeren Belastungsversuchen unterzogen. Aufgrund größerer Wirtschaftlichkeit entschied man sich für die Verwendung von Rechteckquerschnitten. Ob der positiven Ergebnisse der Bauweise[50] entstanden in den darauffolgenden Jahren viele Kirchendächer, Schulturnhallen, Fabrik- und Veranstaltungshallen.

ion was in collaboration with the Thompson Boat Manufacturing Company in Peshtigo. The manufacture of glulam structures enabled the company to compensate for the seasonal fluctuations in boat-building. This cooperation led to the formation of the first glulam company in North America – Unit Structures, Inc., managed by Peter Thompson and Max Hanisch.[49]

Responsible for the checking of construction projects was Wisconsin Industrial Commission, but as the Commission had little experience of glued building components, it called for additional mechanical fasteners such as bolts and metal straps. This induced Unit Structures to sponsor more precise studies, which were carried out by USDAFPL. The beams fabricated by Unit Structures were used in a test structure and subjected to long-term loading tests. Rectangular sections were favoured owing to the better economy. The positive results of this form of construction[50] led to many church roofs, school gymnasiums, factory and other shed-type structures being erected in the following years.

Vorige Doppelseite **Unit Structures, Versuchsgebäude für die USDAFPL, Madison, Wisconsin, 1934-1935.**
Previous double page US Department of Agriculture Forest Products Laboratory, test building, 1934-1935.

Mit dem Kriegseintritt Amerikas wurden ab 1941 militärisch genutzte Gebäude wie der Flugzeughangar in Fargo, North Dakota, für die St. Paul's Nordwest Airlines gebaut. Dieser stellte mit 46,7 m Spannweite die damals größte Halle dieser Art dar. 1942 folgten in St. Paul zwei Flugzeughangars mit 52,6 m Spannweite.

Seit 1970 firmiert der Betrieb der Unit Structures unter dem Namen Sentinel Structures und produziert noch heute Dach- und Hallentragwerke wie auch Brücken und gebogene Spanten in Holzleimbauweise für den Schiffsbau.

Obwohl die Produktion von Holzleimbindern erst spät in Nordamerika einsetzte, verbreitete sie sich rasch durch verschiedene neue Firmengründungen. 1938 begann die Rock Island Lumber Company in Blue Earth, Minnesota, mit ihrer Produktion. Im Juni 1939 nahm die Rilco Laminated Products, Inc. die Herstellung von Holzleimträgern in der neuen Fabrik in Albert Lea, Minnesota auf, wo Scheunendächer in großer Anzahl vorfabriziert wurden. Der Betrieb bestand bis zu Beginn der sechziger Jahre.

America's entry into the war in 1941 saw the construction of military buildings such as the aircraft hangar in Fargo, North Dakota, for St Paul's Northwest Airlines. With a span of 46.7 m this was at the time the largest single-storey shed of its kind. In 1942 two further hangars were built in St Paul, each with a span of 52.6 m. Since 1970 the company has operated under the name of Sentinel Structures and today still produces roof and shed-type structures as well as bridges and curved glulam ribs for the shipbuilding industry.

Although the production of glulam beams started late in North America, the technique spread rapidly due to various new company start-ups. The Rock Island Lumber Company in Blue Earth, Minnesota, began their production in 1938. In June 1939 Rilco Laminated Products, Inc. started fabricating glulam beams in a new factory in Albert Lea, Minnesota, where barn roofs were prefabricated in great numbers. This company existed until the start of the 1960s.

Hetzer AG, Tragwerksübersicht
a gerader Dreigelenkbinder mit Zugband
b gebogener Zweigelenkbinder mit Zugband
c Dreigelenkbogen mit Satteldach
d Dreigelenkrahmen
e abgewinkelter Dreigelenkbinder mit angehobenem Zugband und Satteldach
f abgewinkelter Dreigelenkbinder mit angehobenem Zugband
g Dreigelenkbogen mit runder Dachhaut
h Dreigelenkspitzbogen

Hetzer AG, catalogue of loadbearing structures.
a straight three-pin frame with collar
b curved two-pin frame with collar
c three-pin arch with pitched roof
d three-pin frame
e cranked three-pin frame with raised collar and pitched roof
f cranked three-pin frame with raised collar
g three-pin arch with curved roof covering
h three-pin pointed arch

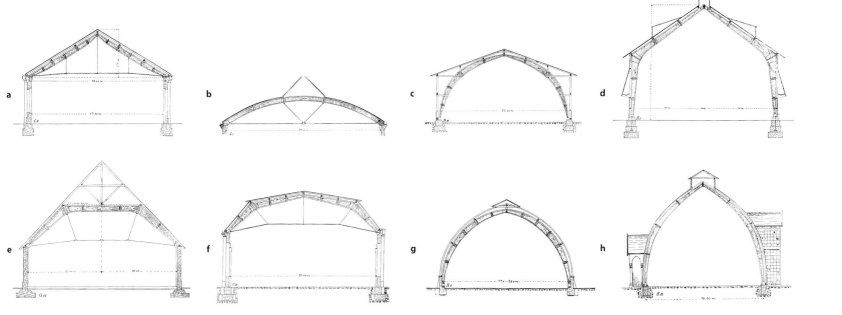

Verarbeitungstechnologie
Production technology

Querschnittsform und Material

Mit der Möglichkeit des lamellierten Querschnittes ergibt sich die Möglichkeit verschiedener Querschnittsformen und Lamellendicken. Gemäß seiner Belastung im Querschnitt unter einer Biegebeanspruchung werden die äußeren Lamellen maximal beansprucht und sollten daher eine höhere Festigkeit besitzen. Die Verwendung von Buchenholz-Lamellen ist schon von Hetzer bekannt, wobei auch von ihm in der Regel aus Kostengründen Fichtenholzlamellen benutzt wurden.

Der in der Anfangszeit des Holzleimbaus vielfach verwendete doppel-T-förmige Querschnitt wurde entsprechend seiner Belastung wie im Stahlbau ausgebildet. Ober- und Untergurte bestanden in der Regel aus drei bis vier Lamellen mit 20 cm Breite. Der Stegbereich hatte eine Breite von etwa 6 cm. Die Dicke der Lamellen variierte abhängig vom Krümmungsradius zwischen 2 und 4 cm. Später setzte sich immer mehr der Rechteckquerschnitt durch, welcher in der Herstellung einfacher zu verleimen war.

Mit dem Verleimen von Holzlamellen stellte sich von Anfang an das Problem der Stoßausbildung. Bei den durch die Otto Hetzer AG ausgeführten Bauten wurde dieses Problem durch bauteillange Lamellen bis zu 15 m in den Ober- und Untergurten umgangen, so daß nur in den gering belasteten Stegbereichen Vollstöße erforderlich waren. Diese Vollstöße können aber im besten Fall nur als druckkraftschlüssig bezeichnet werden. Die biegesteifen Bauteilstöße wurden durch seitlich mittels Schrauben oder Bolzen befestigte Platten erzielt.

Erst in der DIN 1052 vom August 1943 wird unter § 18.1 die Stoßausbildung einzelner Lamellen als Schäftung mit Neigungsverhältnis 1:5 bis 1:10 für zweckmäßig empfohlen. Sie muß auch heute noch als wirksamste Verbindung angesehen werden. Aufgrund der aufwendigeren Herstellung von Schäftungen kam es zur Weiterentwicklung als Keilverzinkung, die 1959 in der DIN 68140 festgelegt wurde. Bereits 1942 wurde die erste Schaftzinkenfräsmaschine von der Firma Knorrnagel in Hannover gebaut.[51] Heute verläuft das Herstellen und Verleimen von Keilzinkenstößen vollautomatisch.

Die Tabelle gibt einen Überblick über die zulässigen Spannungen von Nadelholz von 1910 bis zur heute gültigen Vorschrift. Es ist fast überraschend, wie wenig sich die einzelnen Normen voneinander unterscheiden. Eine Steigerung der zulässigen Spannungen konnte im

Cross-section and material

The option of a laminated section brings with it the possibility of various profiles and lamination thicknesses. Subjecting a section to bending causes maximum stresses in the outer laminations and so these should be of a higher strength. The use of beechwood laminations was already known from Hetzer's work, although he generally employed laminations of spruce for reasons of cost.

The concept behind the I-section so popular in the early years of glued laminated timber construction was similar to that of steel I-sections. Top and bottom flanges normally comprised three or four laminations 200 mm wide and the web section was about 60 mm thick. The thickness of the laminations varied between 20 and 40 mm depending on the radius of curvature. Later, the rectangular section, which was easier to fabricate, came to dominate the scene.

The design of splices proved a problem right from the start of gluing together timber laminations. In the structures of Otto Hetzer AG this problem was overcome by using laminations the full length of the member – up to 15 m – in the top and bottom flanges, so that splices were only necessary in the lowly stressed web. At best though, these joints can only be regarded as abutting surfaces capable of transferring compression. Rigid joints could only be achieved by attaching splice plates with mechanical fasteners.

The first recommendations on joining individual laminations appeared with the publication of DIN 1052 in August 1943 (scarf joints with a slope ratio of 1:5 to 1:10 – section 18.1). This must still be regarded today as the most effective form of splice joint. But owing to the cost of fabricating scarf joints, further work was undertaken and this led to the appearance of the finger joint, defined in DIN 68140 in 1959. However, the first finger-joint cutting machine had been built by the Knorrnagel company in Hannover in 1942.[51] Today, the cutting and gluing of finger joints is a fully automatic process.

The table shows the development in permissible stresses for coniferous wood from the 1910 provisions right up to current standards. It is something of a surprise to discover just how little difference there is between the individual standards. The first improvement in permissible stresses was possible in 1943 with the introduction of timber grades in DIN 1052.

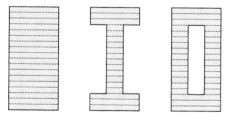

Querschnittsformen: links Vollprofil, mitte Doppel-T-Profil, rechts Kastenprofil.
Possible cross-sections; left: solid; centre: I-section; right: box.

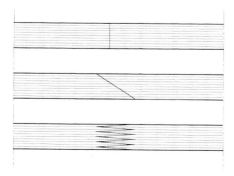

Bauteilstöße: oben Vollstoß, mitte Schäftung, unten Keilzinkenstoß.
Splice joints; top: butt joint; centre: scarf joint; bottom: finger point.

ersten Schritt 1943 in der DIN 1052 durch die Einführung von Holzgüteklassen erreicht werden. Im Verhältnis zur Güteklasse II konnten so in der HGKL I 30% höhere Biegespannungen zugelassen werden. Eine weitere leichte Steigerung erzielte dann die Homogenisierung des Holzes in Verwendung als Brettschichtholz mit HGKL I. Die seit 1996 übliche Einteilung in Sortierklassen brachte eine weitere Steigerung für maschinensortierte Vollhölzer mit Festigkeiten bis zu 18 N/mm^2 (BSH 18).

Diese weitere Homogenisierung des Holzes in Form von Furnierschichtholz oder Furnierstreifenholz führte zu einer Steigerung der zulässigen Biegespannung bis zu 100% im Vergleich zu den Bestimmungen von 1910. Die Steigerung wird durch eine aufwendigere Herstellung ermöglicht, welche einen höheren Leimanteil und Energieaufwand notwendig macht. Diesen gilt es ökologisch im Vergleich zu bewerten.

Bei druck- und biegebeanspruchten Bauteilen führen die möglichen schlankeren Bauteile zu einer höheren Knick- oder Kippbeanspruchung, so daß es nicht zu einer 50%igen Materialersparnis im Bauwerk kommt.

So the bending stresses of a grade I member were allowed to be 30% higher than those of a grade II member. A further small improvement came with the homogenization of the wood through its use as glued laminated timber of grade I. The system of grades in use since 1996 has brought further increases for machine-graded solid timber, which can now reach strengths of 18 N/mm^2 (BSH 18). The further homogenization of the wood in the form of laminated veneer lumber (LVL) or parallel strand lumber (PSL) led to an increase in the permissible bending stress of up to 100% in comparison to the stipulations of 1910. These improvements are made possible by more elaborate production methods which require more adhesive and higher energy. This development should be considered and compared in terms of the ecological impact. With members subjected to compression and bending, the possibility of more slender components leads to higher buckling or overturning stresses, which means that a 50% saving in the material of a structure is not realized.

Übersicht der zulässigen Festigkeiten von Nadelholz gemäß den jeweiligen Zulassungen [N/mm2].
Permissible strengths of coniferous timber according to the respective standards [N/mm2].

	Bestimmungen	SIA	DIN 1052	DIN 1052 / 1943			DIN 1052 / 1988					DIN 1052 / T1 / A1 1996								
	v. 10.01.1910	164/1926	1933																	
		Schweiz		GK III	GK II	GK I	GK III	GKII	GK I	BSH GK II	BSH GK I	S7/MS 7	S10/MS10	S13	MS13	MS 17	BS11	BS 14	BS 16	BS 18
Biegung zul σ$_B$	10-12.	10	10 (9)	7(7,5)	10(11)	13(14)	7	10	13	11	14	7	10	13	15	17	11	14	16	18
Zug II FA zul σ$_{zI}$	10-12.	10	9	0	8,5	10,5	0	8,5	10,5	8,5	10,5	0	7	9	10	12	8,5	10,5	11	13
Zug ⊥ FA zul σ$_{z⊥}$							0	0,05	0,05	0,2	0,2	0	0,05	0,05	0,05	0,05	0,2	0,2	0,2	0,2
Druck II Fa zul σ$_{DII}$	6-8.	7,5	8	6	8,5	11	6	8,5	11	8,5	11	6	8,5	11	11	12	8,5	11	11,5	13
Druck ⊥ Fa zul σ$_{D⊥}$		1,5	2 (3)	2 (2,5)	2 (2,5)	2 (2,5)	2 (2,5)	2 (2,5)	2 (2,5)	2,5 (3)	2,5 (3)	2 (2,5)	2 (2,5)	2 (2,5)	2,5 (3)	2,5 (3)	2,5 (3)	2,5 (3)	2,5 (3)	2,5 (3)
Abscheren zul τ$_a$	1-1,5	1,2	1,2	0,9	0,9	0,9	0,9	0,9	0,9	0,9	0,9	0,9	0,9	0,9	1	1	0,9	0,9	1	1
Schub aus Q zul t$_a$	6-7.						0,9	0,9	0,9	1,2	1,2	0,9	0,9	0,9	1	1	1,2	1,2	1,3	1,5
Torsion zul t$_T$							0	1	1	1,6	1,6	0	1	1	1	1	1,6	1,6	1,6	1,6
	Bestimmungen	SIA	DIN 1052	DIN 1052 / 1943			DIN 1052 / 1988					DIN 1052 / T1 / A1 1996								
	v. 10.01.1910	164/1926	1933																	
Elastizitätsmodul		Schweiz		GK III	GK II	GK I	GK III	GKII	GK I	BSH GK II	BSH GK I	S7/MS 7	S10/MS10	S13	MS13	MS 17	BS11	BS 14	BS 16	BS 18
E$_B$		9000			10000			10000				8000	10000	10500	11500	12500	11000	11000	12000	13000
E$_{zI}$		11000	10000		1000			10000			11000	8000	10000	10500	11500	12500	11000	12000	13000	14000
E$_{DII}$	10000	11000																		
E$_{D⊥}$					300			300				250	300	350	350	400	350	400	400	450
G								500				500	500	500	550	600	550	600	650	700

Leime

Im folgenden soll eine Auswahl an Leimen vorgestellt werden, welche für den Holzleimbau relevant sind. Die Voraussetzung für die Verleimung zweier Hölzer, welche als ein gemeinsamer Querschnitt tragen sollen, ist die höhere Belastbarkeit der Leimfuge gegenüber den angrenzenden Holzquerschnitten. Die Kraftübertragung erfolgt durch die mechanische Verankerung, durch Adhäsion zwischen Holz und Leim und durch Kohäsion im Leim selbst. Als Leime im Holzbau dienen hochmolekulare, organische Stoffe, welche mit Dispersionsmitteln wie Wasser oder organischen Lösungsmitteln verdünnt werden.

Der Abbindevorgang erfolgt unter Abgabe dieser Dispersionsmittel bei gleichzeitiger Abkühlung, durch Gerinnung oder chemische Reaktion je nach den betreffenden Leimstoffen. Dieser Übergang vom Sol- zum Gelzustand ist mechanisch sehr anfällig und ohne erneute Verflüssigung irreversibel. Die Aufnahme des Dispersionsmittels, im allgemeinen Wasser, erfolgt hauptsächlich durch das Holz, welches daher mit geringer Eigenfeuchte verarbeitet werden muß (9–12%). Aus diesem Grund sind solche Leime auch nicht für die Verarbeitung von Furnieren (1 mm) geeignet. Der Anteil des Dispersionsmittels kann auch durch Verdunstung bei offener Leimfuge (Wartezeit 15–30 Min) reduziert werden.

Die Entwicklung der Leime steht im engen Zusammenhang mit ihrer Verwendung. So stellte die Verwendung von Leimen im Hochbau oder auch im Flugzeugbau wesentlich höhere Ansprüche in bezug auf Feuchtigkeitsbeständigkeit, Festigkeit und Dauerfestigkeit. Im folgenden sollen nur die im Holzleimbau am häufigsten angewandten Leime näher beschrieben werden.

Kasein-Leime

Kasein-Leime gehören mit zu den ältesten Leimen. So gibt es ein um 1400 in Mitteldeutschland verfaßtes Leimbüchlein mit Rezepten, welches dem späteren deutschen Reichspatent sehr nahe kommt:

„Leym sieden: Wyltu leym machen, der in dem waßßer helth, nym ungeleschten kalg 1 teyl und rynderkeße 2 teyl, reyp den und lege yn in warm waßßer, daß die feuchtickeyt daraus gehet und reyb das off eynem steyne undereynander oder stos es in eynem merßßel (Mörser) und leyme den steyn und steyn, holcz oder steyne czußammen oder holcz und holcz; her (er) helt sich".[52]

Adhesives

The following section presents a selection of adhesives which are relevant for glued laminated timber construction. The prerequisite for gluing together two pieces of wood which are to carry loads as a composite section is that the glue joint should be stronger than the adjoining timber. The transfer of forces takes place through the mechanical anchorage, the adhesion between the wood and the adhesive, and the cohesion within the adhesive itself. Adhesives for timber make use of high-molecular, organic substances which are diluted with dispersing agents like water or organic solvents.

The setting process involves the release of the dispersing agent with simultaneous cooling, through coagulation or a chemical reaction, depending on the type of adhesive used. This transition from the sol to the gel state is very vulnerable in mechanical terms and irreversible without renewed liquefaction. The dispersing agent, generally water, is mainly absorbed by the wood, which therefore has to be processed with a low moisture content (9-12%). For this reason, such adhesives are not suitable for the processing of veneers (1 mm). The proportion of dispersing agent can also be reduced by encouraging evaporation from an open joint (waiting time 15-30 min).

The development of adhesives is closely tied to their applications. For instance, the use of adhesives in the building industry – like in the aircraft industry – presented considerably higher demands in terms of moisture resistance, strength and durability. Only those adhesives commonly used in laminated timber construction are described in the following.

Casein glues

Casein glues are among the oldest types of adhesive. For example, a booklet containing recipes for glues – which come very close to those of German patent of several centuries later– was written around 1400 in Germany:

"Boiling of glue: If you wish to make a glue that withstands water, take 1 part undissolved lime and 2 parts cow's milk cheese, grate them and lay them in warm water so that the moisture is removed, and rub this on a stone or pound it in a mortar and glue the stone and stone, wood or stone together or wood and wood; it will hold."[52]

Kasein ist in der Kuhmilch enthalten und wird durch Säuerung oder Zugabe von Lab, einem Sekret der Magenschleimhaut von Rindern, gewonnen. Ähnlich wie Glutin ist Kasein eine hochmolekulare Eiweiß-Phosphor-Verbindung, welche getrocknet lagerfähig wird.

Mit gelöschtem oder gebranntem Kalk vermischt, wird Kasein wasserlöslich, wobei sich unter Wärmeentwicklung die chemische Umwandlung in Kalziumkasenit vollzieht. Der Leim geht dann je nach Zusammensetzung langsam in den Gel-Zustand über und ist nicht mehr wasserlöslich. Während dieser Zeit muß das vorhandene Wasser in das Holz diffundieren, weshalb eine vorherige Wartezeit bei offener Leimfuge von 5–10 Minuten günstig ist, ohne daß sich eine Haut bildet.

Folgende Schubfestigkeiten können erwartet werden:
Buche–Buche t = 1,00–1,25 KN/cm^2
Kiefer–Kiefer t = 0,65–0,75 KN/cm^2

Das Reichspatent (DRP No. 60156) wurde Rudolf Piek für die Zugabe von Wasserglas (Kalzium- oder Natriumsilikat) erteilt, die zu einer Verzögerung der Sol-Gel-Umwandlung führt. Der Abbindeprozeß wird dann durch Druck und Hitze ausgelöst.

Die Feuchtigkeitsbeständigkeit ist gering einzuschätzen. Obwohl die erneute Trockenfestigkeit des Leimes fast den ursprünglichen Festigkeiten entspricht, kommt es oft zu einem Öffnen der Fugen infolge Eigenspannungen, da der erforderliche Anpreßdruck fehlt.

Harnstoff-Formaldehyd-Kunstharzleime

Seinen Namen hat Harnstoff durch die Tatsache, daß er zu geringen Mengen auch im tierischen und menschlichen Harn vorkommt. Auf synthetischem Wege wird Harnstoff unter Druck aus Ammoniak und Kohlensäure hergestellt. Dieser Harnstoff wird dann in 40%iger wässriger Formaldehydlösung bei Zugabe von Katalysatoren erhitzt, wodurch der Kondensationsprozeß ausgelöst wird. Bei der Verarbeitung wird die vorher unterbrochene Kondensation vor der Abbindung durch einen Härter – z.B. Salze wie Ammoniumchlorid – wieder angestoßen. Diese Säurehärtung stellt den chemischen Teil der Reaktion dar, währenddessen sich der physikalische Teil durch die Entfernung des Lösungsmittels vollzieht – die Gelbildung.

Je nach Verarbeitungsverfahren wird der Härter untergemischt (für Kalt- und Heißhärtung) oder als Vorstreichverfahren aufgebracht (Kalthärter).

Die Spannzeit der Bauteile ist temperaturabhängig, wobei die Temperatur aber nicht unter 10°C fallen darf.

Casein is a constituent of cow's milk and is obtained by ripening or by adding rennet, a secretion of the gastric mucosa of cattle. Like gluten, casein is a high-molecular protein-phosphorus compound which, when dried, can be stored. Mixed with hydrated or burnt lime, casein becomes soluble in water, with the full chemical transformation to calcium salt taking place with the evolution of heat. The glue then slowly changes to the gel state, depending on its mixture, and is no longer water-soluble. During this time, the water present soaks into the wood, which is why an initial waiting time of 5-10 min with an open joint is advantageous, provided that a skin does not form.

The following shear strengths can be expected:
beech-beech t = 1.00-1.25 kN/cm^2
pine-pine   t = 0.65-0.75 kN/cm^2

Patent No. DRP 60156 was granted to Rudolf Piek for the addition of water glass (calcium or sodium silicate), which delays the sol-gel transformation. The setting process is then triggered by pressure and heat. The moisture resistance of such glues is low. Although the regained dry strength of the glue almost reaches the original strength, internal stresses frequently cause an opening of the joint because the contact pressure is inadequate.

Urea-formaldehyde adhesives

Urea owes its name to the fact that small quantities of it appear in human and animal urine. It is produced synthetically from ammonia and carbonic acid under pressure. This urea is then heated in a 40% formaldehyde-water solution by adding catalysts, whereupon the condensation process is triggered. During production the previously interrupted condensation is restarted prior to curing by using a hardener, e.g. a salt like ammonium chloride. This acid hardening represents the chemical part of the reaction, while the physical part is completed by the removal of the solvent – the gel formation.

The hardener is either mixed in (for cold and hot curing) or spread on (cold curing), depending on the process being used.

The clamping time for the components depends on the temperature, which should never be allowed to fall below 10°C. As urea-formaldehyde adhesives have poor gap-filling properties, without additives

Da der Harnstoff-Formaldehyd-Leim nur eine geringe Fugenbeständigkeit hat, ist er ohne Zusätze nur für Furniere geeignet. Für alle anderen Zwecke sind z.B. gehärtete Kunstharze in Pulverform als Zusätze zu verwenden, wofür H. Klemm am 13.12.1936 das DRP 736618 erhielt (Markenname Kaurit WHK, Melocol-Leim). Nach einer Wartezeit bei offener Leimfuge von 5 bis 15 Minuten sind je nach Temperatur und Härter Spannzeiten bis zu 6 Stunden einzuhalten. Die Beständigkeit der Leimfuge bei Feuchtigkeit ist befriedigend.

Phenol-Formaldehyd-Kunstharzleime

Der Hauptrohstoff neben dem Formaldehyd ist das Phenol, auch Karbolsäure genannt, das bei der Destillation des Stein- und Braunkohlenteers anfällt. Besonders das Phenolprodukt Resorzin findet heute eine weite Verbreitung.

Die Phenole werden mit Formaldehyd, Kondensationsmitteln und Lösungsmitteln (Wasser, Azeton) vermischt, wobei die Reaktion durch höhere Temperaturen ausgelöst wird. Als Katalysator dient Natronlauge. Die Kondensation vollzieht sich unter Austritt von Wasser. In diesem sogenannten „Resol"-Zustand ist das Harz noch in Wasser und organischen Lösungen löslich. Die Reaktion wird durch Abkühlung und Stabilisatoren unterbrochen und kann dann nach Auftrag in der Leimfuge, um auszuhärten, durch Hitze wieder angestoßen werden (Resit-Zustand). Beim Kaltverfahren gibt man eine Säure (z.B. Paratoluolsulfonsäure) als Härter hinzu, die im Harz gebunden wird. Freie Säuren können bei zu hoher Dosierung zur Zerstörung des Holzes und der Leimfuge führen. Die Wartezeit bei offener Leimfuge ist entsprechend dem Härteranteil länger als bei anderen Leimen, da sich die Entfernung des Lösungsmittels nur sehr langsam vollzieht.

Die Festigkeit und Beständigkeit gegen Nässe, Hitze und Feuchtigkeit ist höher als bei anderen Leimen und dabei koch-, schimmel-, und pilzbeständig, tropenfest und termitensicher. Durch den Kontakt mit Phenolen kann es im Einzelfall zu Gesundheitsschäden wie Hautekzemen kommen. Die Gefahr bei Resorzin scheint geringer zu sein.

Melamin-Formaldehyd-Kunstharzleime

Melamin wird aus Kalkstickstoff gewonnen, wobei die Zwischenprodukte – Zyanamid und Dizyandiamid – in Ammoniakatmosphäre unter Druck erhitzt werden. Zusammen mit Formaldehyd beginnt er zu kon-

they are only suitable for veneers. All other applications require the addition of, for example, hardened synthetic resins in powder form, for which H. Klemm was granted patent No. DRP 736618 on 13 December 1936 (brand-names: Kaurit WHK, Melocol-Leim). After a waiting time of 5-15 min with an open joint, clamping times of up to 6 h have to be maintained depending on temperature and hardener. The moisture resistance of this type of adhesive joint is satisfactory.

Phenol-formaldehyde adhesives

The main ingredient besides formaldehyde is phenol, also known as carbolic acid, which is obtained from the distillation of coal and lignite tar. The phenol product resorcinol is widely used today. The phenols are mixed with formaldehyde, condensing agents and solvents (water, acetone), with the reaction being triggered by high temperatures. Sodium hydroxide solution serves as a catalyst. The condensation is completed with the discharge of water. In this so-called resol state the resin is still soluble in water and organic solvents. The reaction is interrupted by cooling and by stabilizers and can be restarted, for the curing process, after being applied to the joint by the application of heat (resite state). In the cold process an acid (e.g. p-toluenesulphonic acid) is added as a hardener; this acid bonds with the resin. Unbonded acids resulting from the addition of too much acid can destroy the wood and the glue joint. The waiting time with an open joint is longer than with other adhesives, corresponding to the proportion of hardener, because the solvent is only removed very slowly.

The strength and resistance to water, heat, and moisture is higher than other adhesives and so this glue is boilproof as well as resistant to mould and fungal attack, remains stable under tropical conditions and is resistant to termites. Contact with phenols can cause skin eczemas or other health problems in some instances. The risk with resorcinol seems to be lower.

Melamine-formaldehyde adhesives

Melamine is obtained from calcium cyanamide, with the intermediate products – cyanamide and dicyandiamide – being heated in an ammonia atmosphere under pressure. Together with formaldehyde

densieren und härtet entweder unter Hitze oder mit Säuren als Härtern kalt aus. Die Eigenschaften dieses Leimes sind denen von Phenol-Formaldehyd-Leimen vergleichbar. Sie werden ebenfalls bei stark schwankenden Klimabedingungen eingesetzt. Heute werden im Holzleimbau vor allem Resorzin- und Melamin-Formaldehyd-Leime verwendet.

Epoxid-Harze

Dieser Leim besteht aus Epichlorhydrin und Diphenolen, die miteinander kondensieren. In der Regel sind Epoxid-Harze je nach Ausgangsstoffen kalthärtend. Aufgrund der hohen Fugenbeständigkeit bei hoher Festigkeit eignen sich diese Harze auch besonders für die Verstärkungsmaßnahmen bei Sanierungen wie zum Beispiel das Austauschen von Balkenköpfen und nachträgliches Schließen offener Leimfugen.

it begins to condensate and hardens either upon the application of heat or in a cold process using acids as hardeners. The properties of these adhesives are comparable to those based on phenol-formaldehyde. They are also used under severely fluctuating climatic conditions. Today, resorcinol and melamine-formaldehyde adhesives are the most widely used types in laminated timber construction.

Epoxy resins

This type of adhesive consists of epichlorohydrin and diphenols, which condense with each other. As a rule, epoxy resins are cold curing, depending on the ingredients. Owing to the high gap-filling ability combined with high strength, these resins are also particularly suitable for strengthening measures during refurbishment work, e.g. the replacement of beam ends and subsequent closing of open glue joints.

Sanierung von Holzleimbauten
The refurbishment of glulam structures

Ein wichtiges Thema beim Holzleimbau ist die Sanierung von Schäden, wobei hier nur ein erster Überblick möglich ist.

Bei der Untersuchung eines Schadens muß grundsätzlich zuerst die Ursache erforscht werden. So können äußere Einwirkungen oder Fehler in der statischen Berechnung bei ordnungsgemäß ausgeführten Tragwerken zu Schäden führen. Darüber hinaus gehende Schäden des Holzes durch Schädlingsbefall oder Fäulnis sind wie im Holzbau zu begutachten und die Ursachen zu beseitigen. Bei der Sanierung von Holzleimbauten liegt das Hauptaugenmerk auf dem Zustand der Holzlamellen und deren Verleimung. Selbst bei alten Holzleimbauten lassen sich die Holzlamellen oft nach optischer Klassifizierung in der Sortierklasse S13 (Holzgüteklasse infolge Astigkeit gemäß DIN) einordnen.

Bei einem Versagen der Leimfuge ist zuerst zu prüfen, ob sämtliche Leimfugen in nicht ausreichender Güte hergestellt wurden und damit eine Sanierung einzelner Fugen nur neue Schadstellen nach sich zieht. Bei einer Schädigung aller Leimfugen kommt aus Kostengründen oft nur ein Komplettaustausch in Frage. Im Fall einer einzelnen gestörten Leimfuge ist auch hier zuerst die Ursachenermittlung vorzunehmen. Der Fehler der Verleimung kann im Herstellungsprozeß oder im Nutzungszustand liegen. So können zum Beispiel Feuchtigkeitsschwankungen zu Eigenspannungen im Holz führen, welche durch Querzug zur Faser die Leimfuge versagen lassen. Hiervon sind vor allem die äußeren Bereiche eines Querschnitts betroffen, da hier die Schwankungen größer sind und sich schneller vollziehen, die Verformung durch den inneren Querschnitt aber behindert wird und dadurch Eigenspannungen entstehen. Auch der Knick eines Binders oder eine konzentrierte Lasteinleitung können Querzugspannungen im Querschnitt zur Folge haben, welche zum Aufreißen des Querschnitts führen.

Oberflächige offene Fugen bis 2 cm Tiefe können mit Epoxidharz verspachtelt werden. Bei größeren Tiefen sind die Fugen zu verkleben. Dafür muß ein fugenbeständiges Epoxidharz verwendet werden. Diese Arbeiten müssen bei mindestens 15°C und einer Holzfeuchte von unter 15% ausgeführt werden. Sollten nach einer Sanierung immer noch Querzugspannungen im Tragwerk aufgenommen werden, so müssen außen Furnierschichtholzplatten aufgenagelt und geleimt werden. Aus optischen Gründen sind auch innere eingeleimte Gewindestangen möglich.[53]

One important topic in glued laminated timber construction is the repair of damage. This chapter is only intended to provide an introductory insight.

When examining damage, the cause must always be established first. For example, external influences or errors in the structural analysis might have led to damage in otherwise properly constructed loadbearing structures. Damage to wood caused by insects or rot have to be assessed and the causes eliminated just like with normal timber construction. When refurbishing glulam structures, special attention must be given to the condition of the laminations and their glue joints. Even old glulam structures can often be classified as grade S13 (DIN timber grade for knotty wood) upon visual inspection.

If a glue joint has failed, then the adequacy of all the glue joints must first be questioned in order to avoid successive failures as each individual joint is repaired. Damage to all joints often entails complete replacement for reasons of cost. The first move in assessing damage to a single glue joint must be to determine the cause. The failure of the glue may be due to the production process or the type of use. For example, fluctuations in the moisture level can lead to internal stresses in the wood which, as tension perpendicular to the grain, can cause failure of the glue joint. It is primarily the outer zones of the cross-section which are affected because it is here that the fluctuations are greater and take place more quickly. The outer section wants to deform but is hindered by the inner section and this results in the build-up of internal stresses. A crank in a member or an incoming concentrated load can also lead to transverse tensile stresses within the cross-section which cause the section to tear apart.

Superficial open joints up to 20 mm deep can be filled with epoxy resin. Deeper open joints must be glued and pressure applied until "squeeze-out" of the glue occurs. A gap-filling epoxy resin is essential for this. Such repairs must be carried out at a temperature of a minimum of 15°C and with the moisture content of the wood no higher than 15%. If after refurbishment transverse tension must still be accommodated in the member, then laminated veneer lumber (LVL) panels must be nailed and glued to the outside. If this is ruled out on optical grounds, then threaded bars glued into the member are an alternative.[53]

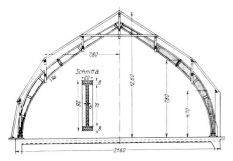

Ing./Ausf.: Hetzer AG, Stallgebäude, Wernesgrün, 1911, spitzer Dreigelenkbogen, Querschnitt, Detail der Gurtsanierung.
Engineers/Contractors: Hetzer AG, barn, Wernesgrün, 1911, pointed three-pin arch, section, detail of flange repair.

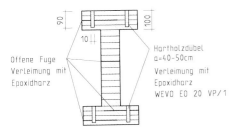

Fäulnisschäden treten häufig im Bereich der Binderfüße auf und müssen in der Regel durch Totalaustausch der betroffenen Binderabschnitte behoben werden. So wurden zum Beispiel einige Binderfüße der Reithalle St. Moritz bereits 1928 durch ausbetonierte U-Profile ersetzt. Diese nicht materialgerechte Sanierung wäre auch in Holz möglich gewesen mit der Gefahr eines erneuten Befalls, da die Binderfüße durch die Balustrade eingepackt und so nicht luftumspült waren.

Eine denkmalgerechte Sanierung eines Holzleimbinders kam bei dem Dachstuhl des Festspielhauses Hellerau zur Ausführung, dessen Dreigelenkbinder 1911 errichtet worden waren. Besonders die Fußpunkte waren durch Pilzbefall stark geschädigt. Bei der Sanierung der Dachkonstruktion im Jahr 2000 wurden die geschädigten Binderfußpunkte ausgewechselt und mit dem neuen Fußpunkt durch Keilzinkenstoß verbunden. Dafür wurden die Dreigelenkbinder abgebaut, getrocknet und dann unter Werkstattbedingungen der Fußpunkt abgetrennt und ersetzt.

Bei älteren Holzleimbauten gilt das Hauptaugenmerk dem Zustand der Leimfugen. Da der damals verwendete Kaseinleim nicht feuchtigkeitsbeständig ist, kommt es bei der Durchfeuchtung der Binder infolge undichter Dachhaut oder hoher Innenraumfeuchte zu offenen Fugen. Durch die Eigenspannungen des Holzes schließen die Fugen sich nicht wieder kraftschlüssig, obwohl die neue Trockenfestigkeit des Kaseinleimes in etwa der ursprünglichen Festigkeit entspricht.

Als Beispiel für eine geglückte Sanierung soll hier auf das Stallgebäude der Firma Gebr. Grünnel von 1911 in Wernesgrün (heute Wernesgrüner Brauerei) näher eingegangen werden. Die horizontalen Auflagerkräfte bei diesem Bau werden von der Geschoßdecke aufgenommen. Nach einem Brand 1918 wurde das Gebäude 1921 ebenfalls durch die Otto Hetzer AG wieder aufgebaut. Hierbei wurde die Gesamthöhe des Binders von 11,55 auf 9,35 m reduziert, wobei die maximale Querschnittshöhe nahezu erhalten blieb. Dafür wurde die Obergurthöhe von 8 cm auf 10 cm erhöht. Besonders ist hierbei auf die durchgehenden, fast 15 m langen Obergurt- und Untergurtlamellen hinzuweisen.

Bei der Sanierung der Scheune wurden in den Ober- und Untergurten offene Leimfugen mit über 50% der Querschnittsbreite festgestellt. Die Leimfugen der Stegbereiche befanden sich in besserem Zustand, da die Feuchtigkeitsschwankungen bei geringerer Dicke zu geringeren Eigenspannungen führen. Diese Schäden

Rot is often a problem at the bases of members and is normally dealt with by replacing the bottom section of the member completely. For example, some of the springings of the arches forming the roof to the riding arena in St Moritz had to be replaced as early as 1928 by concrete-filled steel channel sections. This, in terms of material, inappropriate repair would also have been possible in timber, with the risk of a recurrence of the problem because the springings of the arches are enclosed by the balustrade and therefore not well ventilated.

Refurbishment of a glulam member appropriate to its preserved building status was possible in the roof of the Hellerau Festival Hall, whose three-pin frames were installed in 1911. The bases in particular had been severely damaged by fungal attack. Refurbishment work carried out in 2000 involved replacing the damaged bases with new ones finger-jointed to the remaining sound timber. To do this, the three-pin frames were removed and dried before cutting off the old and attaching the new bases under controlled factory conditions.

In dealing with older glulam structures the condition of the glue joints is the prime concern. As the casein glue used at that time is not water-repellent, leaking roofs or high internal humidity can lead to members becoming saturated and hence to open glue joints. The internal stresses in the wood prevent the joints from closing sufficiently to enable the transfer of forces, although the regained dry strength of the casein glue is roughly equal to its original strength.

One example of a successful refurbishment project is the barn of the Gebr. Grünnel company in Wernesgrün (now Wernesgrüner brewery), built in 1911. The horizontal support reactions in this building are resisted by the floor. After the building burned down in 1918, it was rebuilt in 1921, again by Otto Hetzer AG. The overall height of the frame was reduced from 11.55 to 9.35 m, although the maximum depth of cross-section remained almost the same. To achieve this the depth of the top flange was increased from 80 to 100 mm. The reader's attention is drawn to the continuous laminations of the top and bottom flanges – almost 15 m long!

During refurbishment work glue joints open to 50% of the width of the section were discovered in the top and bottom flanges. The glue joints in the webs were in a better condition because the moisture

waren auf Undichtigkeiten der Dachhaut und eine Dampfhochdruckreinigung der Binder zurückzuführen. Auch die derzeitige Nutzung als Veranstaltungshalle mit bis zu 1000 Zuschauern führt zu starken Feuchtigkeitsschwankungen der Raumluft, die zu Schwankungen der Holzfeuchte führen. So wurden nach einer Veranstaltung im Sommer 1995 eine Holzfeuchte von 16,5% gemessen, was bei 25°C auf eine Luftfeuchtigkeit von 80% schließen läßt. Heute empfohlen wird eine Holzfeuchte bei der Verarbeitung von 8 - 12%.

Bei Fugentiefen über 30% der Querschnittsbreite war eine Sanierung dringend erforderlich. Im vorliegenden Fall hätte die Sanierung der Gurte durch Verpressen aufgrund der Anzahl der offenen Fugen zu großen Kosten geführt, weshalb eine Sanierung der Gurte durch Verdübelung mittels in Epoxidharz eingeleimter Hartholzdübel im Abstand von 50 cm gewählt wurde. Im Versagensfall der Leimfuge ist damit die Knicklänge einer Lamelle begrenzt, so daß es nicht zu einem Totalversagen des Binders kommen kann. Diese Dübel wurden von oben eingeleimt, so daß optisch keine Beeinträchtigung entsteht.

Im Rahmen der Sanierung der Scheune in Wernesgrün stellte sich heraus, daß der Nachweis der Firma Hetzer von 1911 für eine Schneelast von 75 kg/m² erbracht worden war. Diese Schneelast ist für den Standort heute als viel zu gering einzuschätzen und gemäß DIN 1055 auf 150 kg/m² zu erhöhen. Dazu sollte die ehemalige schwere Biberschwanzdeckung wieder aufgebracht werden, für die der Nachweis nicht ohne Verstärkung erbracht werden konnte. Hauptgrund ist die nicht der idealen Stützlinie entsprechende Form des Binders, der durch seine Form schon unter symmetrischer Belastung aus Eigengewicht und Schnee eine Biegebeanspruchung erfährt.

Eine weitere Möglichkeit der Sanierung wie im Fall der Reithalle in St. Moritz stellt den Einbau eines Zugbandes im Bereich der negativen Momente dar, welche auch bei der Halle in Wernesgrün zur Ausführung kam. Diese sehr wirtschaftliche Maßnahme stellt aber eine Beeinträchtigung des Innenraumeindrucks dar, welche im Einzelfall abgewogen werden muß.

Jede Untersuchung vorhandener Tragwerke muß sowohl eine statische Analyse der Lastannahmen, den statischen Nachweis des Tragwerks und eine Ermittlung der Schadensursachen umfassen. Bei Verdacht auf Schäden der Verleimung sind genauere Materialuntersuchungen vorzunehmen.

fluctuations brought about lower internal stresses in the thinner webs. This damage was attributed to leaks in the roof and high-pressure steam cleaning of the members. The building's present use for events with up to 1000 spectators also leads to severe fluctuations in the humidity of the internal air, which in turn causes changes in the moisture content of the wood. For example, after an event in the summer of 1995 the moisture content of the wood was found to be 16.5%, which at 25°C implies an air humidity of 80%. As a comparison, 8-12% is the current recommendation for the moisture content during processing.

With gap depths exceeding 30% of the width of the cross-section, refurbishment was urgently required. In this case repairing the flanges by means of pressing would have led to high costs owing to the number of open joints. Therefore, the use of hardwood dowels inserted at 500 mm centres and fixed with epoxy resin was chosen. If a glue joint fails, then the buckling length of a lamination is limited, so that total failure of the entire member is ruled out. The dowels were inserted from above in order to preserve the appearance of the frames.

The refurbishment of the Wernesgrün barn also brought to light that in 1911 the Hetzer AG had designed the structure for a snow load of 75 kg/m². Today, this snow load is considered to be much too low for this location and according to DIN 1055 should be doubled to 150 kg/m². In addition, the former heavy plain tile roof covering was to be reused, for which strengthening appeared to be necessary. The main reason is the shape of the frame, which does not follow the ideal line of pressure and which is subjected to bending even under symmetrical loading due to dead loads and snow.

Another option during refurbishment, like in the case of the riding arena in St Moritz, was the inclusion of a tie in the zone of the negative moments. Such a tie was also added to the Wernesgrün building. However, this inexpensive measure does impair the impression of the interior. The merits of such ties must be weighed up in each individual case.

Any investigation of an existing structure must encompass a consideration of the loads, a structural analysis of the loadbearing components and the determination of the causes of the damage. If damage to the glue joints is suspected, then detailed material analyses are necessary.

**Stallgebäude, Wernesgrün, 1911,
Außenansicht, Innenansicht nach Sanierung.**
Barn, Wernesgrün, 1911, external view, internal view after refurbishment.

Decken- und Dachkonstruktionen
Roof construction

Verleimte hölzerne Dachkonstruktionen mußten sich zunächst gegen die üblichen zimmermannsmäßigen Holz-, Stahl- und Stahlbetonkonstruktionen durchsetzen. Die Vorteile gegenüber den herkömmlichen Holzkonstruktionen lagen besonders in einer größeren und somit sparsameren Materialausnutzung und einer besseren Nutzbarkeit der Dachräume infolge der Stützenfreiheit. Durch eine einfache Ummantelung der Bauteile konnte auch ein wirksamerer Brandschutz erzielt werden.

Bei gewölbten und gekrümmten Dächern war besonders die leichte Formbarkeit der verleimten Sparren ausschlaggebend. Gegenüber Stahl und Stahlbeton konnten sich die Hetzer-Konstruktionen durch den günstigeren Preis durchsetzen. Entscheidend waren oft auch der hohe Vorfertigungsgrad und somit die kurzen Bauzeiten. In manchen Fällen wie nachträglichen Aufstockungen führte das geringere Eigengewicht auch zu Ersparnissen im Lastabtragungsbereich.

Im folgenden sollen nun die einzelnen Dachkonstruktionen nach ihrer Form und ihrem statischen System dargestellt werden.

Glued timber roof structures first had to establish themselves in the face of competition from traditional jointed timber structures as well as steel and reinforced concrete. The advantages compared to conventional timber construction lay in the better, and hence more economic, use of the material and better use of the roof space thanks to the fewer supports. More effective fire protection was also easily achieved by cladding the components.

It was particularly the ease of shaping that was decisive in making glued rafters the favourite for all forms of curved roofs. And the lower cost of the Hetzer system was a significant advantage when compared to steel and reinforced concrete. The degree of prefabrication, and hence the short on-site assembly times, was often decisive as well. In some cases, e.g. the subsequent addition of further storeys, the lower self-weight also led to savings in the load-bearing structure.

Different forms of roof construction and their structural behaviour will be illustrated in the following.

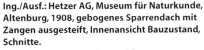

Ing./Ausf.: Hetzer AG, Museum für Naturkunde, Altenburg, 1908, gebogenes Sparrendach mit Zangen ausgesteift, Innenansicht Bauzustand, Schnitte.
Engineers/contractors: Hetzer AG;
Natural History Museum, Altenburg, 1908, curved couple roof braced with collars, internal view under construction, sections.

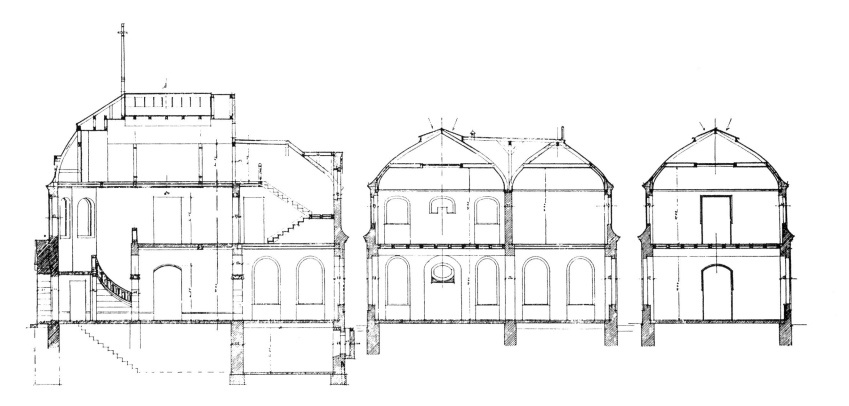

Ing./Ausf.: Hetzer AG, Krematorium Baden-Baden 1910, doppelte Dreigelenkbögen mit aufgesatteltem gebogenem Sparrendach.
Engineers/contractors: Hetzer AG; Baden-Baden Crematorium, double three-pin arch supporting curved couple roof.

Linke Seite und unten **Ing.: Terner und Chopard, Dachkuppel des Hygienischen Instituts, Zürich, 1911, glockenförmige Kuppel aus gebogenen Sparren mit Zangen ausgesteift, Außenansicht und Bauzustand.**
Facing page and below Engineers: Terner & Chopard, roof to the former Hygiene Institute, 1911, now the main building of Zürich university, bell-shaped dome of curved rafters braced by collars, external view and view during construction.

Sparrendächer

Ein sehr schönes Beispiel einer gebogenen Sparrendachkonstruktion mit angehobenem Zugband gemäß dem Patent Nr. 197773 aus dem Jahr 1906 ist der Dachstuhl des Naturhistorischen Museums in Altenburg. Die Sparren haben einen rechteckigen Querschnitt im Abstand von etwa 1 m. Die angehobene hölzerne Zange ermöglichte es, den Saal frei überspannend mit einer entsprechenden Höhe von 4 m auszubilden, ohne das Dach übermäßig hoch werden zu lassen. Das Dach überspannt etwa 8 m, weshalb die Zangen auch nicht überall durchgängig ausgebildet werden mußten und das Oberlicht so von der Konstruktion freigehalten wurde.[54]

Aus Kostengründen wurden in diesem Gebäude auch Hetzer'sche Träger für die Deckenkonstruktion mit 5,5 m Spannweite im Abstand von 80 cm verwendet, welche die hohe Belastung der Steinsammlung aufzunehmen hatten.

Der besonders formschöne Sonderfall einer Sparrenkuppel auf quadratischem Grundriß von 15,7 m entstand um 1911 für den Turm des Hygienischen Instituts in Zürich – heute Hauptgebäude der Universität, Kollegiengebäude 1. Das glockenförmige Sparrendach hat eine Höhe von 8 m. Die gebogenen Sparren (10 x 28 cm im Querschnitt) stehen im Abstand von 90 cm und sind nur im oberen Viertel durch Zangen ausgesteift. Die Kuppel befindet sich heute noch in ausgezeichnetem Zustand. In ähnlicher Art entstanden zur gleichen Zeit eine Reihe von Dachkonstruktionen für Wohnhäuser, da die Konstruktion ohne Stützen flexible Grundrißgestaltung ermöglicht (Baden-Baden, Zürich, Aachen).

Couple roofs

A very elegant example of a curved couple roof design with raised collar according to patent No. 197773 from 1906 can be seen at the Natural History Museum in Altenburg. The rafters have a rectangular cross-section and are spaced at approx. 1 m centres. The raised timber collar enables the space below to be spanned without intermediate columns and with a clear headroom of 4 m, but without needing to make the roof excessively tall. The span of the roof is approx. 8 m, which is why the collars are not required across the full span at every rafter. This also helps to keep the rooflight free from intervening structural members.[54]

For reasons of cost, Hetzer beams were also used for the floors in this building. The beams span 5.5 m and are placed at 800 mm centres – necessary to carry the high loads of the stone collection.

The particularly elegant case of a couple roof on a square base of side length 15.7 m was built in 1911 for the tower of the Hygiene Institute in Zürich – today the main building of the university, College 1. This bell-shaped roof is 8 m tall. The curved rafters (100 x 280 mm) are placed at 900 mm centres and are braced by collars only in the upper quarter. The roof still remains in an excellent condition today. A series of similar roof designs were erected at about the same time and gained favour because the construction without columns allowed a flexible plan layout (Baden-Baden, Zürich, Aachen).

Dreigelenkrahmen

Eine bei der Otto Hetzer AG vielfach verwendete Form der Dachkonstruktion ist der abgewinkelte Dreigelenkrahmen, welcher bei Spannweiten zwischen 10 und 20 m zu sinnvollen Bauteilgrößen führte. Zur Aufnahme der horizontalen Auflagerkraft am Widerlager wurde der Binder mit einem Zugband gehalten, das oftmals angehoben (gesprengt) wurde, um einen leichteren Raumeindruck zu gewinnen. Die Dreigelenkrahmen standen im Abstand von 4-5 m, wobei die Dachhaut von einer Sekundärkonstruktion aus Sparren und Pfetten getragen wurde.

Diese Art des Dachstuhls fand etwa bei der Überdachung von Kirchen und Turnhallen Anwendung. Ein frühes Beispiel stellt das Dach der Turnhalle in Mürwik bei Flensburg von 1907 dar. Als Haupttragwerk dient ein abgewinkelter Dreigelenkrahmen mit angehobenem Zugband. Die Spannweite beträgt 13,83 m bei einer Konstruktionshöhe von 4,15 m.

In der Schweiz verwendete das Ingenieurbüro Terner und Chopard hauptsächlich spitze Dreigelenkrahmen zur Überdachung von Schulturnhallen und Kirchen. Die Schule in Altstetten ist hierfür ein typisches Beispiel. Ebenso wurde 1911 die katholische Kirche in Romanshorn mit unterspannten Dreigelenkbindern im Achsabstand von 4,5 m mit einer Spannweite von 14,2 m überdeckt.[55]

Three-pin arches

One type of roof used frequently by Otto Hetzer AG is the cranked three-pin frame, which led to reasonable component sizes for spans of 10-20 m. To resist the horizontal support reactions, the members were joined by a collar, often raised, in order to create a more lightweight aesthetic impression. Three-pin arches were generally placed 4-5 m apart, which necessitated a secondary construction of purlins and rafters to carry the roof covering.

This type of roof structure was popular for churches and gymnasiums. One early example is the roof to the gymnasium in Mürwik near Flensburg (1907). The primary structure is a cranked three-pin frame with raised collar. The frame spans 13.83 m and rises 4.15 m.

In Switzerland the engineering team of Terner & Chopard mainly preferred pitched roofs for churches and school gymnasiums. The school in Altstetten is a typical example of this style. The Catholic church in Romanshorn was roofed over in 1911 with trussed three-pin arches spanning 14.2 m and placed at 4.5 m centres.[55]

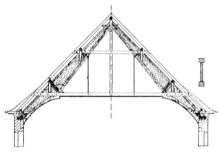

Linke Seite und oben **Ing.: Terner und Chopard, Dach der Turnhalle Zürich-Altstetten, 1911, Innenansicht Dachstuhl, Außenansicht, Querschnitt.**
Facing page and above Engineers: Terner & Chopard; roof structure to gymnasium in Zürich-Altstetten, 1911, internal view of roof structure, external view, section.

Links **Ing./Ausf.: Terner und Chopard, Katholische Kirche, Romanshorn, 1911, unterspannte Dreigelenkbinder, Grundriß und Querschnitt.**
Left Engineers: Terner & Chopard; roof structure to catholic church in Romanshorn, 1911, trussed three-pin frame, plan and section.
Rechts **Ing./Ausf.: Hetzer AG, ehemalige kaiserliche Turnhalle in Mürwik bei Flensburg, 1907, Dreigelenkrahmen mit angehobenem Zugband, Schnitt.**
Right Engineers/contractors: Hetzer AG; former imperial gymnasium in Mürwik near Flensburg, 1907, three-pin frame with raised collar, section.

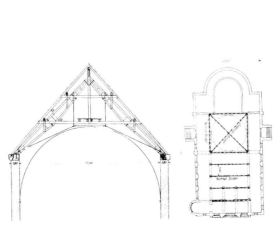

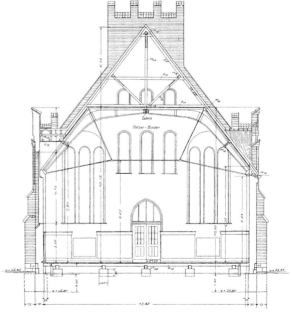

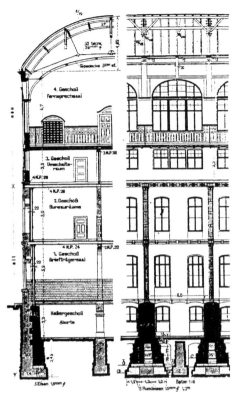

Ing./Ausf.: Hetzer AG, Fernmeldehalle in Trier, 1909, Zweigelenkbogenbinder mit angehobenem Zugband, Quer- und Längsschnitt.
Engineers/contractors: Hetzer AG;
telephone exchange, Trier, 1909,
two-pin arch with raised collar, sections.

Zweigelenkbogen

Bei runden Dachformen fanden ebenso Zweigelenkbogenträger Verwendung, welche mit Zugbändern am Auflager gehalten wurden. Oftmals wurden Unterdecken daran befestigt, um den Raumeindruck nicht zu stören.

In Trier setzte sich 1909 eine Zweigelenkbogen-Konstruktion bei der Überdachung des Fernsprechsaales gegen eine Stahl- und Stahlbetonkonstruktion durch. Entscheidend war hierbei sowohl der Preis von 3700 Reichsmark zu 6500 bzw. 8300 Reichsmark als auch das wesentlich geringere Gewicht (21.000 kg zu 35.000 kg bzw. 100.000 kg), was zu einem geringeren Gründungsaufwand bei dieser nachträglichen Aufstockung führte. Auch die geringe Richtzeit von sieben Arbeitstagen war von Vorteil.[56]

Die doppel-T-förmigen Binder aus Fichtenholz haben eine Höhe von 70 bzw. 50 cm am Rand und 9 Stegverstärkungen. Diese dienten der Sicherung aufgehender Leimfugen. Zur Unterstützung der Pfetten (18 x 24 cm im Querschnitt) sind am Binder abgehängte Kopfbänder vorhanden.

Den Sonderfall der Zweigelenkbogen auf rundem Grundriß stellt die Überdachung des Krematoriums Sihlfeld D in Zürich dar. Die sehr flache Kuppel mit 12 m Spannweite besteht aus vier radial angeordneten Zweigelenkbögen mit angehobener Unterspannung. Die gebogenen Hetzer-Sparren (10 x 15 cm) lagern in den Viertelspunkten auf einer Ringpfette und in der Mitte auf. Die untergehängte halbkugelförmige Deckenkuppel wird von acht am Rand gespreizten Hetzer-Sparren gehalten.

Two-pin arches

Curved roofs also made use of the two-pin arch held by ties between the supports. The ceilings in such buildings were often fixed directly to such arches in order to maintain the impression of open space.

In Trier in 1909 a two-pin timber arch was chosen instead of steel or reinforced concrete for the roof of the telephone exchange. The decisive factors here were the price of 3700 Reichsmark (compared to 6500 and 8300 Reichsmark respectively) and also the substantially lower weight (21 000 kg compared to 35 000 and 100 000 kg respectively), which in turn led to lower costs for the foundations for this subsequent addition of storeys. Another advantage was the short erection time of just seven working days.[56]

The I-shaped beams of spruce are 700 mm deep (500 mm at the edges) and have nine web stiffeners. These served to secure the ascending glue joints. Angle braces suspended from the arch are included to support the purlins (180 x 240 mm).

The special case of a two-pin arch on a circular base can be seen in the roof to the Sihlfeld D Crematorium in Zürich. This very shallow dome with a span of 12 m comprises four radial two-pin arches with raised underslung framing. The curved Hetzer rafters (100 x 150 mm) are supported on a ring purlin at quarter-points and at the centre. Eight Hetzer rafters splayed at the perimeter support the suspended inner hemispherical dome.

Arch.: Fröhlich; Ing.: Terner und Chopard; Krematorium, Sihlfeld, Zürich, 1910, kreisförmige Kuppel aus radial angeordneten Kreisbögen mit angehobener Unterspannung, Schnitt, Grundriß.
Architect: Fröhlich; engineers: Terner & Chopard;
crematorium, Sihlfeld, Zürich, 1910, circular dome
of radial arches with raised underslung framing,
section, plan.

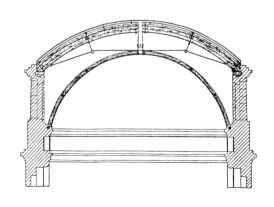

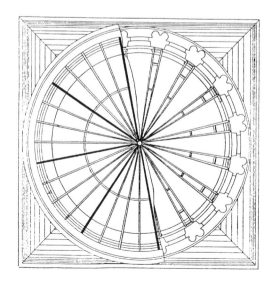

Eine Zweigelenkbogen-Kuppel auf ovalem Grundriß entstand 1909 für die Stadtgartenhalle in Hagen, Westfalen. Sie spannte über eine Fläche von 12,3 m und 17 m. Drei Zweigelenkbinder mit angehobenem Zugband und vier Gratbindern ergeben mit ringförmigen Pfetten die Auflager für die gebogenen Sparren. An der Unterspannung war eine Putzdecke abgehängt. Am 15. März 1945 wurde die Kuppel durch Brandbomben zerstört.

Auf dem Werksgelände der Otto Hetzer AG in Weimar entstand 1915 für die Leimerei eine Dachkonstruktion mit einem Zweigelenkbogen und abgehängtem hölzernen Zugband. Zur Aussteifung liegen diese Bögen auf Fachwerkstützen auf. Dieser Bautypus ist relativ selten und stellt eine Übergangsform zu den reinen Binderhallen dar.

Die Firma Nemaho baute 1924 den Dachstuhl für einen Schlafsaal in Bergen op Zoom unter Verwendung von Zweigelenkrahmen mit einer Spannweite von 11,88 m. Eine vergleichbare Rahmenkonstruktion entstand 1929 für die Dachkonstruktion der Van

A two-pin dome on an oval base was erected in 1909 for the Stadtgartenhalle in Hagen, Westphalia. The area covered measured 12.3 x 17 m. Three two-pin arches with raised collar and four hip trusses with ring purlins provide the supports for the curved rafters. A plaster ceiling was suspended from the underslung framing. The dome was destroyed on 15 March 1945 during an Allied bombing raid.

A two-pin arch with suspended timber collar was built in 1915 for the roof of the glue shop for the Otto Hetzer AG works in Weimar. These arches were supported on battened columns for stability. This type of construction is relatively rare and represents a transitional form to that of the true glulam frame shed.

Nemaho built a roof structure for a dormitory in Bergen op Zoom in 1924 using two-pin frames with a span of 11.88 m. A similar frame construction was erected in 1929 for the roof of the Van Nelle factory in Rotterdam (architects: J. A. Brinkman and L. C. v. d. Vlugt). The unobstructed space which ensued was used for the works canteen.

Ing./Ausf.: Hetzer AG, Stadtgartenhalle, Hagen, 1909, Zweigelenkbogenbinder mit angehobenem Zugband und vier Gratbindern, Längsschnitt, Querschnitt, Abbund auf dem Werksgelände.
Engineers/contractors: Hetzer AG; Stadtgartenhalle, Hagen, Westphalia, 1909, two-pin frame with raised collar and four hip beams, sections, trial assembly at the works in Weimar.

Nächste Doppelseite **Ing./Ausf.: Nemaho, Schlafsaal, Bergen op Zoom, 1924. Bauzustand.**
Next double page Engineers/contractors: Nemaho; dormitory in Bergen op Zoom, 1924, under construction.

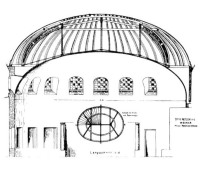

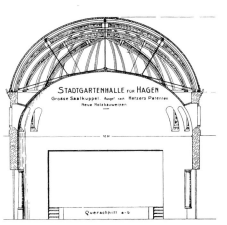

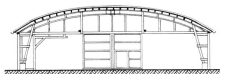

Ing./Ausf.: Hetzer AG, ehemalige Leimerei auf dem Werksgelände, Weimar, 1915, Zweigelenkbogen mit abgehängtem Zugband, Innenansicht, Schnitt.
Engineers/contractors: Hetzer AG; former glue shop at the works in Weimar, 1915, two-pin arch with suspended tie, internal view, section.

Nelle Fabrik in Rotterdam (Architekt J. A. Brinkman und L.C.v.d. Vlugt). Der so entstehende stützenfreie Raum wurde als Speisesaal genutzt.

Dachkonstruktionen aus Holzleimbindern wurden in der Regel bei größeren Spannweiten und Bauaufgaben genutzt, die diesen planerischen Aufwand rechtfertigten. Als normaler Dachstuhl konnten sie die Dachstuhlkonstruktionen aus Vollholz nicht verdrängen. Eine Ausnahme stellen die Scheunendächer in den USA seit Ende der dreißiger Jahre dar, welche praktisch als Bausatz auf die Baustelle geliefert werden konnten und damit höchst wirtschaftlich waren.

Roof structures employing glued laminated timber were primarily used for larger spans and for projects which justified the design work. For normal roofs such constructions could not replace traditional structures made from solid timber sections. One exception was barn roofs in the USA, which since the late 1930s have been delivered to site practically in kit form and hence represent an extremely economic alternative.

Arch.: J. A. Brinkman, L.C. van der Vlugt; Ing./Ausf.: Nemaho, Speisesaal, Van Nelle's Fabrik, Rotterdam, 1929, Innenansicht.
Architects: J. A. Brinkman, L. C. van der Vlugt; engineers/contractors: Nemaho; works canteen, Van Nelle factory, Rotterdam, 1929, internal view.

Bahnsteigüberdachungen
Platform roofs

Linke Seite **Arch.: N. V. Spoorwegopbouw te Utrecht; Ausf.: Nemaho, Bahnsteigüberdachung, Delft, 1950, eingespannte Stütze mit Kragarmen, Pfetten und gebogenen Sparren.**

Facing page Architects: N. V. Spoorwegopbouw te Utrecht; contractor: Nemaho; platform canopy, Delft, 1950, restrained column with cantilevers, purlins and curved rafters.

Nach ersten, teilweise euphorisch kommentierten Tragwerksentwicklungen aus Eisen und Stahl zur Überdachung von Bahnsteigen stellten sich schon bald die ersten Ernüchterungen ein. Die ständige Belastung durch den Ausstoß von Rauchgasen und Wasserdampf resultierte in starken Korrosionserscheinungen, die auch durch schwierige, aufwendige Instandsetzungsmaßnahmen und beste Anstriche kaum zu vermeiden waren. Besonders leichte Konstruktionen wie Wellbleche wurden schon nach kurzer Zeit undicht. Bei ausbleibender Instandsetzung führte diese Korrosion zum Versagen. So wurde der Einsturz der Gleishalle des Bahnhofes Charing Cross in London 1920 auf das Durchrosten der eisernen Zugbänder der Bogenbinder zurückgeführt.[57]

Auch Stahlbetonkonstruktionen konnten sich aus Kostengründen nur selten durchsetzen. Schaechterle berichtet 1924 von ungefähr 50% höheren Aufwendungen für Stahlbetonkonstruktionen im Vergleich zu Holzkonstruktionen. Daraus ergab sich ein verstärkter Einsatz von Holz für Bahnsteigdächer und -hallen; bereits 1912 empfahl die Generaldirektion der Schweizer Bahnen in Bern die Verwendung von Holz.[58]

Erste Bahnsteigüberdachungen aus Holz entstanden in Erfurt, Stuttgart und Essen. Die dabei gemachten Erfahrungen führten zu einer vorsichtigeren Einschätzung besonders im Hinblick auf die Wetterbeständigkeit: „Die seinerzeit von der Hetzer AG in Vorschlag gebrachte zulässige Beanspruchung von 140 kg/cm^2 auf Biegung und 11,5 kg/cm^2 auf Schub waren viel zu hoch gegriffen. Nach unseren Erfahrungen ausgeführter Bauten sollte für das ungünstigste Zusammenwirken der äußeren Kräfte, Eigengewicht, Nutzlast, Schnee, Wind über 80 kg/cm^2, entsprechend vier- bis fünffacher Bruchsicherheit nicht hinausgegangen werden."[59]

After the initial structural engineering developments in iron and steel for the roofs to railway stations were welcomed (sometimes with euphoric comments), it was not long before the first disillusionment set in. The constant deluge of smoke, fumes and steam led to corrosion which was almost impossible to prevent, even with elaborate maintenance measures and the best paints. In particular, lightweight constructions like corrugated sheeting quickly became unserviceable. If maintenance was not carried out, then this corrosion eventually led to failure. For instance, the collapse of the trainshed at Charing Cross station in London in 1920 was attributed to the corrosion of the iron ties to the arches.[57]

And the cost of reinforced concrete meant that it was only used on rare occasions. Schaechterle reported in 1924 that the cost of a reinforced concrete structure was approx. 50% higher than that of a design in timber. All these factors led to an increased use of timber for railway stations, which is why the management of Swiss Railways in Bern decided as early as 1912 to recommend the use of timber.[58]

The first timber platform canopies appeared in Erfurt, Stuttgart and Essen. However, the experience gained with these early roofs led to a more circumspect assessment, particularly with regard to weather resistance: "The permissible stresses of 140 kg/cm^2 for bending and 11.5 kg/cm^2 for shear suggested by Hetzer AG at the time were much too high. According to our experience with real buildings, a figure of 80 kg/cm^2, corresponding to a factor of safety against failure of 4-5, should not be exceeded for the most unfavourable combination of external forces, dead loads, imposed loads, snow, and wind."[59]

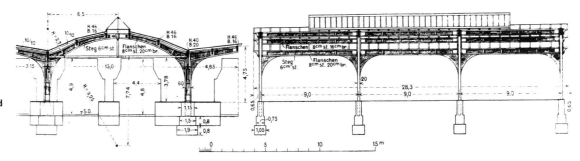

Ing./Ausf.: Hetzer AG, Ladestegüberdachung, Erfurt, 1913, Zweigelenkrahmen mit Zugband und zwei Kragarmen, Quer- und Längsschnitt.
Engineers/contractors: Hetzer AG; goods platform canopy, Erfurt, 1913, two-pin frame with two cantilevers, sections.

Ing./Ausf.: Hetzer AG, Versandschuppen, Stuttgart, 1914, Zweigelenkrahmen mit Zugband mit Einfeldträger und Kragarmen, Quer- und Längsschnitt.
Engineers/contractors: Hetzer AG; forwarding hall, Stuttgart, 1914, two-pin frame with collar, single-span beam and cantilevers.

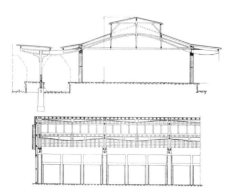

1913 entstand eine heute noch erhaltene Ladestegüberdachung in Erfurt. Die 18 m weit spannende Bogenkonstruktion mit hölzernem Zugband kragt jeweils seitlich um 3,15 m und 4,65 m aus. Die Binder stehen im Abstand von 9 m, weshalb die Pfetten ebenfalls als Doppel-T-Profile ausgebildet wurden. Die Aussteifung erfolgt über biegesteife Eckausbildungen in Längsrichtung und eingespannte Stützen in Querrichtung. Die Einspannung am Fußpunkt diente hauptsächlich der Ableitung der Anprallasten.

Auch in Stuttgart entstand 1914 ein 154 m langer Versandschuppen mit Laderampe. Die Dachkonstruktion überspannte als Bogen mit hölzernem Zugband den 16 m breiten Schuppen stützenfrei. Die im Abstand von 9 m stehenden Binder überspannten die Laderampe, ein Gleis und einen weiteren Bahnsteig, wo sie nochmals aufgelagert waren. Der über den Gleisen befindliche Lüftungsschlitz führte auch zu starken Verwitterungen der Binder durch Feuchtigkeit und Sonneneinstrahlung. So klafften die Leimfugen in der Mitte des Steges über einer Länge von 2 bis 3 m auf. Eine später durchgeführte Erweiterung wurde aufgrund dieser Erfahrungen und aus Kostengründen als Fachwerkkonstruktion ausgeführt.

Für den Bahnhof Interlaken-West entwarf Charles Chopard eine Bahnsteigüberdachung mit kleineren Achsabständen und geringeren Auskragungen, die zu wesentlich schlankerer Ausbildung der Stützen führte. Besonders ist hierbei der geringe Biegeradius von 1,6 m der Lamellen zu beachten, welcher durch gerin-

A goods platform canopy in Erfurt dating from 1913 still exists today. The 18-m-span frame construction with timber collar also cantilevers beyond the supports – 3.15 m on one side, 4.65 m on the other. The frames are positioned every 9 m, which is why the purlins also need to be I-sections. Stability is provided by rigid corners in the longitudinal direction and fixed-based columns transverse. The fixed bases are mainly necessary to accommodate impact loads.

Stuttgart was also the location of a 154-m-long forwarding hall with loading ramp dating from 1914. The roof construction spanned the 16-m-wide hall as a curved beam with timber collar and no intermediate columns. The beams at a spacing of 9 m spanned the loading ramp, one track and another platform, where they rested on a further support. The ventilation opening in the roof above the track also led to the arches being severely exposed to moisture and solar radiation. This caused the glue joints in the middle of the web to split open over a length of 2-3 m. Owing to this, and for reasons of cost, a later extension was realized as a truss.

Charles Chopard designed a platform canopy for Interlaken-West station in which the frames were placed closer together and the cantilevers were shorter, which in turn led to considerably more slender columns. Especially noteworthy here is the tight bending radius of 1.6 m for the laminations, made possible through the use of thin pieces (10-15 mm) instead of the usual 20-30 mm.[60]

Links **Ladestegüberdachung, Erfurt, Bauzustand.**
Mitte **Bahnsteigüberdachung, Essen-Nord, Bauzustand.**
Rechts **Bahnsteigüberdachung, Interlaken-West, Teilansicht.**
Left Goods platform canopy, Erfurt, under construction.
Centre Platform canopy at Essen-Nord station, under construction.
Right Platform canopy at Interlaken-West station, part view.

**Ing./Ausf.: Hetzer AG, Bahnsteigüberdachung, Essen-Nord, 1921,
eingespannte Stütze mit zwei Kragarmen, Quer-, Längsschnitt und Grundriß.**
Engineers/contractors: Hetzer AG; platform canopy at Essen-Nord station, 1921, restrained column with two cantilevers, sections and plan.

gere Lamellenstärken von 10-15 mm (statt 20-30 mm) erreicht wurde.[60]

Eine einstielige, zweiseitig um 6,10 m auskragende Bahnsteigüberdachung entstand am Bahnhof Essen-Nord. Die in zwei U-Profile eingespannten Stützen stehen im Achsabstand von 8,1 m, der von Doppel-T-Pfetten überspannt wird.

Seit dieser Zeit sind nur wenige Bahnsteigüberdachungen als reiner Holzleimbau ausgeführt worden, wie zum Beispiel einige Überdachungen bei der British Railways 1958.[61] Eine Kombination aus Stahlstützen und -trägern mit gebogenen Holzleim-Sparren findet sich in Delft. Die Dauerhaftigkeit der mittlerweile gut 85 Jahre alten Bahnsteigüberdachung in Interlaken-West läßt vermuten, daß nicht mangelnde Beständigkeit, sondern architektonische Fragen der Materialwahl die weitere Verbreitung dieser Bauweise entscheidend verhindert haben.

A single-column platform canopy cantilevering 6.10 m to both sides was built at Essen-Nord station. The columns restrained in pairs of channel sections are spaced at 8.1 m centres, a distance spanned by I-section purlins.

Since then only a few platform canopies have been realized purely in glued laminated timber, e.g. a number of canopies for British Railways in 1958.[61] A combination of steel columns and beams with curved glulam rafters can be seen in Delft. The condition of the platform canopy at Interlaken-West, now more than 85 years old, seems to indicate that it was not inferior durability but rather architectural fashions regarding choice of material that mainly hindered the widespread use of this form of construction.

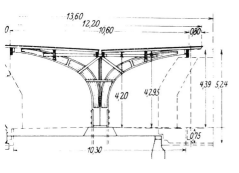

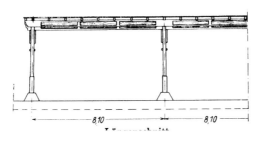

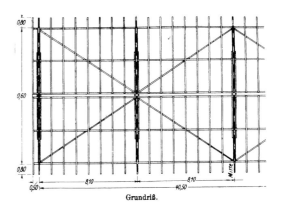

Grundriß.

Hallen
Single-storey sheds

Deutsche Eisenbahnhalle, Außenansicht.
German Railways exhibition hall, external view.

Seit Beginn des Holzleimbaus nahm der Hallenbau eine stürmische Entwicklung bis in die Anfänge der sechziger Jahre, wo Spannweiten von über 100 m erreicht wurden. Damit wurden gleichzeitig technische und wirtschaftliche Grenzen erreicht. Seitdem beschränkt sich der Bau von Binderhallen vor allem auf gewerbliche und sportliche Nutzungen mit Spannweiten bis zu 60 m. Häufig werden hierbei auch Fertighallen verwendet, welche gestalterisch die Anfänge der Entwicklung selten übertreffen.

Daher soll in diesem Kapitel auch eine Anzahl älterer Hallen gezeigt werden, welche besonders architektonisch überzeugend gestaltet wurden. Im Hinblick auf ihre Aufenthaltsqualität bieten sie natürlich belichtete und belüftete Arbeitsplätze, welche noch heute im Bereich des Industriebaus nicht selbstverständlich sind. Um den Überblick über die gezeigten Hallen zu vereinfachen, werden diese in Gruppen nach der Form ihrer Binder (halbkreisförmig, parabelförmig, spitzbogenförmig sowie Rahmenbinder mit Zugband) zusammengefaßt.

From the advent of glued laminated timber, single-storey shed construction developed with lightning speed up to the early 1960s, when spans exceeding 100 m were achieved. This marked the limits in both engineering and economic terms. Since then such buildings have been confined to industrial and sports uses, with spans up to 60 m. Prefabricated constructions are frequently employed which, in terms of aesthetics, are seldom an improvement on the first designs.

Therefore, this chapter will illustrate a number of older shed-type buildings which possess a particular architectural quality. The thus documented structures provide a pleasant, naturally lit and naturally ventilated working environment, something which is, even today, not necessarily a matter of course in industry. In order to simplify this review of single-storey glulam construction sheds, they have been classified according to type of main member (semicircular, parabolic, and pointed arch frame with collar).

Der Entwicklung dieser Hallen gingen umfangreiche statische Untersuchungen voraus:

„Im Gegensatz zu den bisherigen nur auf reinen Erfahrungsgrundsätzen beruhenden Holzkonstruktionen, die unnötig viel Material erforderten und trotzdem nur geringe Tragfähigkeit aufwiesen, haben wir unser besonderes Augenmerk darauf gerichtet, klare und theoretisch richtige Tragwerke zu konstruieren, deren Berechnung sich nach den neuen Methoden der Statik einwandfrei durchführen läßt. Unsere Systeme besitzen eine ungewöhnliche erhöhte Tragfähigkeit und sind dabei unter vollständiger Ausnutzung des Materials besonders sparsam konstruiert."[62]

Am Anfang jeder Berechnung stand natürlich die Wahl einer angemessenen Tragwerksform. Der halbkreisförmige Binder stellt dabei die erste klare Grundform dar, welche durch einen Radius definiert leicht herzustellen war. Aufgrund der erwähnten Abweichungen von der idealen Stützlinie, welche ja bereits Ardant baupraktisch untersucht hatte, mußten die hohen Biegebeanspruchungen durch eine Aufweitung des Querschnitts in den Viertelspunkten bewältigt werden. Damit war die Spannweite eingeschränkt, wenn der Materialverbrauch nicht unwirtschaftliche Ausmaße erreichen sollte.

Die Optimierung als parabelförmiger Binder besaß zwar den Vorteil geringer Biegebeanspruchung und damit schlanker Querschnitte, hatte aber in den Randbereichen eine Einschränkung der Hallenhöhe zur Folge. So fand diese Tragwerksform in rein wirtschaftlich genutzten Gebäuden wie zum Beispiel den Salzlagerhallen Verwendung. Hierbei wurden oft die Hallenwände als Fundamente ins Erdreich eingegraben, um damit einen Gegendruck zu den Horizontalschüben der Binder zu erzeugen. Übergangsformen zwischen halbkreis- und parabelförmig kann man als abgewinkelte Binder bezeichnen, welche die Ausbildung einer Satteldachform erleichterten.

Zur weiteren Steigerung der Tragfähigkeit der halbkreis- und parabelförmigen Binder wurden im Bereich des Firstpunkts auch Zangen vorgesehen oder die Biegebeanspruchung der Binder durch Zugbänder in den Viertelspunkten reduziert. Diese Zugbänder schränkten die Raumwirkung optisch stark ein und wurden nach Möglichkeit vermieden. So fanden sie bei der Reithalle in St. Moritz erst im Rahmen der Sanierung Verwendung, um starke Verformungen und ein Versagen der Konstruktion zu verhindern.

The development of these sheds was preceded by extensive structural engineering studies:

"In contrast to the forms of timber construction used hitherto, which were based exclusively on empirical formulas and which consumed unnecessary quantities of material but still exhibited low loadbearing capacities, we have paid special attention to designing coherent and theoretically correct structures which can be readily analysed according to the new methods of structural engineering. Our systems exhibit an extraordinary improvement in loadbearing capacity but nevertheless represent particularly economical designs which make full use of the material."[62]

The start of any analysis must of course be the choice of an appropriate structural form. The semicircular arch was the first distinct basic form which, defined by a radius, was easy to produce. Owing to the aforementioned deviations from the ideal line of pressure, which Ardant had investigated in practical trials, the high bending stresses had to be resisted by increasing the cross-section at the quarter-points. This limited the possible spans, if consumption of material was not to reach uneconomic proportions.

Optimization of this form leads to a parabolic arch which, although it possesses the advantage of lower bending stresses and hence more slender sections, has only limited headroom at the side of the building. Therefore, this structural form is favoured for salt warehouses and other similar uses. The walls are often sunk into the ground to form the foundations and hence resist the horizontal thrust of the arch. Transitional forms between semicircle and parabola are designated "cranked frames." These allow the construction of a pitched roof.

The loadbearing capacities of semicircular and parabolic arches are increased by adding a collar near the crown, or the bending stresses can be reduced by including ties at the quarter-points. However, such ties seriously impair the appearance of the interior and should be avoided whenever possible. Ties had to be added to the riding arena in St Moritz during refurbishment work in order to curtail severe deformations and prevent failure of the structure.

Both of these structural forms are very tall in relation to the span. Such headroom is usually unnecessary for commercial purposes and only leads to heating problems. Specifications calling for straight walls

Arch.: Peter Behrens; Ing.: Herrmann Kügler, München; Ausf.: Steinbeis & Cons., Rosenheim; Deutsche Eisenbahnhalle zur Weltausstellung, Brüssel, 1910, Zweigelenkrahmen mit abgehängtem Zugband, Bauzustand.
Architect: Peter Behrens; engineer: Herrmann Kügler, Munich; contractor: Steinbeis & Cons., Rosenheim; German Railways exhibition hall, World Exposition, Brussels, 1910, two-pin frame with suspended tie, under construction.

Deutsche Eisenbahnhalle, Querschnitt, Schnitt durch Oberlicht, Grundriß.
German Railways exhibition hall, section, section through rooflight, plan.

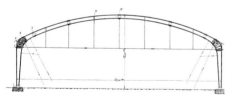

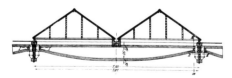

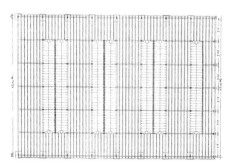

Beide Tragwerkstypen besaßen im Verhältnis zu ihrer Spannweite eine große Höhe, welche für eine gewerbliche Nutzung meist nicht gebraucht wurde und nur unnötige Beheizungsprobleme erzeugte. Aus der notwendigen Anforderung gerader Wände und einem Dachgefälle für die Entwässerung entstand die Rahmenbauweise, welche aber große Biegebeanspruchungen in den Eckbereichen ergab. Um diese auf ein Minimum zu begrenzen, wurden abgehängte Zugbänder in Holz vorgesehen, welche den Horizontalschub aus Eigengewicht und Schnee aufnahmen. Die Biegesteifigkeit des Rahmens wurde vor allem zur Abtragung der Windlasten quer zur Halle benötigt und ließ sich dann mit wirtschaftlichen Querschnitten bewältigen.

Als statische Systeme fanden sowohl Zweigelenk- und Dreigelenkbinder Anwendung. Die Dreigelenkbinder waren als statisch bestimmte Systeme unempfindlich gegen Setzungen und Verschiebungen. Trotz dieses Vorteils fanden die zweifach statisch unbestimmten Rahmenbinderhallen häufig Verwendung.

Hallen aus Rahmenbindern mit Zugband

Die erste nachzuweisende Halle in Hetzer-Bauweise entstand 1910 als Deutsche Eisenbahnhalle für die Weltausstellung in Brüssel. Sie bestand zwar nur als temporäres Gebäude, hatte aber mit ihren 43 m Spannweite ein erst sehr viel später wieder erreichtes Ausmaß. Der Zweigelenkrahmen mit 14 m Scheitelhöhe hatte in 8,2 m Höhe ein eisernes Zugband.[63] Die im Querschnitt vorhandenen Spannungen wurden mit 136 kg/cm² (=1,36KN/cm²) angegeben, die auch heute mit Brettschichtholz, BS14, zulässig wären. Aufgrund der Größe der Binder waren für den Transport fünf Montagestöße erforderlich, die biegesteif ausgebildet waren.

Die Berechnung des zweifach statisch unbestimmten Systems wurde von dem Ingenieur Hermann Kügler aus München erstellt und aufgrund der erstmaligen Verwendung im Holzbau vollständig veröffentlicht.[64] Der Entwurf der Halle stammt von Peter Behrens und läßt äußerlich wenig von der Leichtigkeit der Konstruktion, geschweige denn seiner außerordentlichen Spannweite vermuten. Dies spiegelt ein gestalterisches Grundproblem der damaligen Architekten mit dem reinen Tragwerk wieder. Das reine Tragwerk aus Holz wird erst durch eine massive Fassade als Dekoration zur Architektur.

and a roof sloped just enough to provide drainage led to the development of the frame. However, this form suffers from high bending stresses at the corners which are minimized by timber ties on hangers to resist the horizontal thrust caused by dead loads and snow. The bending strength of the frame is primarily required to resist transverse wind loads and can be realized with economically sized sections.

Other structural forms in use include the two-pin and three-pin arches. The latter, as statically determinate systems, are not vulnerable to settlement and displacements of the supports. Despite this advantage, the frame with two degrees of indeterminacy has been used on many occasions.

Single-storey sheds with tied frames

The first shed known to use the Hetzer system was built in 1910 as an exhibition hall for German Railways at the World Exposition in Brussels. Although it was only a temporary structure, its span of 43 m set a record which was not beaten until many years later. The two-pin frame was 14 m to the crown and had an iron tie at a height of 8.2 m.[63] The stresses present in the section were given as 136 kg/cm² (= 1.36 kN/cm²), which even today would be permissible with grade BS14 glued laminated timber. To facilitate transport, each frame was divided into six segments which were rigidly joined on site.

The analysis of the system with two degrees of indeterminacy was entrusted to the engineer Hermann Kügler from Munich and published in full as this was a first at the time for timber construction.[64] The architect Peter Behrens was responsible for the design of the building, the exterior of which hardly reflects the lightness of the construction and quite ignores the exceptional span. This illustrates a fundamental design problem that the architects of that period had in dealing with pure structure. The pure timber structure apparently only becomes architecture when concealed behind a massive decorative facade.

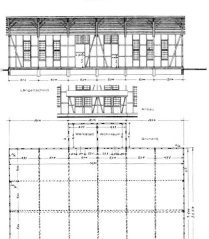

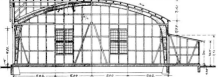

Die Form der Rahmenbinder übernahm die Otto Hetzer AG 1912 beim Bau der Flugzeughallen in Weimar. Die Zweigelenkbinder mit angehobenem hölzernem Zugband besaßen eine Spannweite von 21 m mit einem Binderabstand von 5 m.[65] Im Bereich der Tore wurden die Binder als einhüftige Rahmen ausgebildet und durch einen Torbinder abgefangen. Die Lastannahmen wurden gemäß den ministeriellen Bestimmungen vom 31. Januar 1910 mit 150 kg/m² Grundfläche für Eigengewicht, Schnee und Wind angesetzt, was nach heutiger DIN 1052 besonders im Lastfall Wind als grobe, symmetrische Vereinfachung anzusehen ist, welche zu geringeren Schnittkräften in den Rahmenecken führte.[66] Im Rahmen des Versailler Vertrages 1919 mußten drei der vier Hallen abgebaut werden, die letzte Halle verschwand Mitte der achtziger Jahre durch Abriß. In gleicher Bauart entstanden 1914 vier Flugzeughallen, die nach Chile verkauft wurden. In vergleichbarer Bauweise wurde 1912 in Weimar ein ringförmiger Lokomotivschuppen als einhüftige, unterspannte Binderkonstruktion mit 23 m Spannweite ausgeführt.[67]

The frame form was used by Otto Hetzer AG in 1912 for the construction of the aircraft hangars in Weimar. The two-pin frames with raised timber ties were placed at 5 m centres and had a span of 21 m.[65] At the doors the frames were designed to be supported on one side by a door beam. The loads were according to the ministry stipulations of 31 January 1910 and were assumed as 150 kg/m² for dead loads, snow, and wind, which from the modern viewpoint of DIN 1052 can be regarded as a rough, symmetrical simplification, particularly in the case of wind. These loads led to lower internal forces in the corners of the frames.[66] Three of the four hangars had to be demolished as part of the Treaty of Versailles of 1919 and the last one disappeared in the mid-1980s. Four identical hangars were built in 1914 and exported to Chile. In 1912 an engine roundhouse in Weimar employed a trussed beam construction supported on one side. The span was 23 m.[67]

Oben **Hetzer AG, Typenentwurf einer Flugzeughalle, 1912, Seitenansicht, Schnitte, Grundriß.**
Above Hetzer AG, design for an aircraft hangar, 1912, side elevation, sections, plan.

Rechts **Ing./Ausf.: Hetzer AG, Flugzeughalle, Weimar, 1912, Zweigelenkrahmen mit abgehängtem Zugband, Außenansicht.**
Right Engineers/contractors: Hetzer AG; aircraft hangar, Weimar, 1912, two-pin frame with suspended tie, external view.

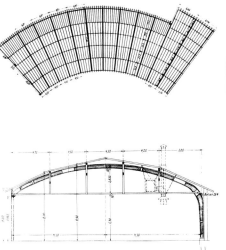

Ing./Ausf.: Hetzer AG, Lokomotivschuppen, Weimar, 1912, Zweigelenkrahmen mit abgehängtem Zugband, Schnitt, Draufsicht, Bauzustand.
Engineers/contractors: Hetzer AG; engine shed, Weimar, 1912, two-pin frame with suspended tie, section, roof plan, under construction.

Ing./Ausf.: Hetzer AG, Abbundhalle, Weimar, 1915, Zweigelenkrahmen mit abgehängtem Zugband, Innenansicht, Schnitt.
Engineers/contractors: Hetzer AG; assembly shop at the works in Weimar, 1915, two-pin frame with suspended tie, internal view, section.

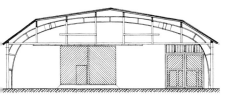

Auf dem Werksgelände der Otto Hetzer AG entstand 1915 die heute noch erhaltene Abbundhalle. Der Zweigelenkrahmen besteht aus drei Bauteilen mit zwei Stößen. Der große Binderabstand von 9 m wird durch die Verwendung von doppel-T-förmigen Pfetten erreicht. Aufgrund des Gleisanschlusses besitzt die Halle eine schräge Stirnseite.

Eine neue Halle dieses Typs ohne Zugbänder entstand als Rahmenkonstruktion für das Firmengebäude Tobias Grau in Hamburg-Rellingen. Die Rahmen mit einer Spannweite von 20 m stehen im Abstand von 5 m und sind mit einer Aluminiumaußenhaut aus Alucobondtafeln verkleidet. Das Gebäude besitzt an seinen Stirnseiten großflächige Verglasungen. Die seitlichen Verglasungen sind mit gebogenen bedruckten Sonnenschutzlamellen verschattet. Im Innern bildet eine Stahlbetonkonstruktion eine zweite Ebene, welche gleichzeitig der Aussteifung dient. Trotz einer sehr schlichten Tragwerksform entsteht durch die Klarheit des Grundrisses und die Materialwahl ein überzeugend modernes Firmengebäude mit Wiedererkennungswert.

The assembly shop of Otto Hetzer AG, which still stands today, was built in 1915. The two-pin frames consist of three parts with two joints. The large centre-to-centre spacing of 9 m was rendered possible by the use of I-section purlins. One gable wall is positioned at an angle to accommodate the adjacent railway siding.

A new building of this type but without ties was built in frame construction for the Tobias Grau company in Hamburg-Rellingen. The frames span 20 m and are placed at 5 m centres. Aluminium Alucobond panels are used for the external cladding. The gables incorporate large expanses of glass which are shaded by curved, printed louvres. A reinforced concrete structure forms a second level internally, which at the same time serves to stabilize the structure. Despite a very simple structural form, the clarity of the layout and the choice of material has created a very confident, identifiable, modern corporate structure.

Arch.: Bothe Richter Teherani, Hamburg; Ing.: Wetzel und von Seht; Firmengebäude Tobias Grau, Hamburg-Rellingen, 1998, Zweigelenkrahmen, Südfassade (vorige Doppelseite), Ostfassade, Schnitt, Grundriß.
Architects: Bothe Richter Teherani, Hamburg; engineers: Wetzel & von Seht; Tobias Grau premises, Hamburg-Rellingen, 1998, two-pin frame, south elevation (previous double page), east elevation, section, plan.

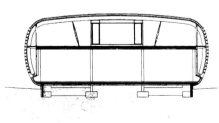

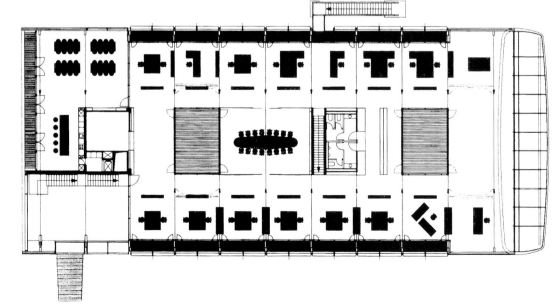

Hallen aus halbkreisförmigen Bindern

Aufgrund der schon erwähnten hohen Biegebeanspruchung halbkreisförmiger Binder finden wir diesen Bautypus nur relativ selten bei Bauwerken mit besonderem gestalterischen Anspruch.

Ein besonders schönes, vorbildliches Beispiel aber ist die Reithalle in St. Moritz. Die Zusammenarbeit zwischen der Firma Nik. Hartmann & Cie und den Ingenieuren Terner und Chopard führte hier zu einem alle Möglichkeiten der neuen Holzbauweise ausschöpfenden Trag- und Bauwerk. Auch die „Kinderkrankheiten" einer neuen Bauweise und das übergroße Vertrauen darin können hieran anschaulich verdeutlicht werden.

Auf einem rechteckigen Grundriß von 19,8 m x 34,5 m überspannen im mittleren Bereich vier halbkreisförmige Dreigelenkbogenbinder im Abstand von 4,9 m mit unterschiedlichem Doppel-T-Querschnitt den Raum. Die Giebelseiten werden durch 14 m weit spannende Gratbinder und Halbbinder überspannt, welche über eine verstärkte Firstpfette die Horizontalkräfte der gegenüberliegenden Giebelseite ausgleichen.

Single-storey sheds with semicircular arches

Owing to the aforementioned high bending stresses in semicircular arches, this structural form is found only rarely, for buildings with exceptional aesthetic demands.

One particularly elegant, exemplary specimen is the riding arena in St Moritz. The collaboration between Nik. Hartmann & Cie and the engineering practice of Terner & Chopard led in this instance to a structure which exploited all the possibilities of the new form of timber construction. But the "teething troubles" of a new construction technique and the excessive faith in the new are also clearly evident in this building.

Above the centre section of a rectangle measuring 19.8 x 34.5 m there is a roof structure comprising four semicircular three-pin arches of varying I-section at a spacing of 4.9 m. The gable ends are formed by 14-m-span hip beams and half-arches which counterbalance the horizontal forces of the opposite gable via a strengthened ridge purlin.

**Ing.: Terner und Chopard;
Ausf.: Nik. Hartmann & Cie; Reithalle, St. Moritz, 1910, Dreigelenkbogen mit abgehängtem Zugband, Bauzustand, Innenansicht.**
Engineers: Terner & Chopard;
contractor: Nik. Hartmann & Cie; riding arena, St Moritz, 1910, three-pin arch with suspended tie, under construction, internal view.

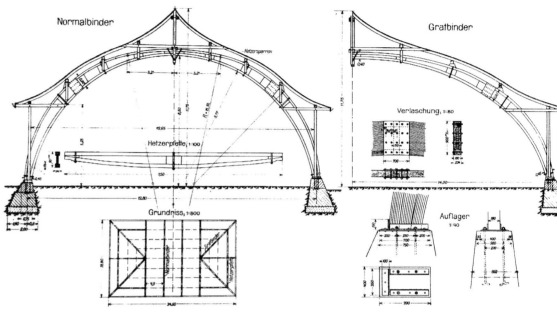

Reithalle, St. Moritz, Ansicht, Schnitte (links Normalbinder, rechts Gratbinder), Grundriß, Details (Verlaschung oben, Auflager unten).
Riding arena, St Moritz, external view, sections (left: standard member; right: hip member), plan, details (top: fish-plate joint; bottom: support).

Da zum einen die halbkreisförmige Binderform nicht der idealen Stützlinie für gleichmäßige ständige Lasten entspricht und darüber hinaus die Schneelasten mit 180 kg/m² Grundfläche im Vergleich zur heutigen Norm als zu gering angesetzt waren, wurden die errechneten Spannungen von ca. 130 kg/cm² (=1,3KN/cm²) sicher erreicht, wenn nicht sogar überschritten. Im Jahr 1917 wurden dann aufgrund der großen Verformungen 32 mm starke Stahl-Zugbänder in 6 m Höhe eingebaut. Auch die schlecht belüfteten und fäulnisgeschädigten Binderfußpunkte mußten 1928 saniert werden. Hierbei wurden die abgesägten Bereiche durch ausbetonierte Stahlprofile ersetzt. Im Eckbereich der Halle wurden ebenfalls 7,5 m weit spannende doppel-T-förmige Pfetten eingesetzt. Das doppelt gekrümmte Walmdach wurde durch gebogene Hetzer-Sparren (10 x 8 cm) erzielt. Das Gebäude wird auch heute noch als Reithalle genutzt, auch wenn die Außenansicht durch einen überdimensionierten Anbau stark beeinträchtigt ist.

As the semicircular arch form does not correspond to the ideal line of pressure for uniformly distributed permanent loads and, furthermore, was only designed for a snow load of 180 kg/m² (too low by modern standards), the calculated stresses of approx. 130 kg/cm² (= 1.3 kN/cm²) are certainly reached, indeed probably exceeded. In 1917 steel ties 32 mm thick were incorporated at a height of 6 m to limit the severe deformation. And the poorly ventilated springings of the arches had rotted badly by 1928 so had to be refurbished. The pieces cut out were replaced by concrete-filled steel sections. I-section purlins spanning 7.5 m were also used in the corners of the arena. The double-curvature hipped roof was achieved through the use of curved Hetzer rafters (100 x 80 mm). The building is still used as a riding arena, although the external elevation has been spoiled by an oversize extension.

Hallen aus spitzbogenförmigen Bindern

Der erste spitze Dreigelenkbogen mit doppel-T-förmigem Querschnitt wird durch die Hetzer AG 1911 als Stallgebäude der Firma Gebr. Grünnel in Wernesgrün (heute Wernesgrüner Brauerei) ausgeführt. Zur Leipziger Baufachausstellung entstand bereits 1913 eine ähnliche Konstruktion als Sporthalle. Die sieben etwas schwächer gekrümmten Dreigelenkrahmenbinder standen im Abstand von 6,25 m und spannten über 25 m. Die Binder hatten einen doppel-T-förmigen Querschnitt (max h =1,1 m). Die horizontalen Auflagerkräfte werden durch ein unter dem Fußboden befindliches Zugband aufgenommen. First- und Mittelpfetten waren doppel-T-förmig ausgebildet. Die Hallenlängsaussteifung erfolgte über diese Pfetten, welche durch die Gratbinder an den Giebelseiten gehalten wurden. Besondere Ausführung verlangten die zweifach gebogenen Kehlsparren der Dachfenster, die ebenfalls mit verleimtem Querschnitt ausgebildet waren. Die Herstellung benötigte drei Wochen, die Zeit der Aufstellung nur eine Woche.

Single-storey sheds with pointed arches

The first pointed three-pin I-section arch was built by Hetzer AG in 1911 as a barn for the Gebr. Grünnel company in Wernesgrün (today the Wernesgrüner brewery). At the Leipzig Building Fair of 1913 there was a similar construction in the form of a sports hall. The seven slightly less curved I-section three-pin arches (max. depth 1100 mm) were placed at 6.25 m centres and spanned more than 25 m. The horizontal support reactions were resisted by a tie positioned below floor level. Ridge and middle purlins were likewise I-sections. Longitudinal stability was provided by these purlins, which were held by the hip beams at the gable ends. Special care was required at the valley rafters which curved in two directions to accommodate the dormer windows; these also made use of glulam sections. Fabrication took three weeks, the erection took only one.

Ing./Ausf.: Hetzer AG, Sporthalle auf der Baufachausstellung, Leipzig, 1913, Dreigelenkrahmen, Längsschnitt, Ansicht, Grundriß, Innenansicht.
Engineers/contractors: Hetzer AG; sports hall, Leipzig Building Fair, 1913, three-pin frame, section, elevation, plan, internal view.

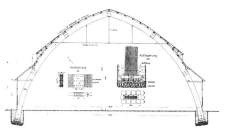

Ing.: Terner und Chopard; Ausf.: B. Zöllig, Arbon; Sängerfesthalle, Küsnacht bei Zürich, 1911, Dreigelenkbogen, Bauzustand, Querschnitt.
Engineers: Terner & Chopard; contractor: B. Zöllig, Arbon; Choirs Festival Hall, Küsnacht near Zürich, 1911, three-pin arch, under construction, section.

In Spitzbogenform wurde auch die temporäre Sängerfesthalle in Küsnacht bei Zürich mit einer Spannweite von 30 m erstellt. Die Dreigelenkspitzbögen mit rechteckigem Querschnitt (18 x 80 cm) standen im Abstand von 5 m und hatten zusätzlich ein Zugband im oberen Drittel.[68] Die Wahl dieser Tragwerksform erfolgte nicht zufällig, sondern war der idealen Stützlinie stärker als der des Halbkreisbogens angepaßt, wodurch geringere Momente auftraten und so eine günstigere Ausnutzung des Querschnittes bei großer Spannweite ermöglicht wurde. Die Gründung erfolgte aufgrund der befristeten Standzeit auf einem hölzernen Balkenrost.

Aus den spitzbögigen Bindern entwickelten sich spitze Dreigelenkrahmen, welche eine Satteldachform ermöglichten. Nach den bereits erwähnten Korrosionsproblemen bei der Verwendung von Stahl bei Eisenbahnbauten kam es zur verstärkten Verwendung von Holz und Holzleimbindern.[69] Ein besonders schönes Beispiel für diesen Typus ist die Lokomotivremise der Schweizer Bundesbahn auf dem Äbigut in Bern. Hierbei wurden spitze Dreigelenkrahmen ohne stählernes Zugband bei einer Spannweite von 20,79 m, 21,59 m und 24,82 m verwendet. Die Binder mit rechteckigem Querschnitt (bis 20 x 105 cm) stehen im Abstand von 5 m.[70] Die Anlage befindet sich heute noch in sehr gutem Zustand, obwohl sie teilweise ohne Holzschutzanstrich ausgeführt wurde.

The pointed arch shape (span 30 m) was also employed for the temporary Choirs Festival Hall in Küsnacht near Zürich. The pointed three-pin arches with a rectangular cross-section (180 x 800 mm) were placed at 5 m centres and also included a tie in the upper third.[68] The choice of this structural form was not arbitrary but instead followed the ideal line of pressure somewhat better than the semicircular arch, leading to lower bending moments and hence to better use of the cross-section for a long span. Owing to the temporary nature of the construction, a timber grillage was adequate for the foundation.

The pointed arch form spawned the pointed three-pin frame, which allowed the inclusion of a pitched roof. Steel used for railway structures suffered from serious corrosion problems, as mentioned above; after this drawback was recognized, timber and glulam were increasingly used as substitutes.[69] One particularly elegant example of this type is the Swiss Railways engine shed at Äbigut in Bern. Pitched three-pin frames with a rectangular section (max. 200 x 1050 mm) were employed here without steel ties; the spans were 20.79 m, 21.59 m and 24.82 m, and the frames were spaced at 5 m centres.[70] The facility is still in remarkably good condition today, even though not all of the wood was treated with preservative.

Ing.: Terner und Chopard; Ausf.: Gribi & Cie., Burgdorf; Lokomotivremise, Bern, 1911, Dreigelenkrahmen, Schnitt.
Engineers: Terner & Chopard; contractor: Gribi & Cie., Burgdorf; engine shed, Bern, 1911, three-pin frame, section.

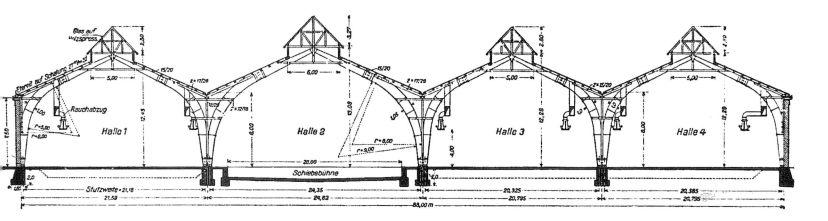

Lokomotivremise, Bern, 1911, Bauzustand, Innenansichten.
Engine shed, Bern, 1911,
under construction, internal views.

Unten **Ing./Ausf.: Hetzer AG, Schiebebühnenhalle am Rosenstein, Stuttgart, 1915, Quer- und Längsschnitt.**
Bottom Engineers/contractors: Hetzer AG; traverser hall, Rosenstein, Stuttgart, sections.

Aufgrund der in Bern gemachten guten Erfahrungen entschied man sich 1915 in Stuttgart bei der Überdachung der Schiebebühnenhalle am Rosenstein für dieselbe Bauweise bei einer Spannweite von 25 m. Nach Kostenvergleichen lagen Holzkonstruktionen etwa 50 % günstiger als Stahl- und Stahlbetonkonstruktionen (12,- zu 20,- bzw. 22,- RM/m²).[71] Um den Aufwand des Tragwerkes noch zu minimieren, wurden die Binderabstände auf 10 m verdoppelt und mit doppel-T-förmigen Hetzerpfetten überspannt, welche zugleich die gedrückten Binderuntergurte gegen Kippen aussteiften. Der feuerfeste Anstrich (Wetterfestonat) hielt aber dem starken Feuchtigkeitsanfall nicht stand. Korrosionserscheinungen an Stahlschrauben traten nur im luftzugänglichen Bereich, nicht dagegen im Holz auf. Die Halle fiel den Zerstörungen des Zweiten Weltkriegs zum Opfer.

The good experiences in Bern led to the decision to use the same form of construction in 1915 for the roof to a 25-m-span traverser hall at Rosenstein in Stuttgart. A comparison of costs revealed that timber would bring savings of about 50 % compared to steel or reinforced concrete (12, 20 and 22 Reichsmark/m² respectively).[71] In order to minimize the cost of the structure, the spacing of the frames was doubled to 10 m and this distance spanned with I-section Hetzer purlins, which at the same time provided lateral restraint to the lower (compression) flanges of the frames. The fire-resistant finish (Wetterfestonat) could not withstand the high moisture levels, however, and the steel bolts started to corrode, albeit only at places exposed to the air, not within the timber itself. The building was destroyed during World War II.

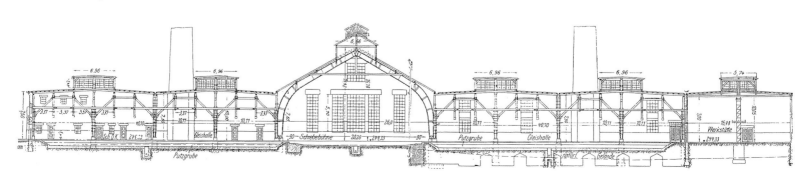

Ing./Ausf.: Hetzer AG, Rohsalzspeicher, Staßfurt, 1914, Zweigelenkbögen, Detailansicht des Dachs, Querschnitt, Längsschnitt, Innenansicht.
Engineers/contractors: Hetzer AG; crude salt store, Berlepsch Mine, Stassfurt, 1914, two-pin arch, detail of roof, section, longitudinal section, internal view.

Hallen aus parabelförmigen Bindern

Die parabelförmigen Binder stellen ein sehr wirtschaftliches Tragwerk mit geringer Biegebeanspruchung dar, welches daher besonders häufig bei Lagerhallen benutzt wird. Diese Binder werden in der Regel als Zweigelenkbinder mit biegesteifen Bauteilstößen ausgebildet. Ein großer Verwendungsbereich für Holzhallen stellt durch ihre Korrosionsbeständigkeit die Kaliindustrie dar. So entstand 1914 ein 96 m langer Rohsalzspeicher für das Königliche Salzwerk Staßfurt auf dem Gelände des Berlepsch-Schachtes. Die Zweigelenkbinder haben eine Spannweite von 30 m und stehen im Achsabstand von 5 m. Die Binder ruhen auf massiven 5 m hohen Widerlagern, wodurch zusätzlicher Raum geschaffen werden konnte und die Binderfußpunkte trocken gelagert sind. Gleiche Salzlagerhallen entstanden für das Kaliwerk der Steinförde AG in Wathlingen bei Celle und in Velsen, Holland. Die Bauaufgabe hat sich bis heute nahezu unverändert erhalten, wobei die Spannweiten sich etwas erhöhten.

Flachere parabelförmige Binder finden sich als Dreigelenkbögen bei dem Tramdepot in Basel von 1915. Die 92 m lange und 43 m breite zweischiffige Halle wird durch zwei parabelförmige Dreigelenkbogenbinder mit abgehängtem stählernen Zugband überspannt. Die Binder stehen im Abstand von 7 m und haben einen Rechteckquerschnitt von 18 x 60 cm. Der Binderabstand wird ebenfalls mittels Hetzer-Pfetten (15 x 32 cm) überspannt. Noch heute befindet sich das Depot in bestem Zustand und voller Benutzung.

Bei dem Neubau des schiffsarchäologischen Instituts in Lelystad wurde eine 140 m lange Halle aus parabelförmigen Dreigelenkbindern errichtet. Aufgrund der großen Lasten durch den Kranbahnbetrieb mußten die Binder relativ stark dimensioniert werden.

Single-storey sheds with parabolic arches

The parabolic arch represents a very economic structural form with low bending stresses; therefore, it is particular popular for warehouses. These structures are normally designed as two-pin arches with rigid joints. Owing to the corrosion resistance of wood, the potash industry is a major user of timber sheds. In 1914 a 96-m-long crude salt store was built for the Stassfurt Royal Saltworks on the site of the Berlepsch Mine. The two-pin arches span 30 m and are positioned at 5 m centres. They are founded on 5-m-high masonry supports, thereby creating extra storage space and helping to keep the springings of the timber arches dry. Identical salt storage sheds were built for the potash works of Steinförde AG in Wathlingen near Celle, and in Velsen, Netherlands. This application has remained practically unchanged to this day, although the spans have increased somewhat.

Shallower parabolic three-pin arches were used for the tram depot in Basel in 1915. The roof structure to the 92 x 43 m two-bay building is formed by two parabolic three-pin arches having a rectangular section (180 x 600 mm) with steel ties on hangers. Hetzer purlins (150 x 320 mm) span the 7 m between each arch in order to carry the roof. The depot is still in excellent condition and remains in full use.

A 140-m-long shed employing parabolic three-pin arches formed the new building for the Institute for Ship Archaeology in Lelystad. The heavy loads from the crane rails necessitated relatively large members.

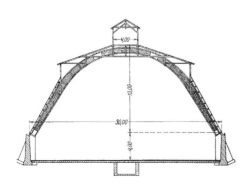

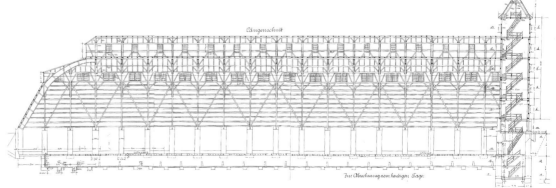

Links Ing./Ausf.: Hetzer AG, Rohsalzspeicher,
Wathlingen, ca. 1912, Bauzustand.
Rechts Ing./Ausf.: Nemaho, Salzlagerhalle, Velsen,
1928-1929, Bauzustand.
Left Engineers/contractors: Hetzer AG;
crude salt store, Steinförde AG, Wathlingen, c. 1912,
under construction.
Right Engineers/contractors: Nemaho; salt store,
Velsen, 1928-1929, under construction.

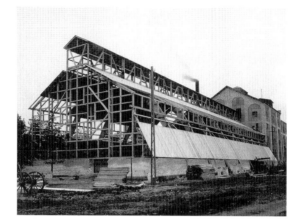 

Arch.: R. Leisinger; Ing.: Terner und Chopard; Ausf.:
Schweizer AG für Hetzer'sche Holzbauweisen;
Straßenbahndepot Dreispitz, Basel, 1915,
Dreigelenkbogen mit Zugband.
Schnitt, Innenansichten.
Architect: R. Leisinger; engineers: Terner & Chopard;
contractor for Hetzer system: Schweizer AG; Dreispitz
tram depot, Basel, 1915, three-pin arch with tie.
Section, internal views.

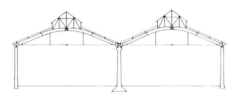

Arch.: Kees Christiaanse; Ausf.: Nemaho; Schiffsarchäologisches Institut, Lelystad, Holland, 1998, Dreigelenkbogen, Querschnitte, Bauzustand, Längsschnitt, Grundriß, Außenansicht, Innenansicht.
Architect: Kees Christiaanse; contractor: Nemaho; Institute for Ship Archaeology, Lelystad, Netherlands, 1998, three-pin arch, sections, under construction, longitudinal section, plan, external view, internal view.

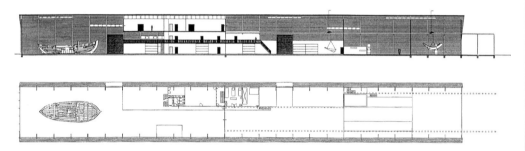

Mehrschiffige Binderhallen

Eine der ersten mehrschiffigen Binderhallen wurde 1922 in Zusammenarbeit der Nemaho und der Otto Hetzer AG in Weimar für die R.A.I. in Amsterdam gebaut. Die dreischiffige Halle besaß eine Länge von 187 m und eine Gesamtbreite von 55,1 m. Das Hauptschiff der Halle hatte zwar nur 30 m Spannweite, aber dies bei einer Höhe von nur 11,25 m. Die Binder standen im Abstand von 6,75 m. Eine ähnliche Halle mit etwas kleineren Ausmaßen entstand für die Blumenausstellung in Utrecht, deren größte Spannweite 24 m betrug. Zum Bau einer dreischiffigen Viehmarkthalle in s'Hertogenbosch kam es 1930, deren Abmessungen 70 x 87,5 m betrugen. Die parabelförmigen Binder hatten eine Spannweite von 30 und 20 m und standen im Abstand von 6,75 m. Im Jahr 1939 wurde die Anlage durch eine 50 m weit spannende Halle mit 13 m Höhe erweitert. Die maximale Binderhöhe betrug 1,42 m. Aufgrund der hohen Feuchtigkeit beim Reinigen der Hallen mußten später die Binderfußpunkte in Stahlbeton ersetzt werden. Die Widerstandsfähigkeit der Binder wurde 1947 bei einem Brand unter Beweis gestellt. Die Halle steht heute noch.

Multi-bay single-storey sheds

One of the first multi-bay single-storey sheds was built in 1922, the outcome of a joint venture between Nemaho and Otto Hetzer AG, Weimar, for the R.A.I. in Amsterdam. The three-bay shed was 187 m long and 55.1 m wide over all three bays. The main bay had a span of only 30 m but it achieved this with a height of just 11.25 m. The frames were placed at 6.75 m centres. A similar but slightly smaller building (max. span 24 m) was erected for the flower show in Utrecht. A three-bay cattle market measuring 70 x 87.5 m was built in s'Hertogenbosch in 1930. The parabolic arches at 6.75 m centres spanned 30 m and 20 m. An extension with a span of 50 m and a rise of 13 m was added in 1939. Maximum depth of the members was 1420 mm. However, the high humidity in the hall caused by cleaning operations led to the springings of the arches having to be replaced by reinforced concrete ones at a later date. The arches were really put to the test during a fire in 1947. The building still stands today.

Linke Seite **Ing./Ausf.: Nemaho, Hetzer AG; Ausstellungshalle für die R.A.I., Amsterdam, 1922, Dreigelenkrahmen, Innenansicht.**
Facing page Engineers/contractors: Nemaho, Hetzer AG; exhibition hall for the R.A.I. in Amsterdam, 1922, three-pin frame, internal view.

Arch.: Gemeentewerken Utrecht; Ing./Ausf.: Nemaho; Blumenhalle, Utrecht, 1928, Dreigelenkrahmen, Bauzustand, Innenansicht.
Architects: Gemeentewerken Utrecht; engineers/contractors: Nemaho; flower show building, Utrecht, 1928, three-pin frame, under construction, internal view.

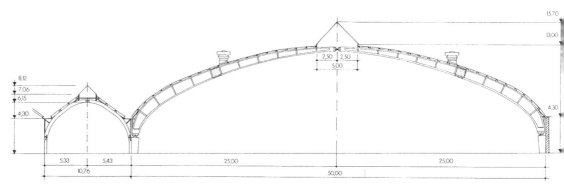

Arch.: Gemeentewerken Middenhal Rundermarkt; Ing./Ausf.: Nemaho; Viehmarkthalle, s'Hertogenbosch, 1930, Erweiterung 1939, parabolischer Dreigelenkrahmen, teilweise mit Zugband, Schnitt.
Architects: Gemeentewerken Middenhal Rundermarkt; engineers/contractors: Nemaho; cattle market, s'Hertogenbosch, 1930, extension 1939, parabolic three-pin frame, partly with tie, section.

Viehmarkthalle, s'Hertogenbosch, 1930, Bauzustand (links), nach Brand 1947 (rechts).
Cattle market, s'Hertogenbosch, 1930, under construction (left), after the fire in 1947 (right).

Viehmarkthalle, s'Hertogenbosch, Erweiterung 1939.
Cattle market, s'Hertogenbosch, extension 1939.

Auktionshallen

Im Rahmen der landwirtschaftlichen Entwicklung der Polder wurden in Holland seit 1920 eine Reihe von Gemüseauktionshallen errichtet, welche sowohl vom Wasser, als auch von Land beliefert werden konnten. Die Auktionshalle in Noord-Scharwoude wurde zu ihrer Entstehungszeit hauptsächlich über Kanäle beliefert, so daß die Halle praktisch eine überdachte Wasserfläche darstellte. Diese wurde mit zunehmender Lieferung per LKW dann später zugeschüttet. 1957 wurde die Halle um eine 38,5 m weit spannende Halle erweitert. Die Halle soll in den nächsten Jahren abgerissen werden und einem Wohngebiet mit Supermarkt weichen.

Auction halls

Since 1920 agricultural developments on the Dutch polders included the building of a series of vegetable auction halls which could receive deliveries by road or canal. When it was built, the auction hall in Noord-Scharwoude received most of its goods via the canals; the hall itself was virtually a covered pond. This was later filled in as more and more produce arrived by road. In 1957 the building was extended by the addition of a hall with a span of 38.5 m. Unfortunately, the building will soon have to be demolished to make way for a new residential estate and supermarket.

Arch.: H. A. Pothoven; Ing./Ausf.: Nemaho; Auktionshalle, Ter Aar, 1953, parabelförmiger Zweigelenkbogen mit Kragarmen,
Oben **Eröffnung der Auktionshalle durch Königin Juliana.**
Unten **Außenansicht.**
Architect: H. A. Pothoven; engineers/contractors: Nemaho; auction hall, Ter Aar, 1953, parabolic two-pin arch with cantilevers.
Above Opening ceremony with Queen Juliana.
Below External view.

**Arch.: A. Vis, Oudkarspel, H. Tauber;
Ing./Ausf.: Nemaho; Gemüseauktionshalle,
Noord-Scharwoude, 1928, Erweiterung 1957,
parabelförmiger Dreigelenkrahmen mit Zugband, Innenansichten, oben 1957, rechts 1928.**
Architects: A. Vis, Oudkarspel, H. Tauber;
engineers/contractors: Nemaho; vegetable auction
hall, Noord-Scharwoude, 1928, extension 1957, parabolic three-pin frame with tie, internal views, above
1957, right 1928.

Kirchen

Die Reihung der Binder erinnert in vielen Hallen an sakrale Räume, wie sie durch romanische und gotische Kirchen bekannt sind. Es ist also naheliegend, daß diese Holzleimbinder auch zur Überdachung von Kirchen genutzt wurden. Die Kirche in Amsterdam soll hier nur als Beispiel dienen. In den Vereinigten Staaten entstanden seit 1935 Kirchendächer mit Holzleimbindern, wie zum Beispiel die Kirchen in Laona und Middleton, Wisconsin.

Churches

The rows of frames in many halls remind the observer of sacred buildings, like Romanesque and Gothic churches. Therefore, it was only logical that such glued laminated timber should find favour for church roofs too. The church in Amsterdam is only intended to serve as one example. In the USA church roofs with glulam beams have been built since 1935, e.g. the churches in Laona and Middleton, Wisconsin.

Linke Seite **Arch.: E. Drewes; Ing./Ausf.: Nemaho; Kirche, Buiksloot, Amsterdam, 1928, parabelförmiger Zweigelenkrahmen, Innenansicht.**
Facing page Architect: E. Drewes; engineers/contractors: Nemaho; church, Buiksloot, 1928, parabolic two-pin frame, internal view.

Arch.: Max Hanisch sen., Marinette, Wisconsin; Ing./Ausf.: Unit Structures, Peshtigo, Wisconsin; Katholische Kirche St. Leonhard's, Laona, Wisconsin, 1936, spitzer Dreigelenkbogen, Innenansicht.
Architect: Max Hanisch sen., Marinette, Wisconsin; engineers/contractors: Unit Structures, Peshtigo, Wisconsin; Catholic church, St Leonhard's, Laona, Wisconsin, 1936, pointed three-pin arch, internal view.

Arch.: John Flad; Ing./Ausf.: Unit Structures; Katholische Kirche, Middleton, Wisconsin, 1950, parabolischer Bogen, Innenansicht.
Architect: John Flad; engineers/contractors: Unit Structures; Catholic church, Middleton, Wisconsin, 1950, parabolic arch, internal view.

Fabrik- und Lagerhallen

Die Anwendungsmöglichkeiten der Holzleimbauweise im Fabrik- und Lagerhallenbereich ist von großer Vielfalt. Mehrere Autoreparaturwerkstätten entstanden als Binderhallen aus parabelförmigen Zweigelenkrahmen, zum Beispiel in Amersfoort und in Waremme. Die Citroën Garage in Waremme in Belgien wurde 1950 gebaut und unterscheidet sich vor allem in der Verwendung eines rechteckförmigen Querschnitts, quer liegenden Oberlichtern und einer geringeren Spannweite.

Beim Bau von Lagerhallen wurden oftmals, wie beispielsweise in Deventer, aufgrund der günstigen Raumhöhen Dreigelenkrahmen verwendet. Das Besondere dieser Halle sind die Dachluken, welche ein einfaches Absetzen der per Kran aus dem Schiff gehobenen Waren ermöglichten.

Factories and warehouses

The potential applications for glued laminated timber for factory buildings and warehouses is very diverse. Several vehicle repair workshops were constructed as glulam sheds with parabolic two-pin arches, e.g. in Amersfoort and in Waremme. The Citroën garage in Waremme, Belgium, was built in 1950 and is distinctive because of its use of rectangular sections, the transverse rooflight arrangement and the short span.

Three-pin frames are often used for warehouses, e.g. in Deventer, owing to the beneficial internal headroom. The special feature of the warehouse in Deventer is the roof openings, which enable goods to be transferred by crane directly from ship to building.

Oben **Arch.: H. A. Pothoven; Ing./Ausf.: Nemaho; Garage Pon, Amersfoort, 1928, parabelförmiger Dreigelenkrahmen, Innenansicht.**
Above Architect: H. A. Pothoven; engineers/contractors: Nemaho; Pon garage, Amersfoort, 1928, parabolic three-pin frame, internal view.

Rechts **Arch.: Fernard Lognard, Waremme; Ing./Ausf.: Nemaho; Citroën Garage, Waremme, 1950, parabelförmiger Dreigelenkrahmen, Innenansicht.**
Right Architect: Fernard Lognard, Waremme; engineers/contractors: Nemaho; Citroën garage, Waremme, 1950, parabolic three-pin frame, internal view.

Ing./Ausf.: Nemaho, Hafenlagerhalle, Deventer, 1950, Dreigelenkrahmen, Außenansicht geschlossen, Außenansicht offen, Innenansicht Dachfenster.
Engineers/contractors: Nemaho; port warehouse, Deventer, 1950, three-pin frame, external view with openings closed, external view with openings open, internal view showing roof openings.

Die Rohkohlemischhalle in Marl von 1981 stellt eine sehr wirtschaftliche Form der Überdachung dar. Die Halle besteht aus 36 Dreigelenkrahmen mit einer Spannweite von 60,5 m. Je sechs Rahmenhalbachsen wurden incl. Pfetten und Aussteifungsverbänden am Boden vorgefertigt und innerhalb von drei Tagen aufgerichtet. Die dafür notwendige gelenkige Lagerung erfolgte durch eine zweiteilige Stahlkonstruktion, welche mittels eines Gelenkbolzens verbunden war. Diese Lagerung setzte auf wandartigen Stahlbetoneinzelfundamenten auf, welche gleichzeitig einen Anprallschutz für die Holzkonstruktion überflüssig machte.

Weitere Hallen mit Dreigelenkrahmen entstanden 1935 in Willemstad, Curaçao, und 1939 in Durban, Südafrika.

1946-1948 wurde in Bogotá die seinerzeit größte Fabrikhalle mit 68 m Spannweite gebaut. Die Höhe der Halle betrug 15 m. Die aus 6 Bauteilen zusammengesetzten parabelförmigen Binder standen im Abstand von 6,57 m. Eine etwas kleinere Halle wurde 1952 als Flugzeughangar in Barranquilla, Kolumbien, mit 51,3 m Spannweite im Abstand von 6 m gebaut.[72]

The raw coal mixing shed in Marl dating from 1981 represents a very economic form of roofing-over an area. The building consists of 36 three-pin frames with a span of 60.5 m. Groups of six half-frames, including purlins and bracing, were assembled on the ground and erected within three days. The hinged supports required were realized as two-part steel elements connected by means of hinge pins. These supports are mounted on reinforced concrete pad foundations in the form of plinths, thereby rendering unnecessary any form of impact protection for the timber construction.

Further single-storey sheds with three-pin frames were built in 1935 in Willemstad, Curaçao, and in 1939 in Durban, South Africa.

The, at the time, largest factory building of its kind (span 68 m) was constructed in 1946-1948 in Bogotá, Colombia. The parabolic arches rose 15 m and were each made up of six segments and placed at 6.57 m centres. A slightly smaller building was erected in Barranquilla, Colombia, in 1952 as an aircraft hangar; the frames at 6 m centres spanned 51.3 m.[72]

Ing.: Kirschner, Dülmen; Ausf.: Nemaho; Rohkohlemischhalle, Marl, 1981, Dreigelenkrahmen, Bauzustand.
Engineer: Kirschner, Dülmen; contractor: Nemaho; raw coal mixing shed, Marl, 1981, three-pin frame, under construction.

Ing./Ausf.: Nemaho; Kunstdüngerhalle, Durban, 1939, parabelförmiger Dreigelenkbogen, Außenansicht.
Engineers/contractors: Nemaho; artificial fertilizer plant, Durban, 1939, parabolic three-pin arch, external view.

Rechts **Arch.: Manuel de Vengoechea, Bogotá; Ing./Ausf.: Nemaho; Fabrikhalle, Bogotá, 1947-1948, parabelförmiger Dreigelenkrahmen aus sechs Stößen, Bauzustand.**
Right Architect: Manuel de Vengoechea, Bogotá; engineers/contractors: Nemaho; factory in Bogotá, Colombia, 1947-1948, parabolic three-pin frame (in six segments), under construction.

Unten **Ing./Ausf.: Nemaho; Flugzeughangar, Barranquilla, Kolumbien, 1952, parabelförmiger Dreigelenkrahmen, Schnitt, Sparren- und Pfettenplan.**
Below Engineers/Contractors: Nemaho; aircraft hangar, Barranquilla, Colombia, 1952, parabolic three-pin frame, section, plan on rafters and purlins.

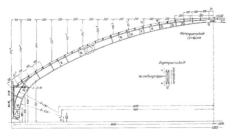

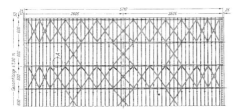

Hafenlagerhalle, Willemstad, Curaçao, 1950, Dreigelenkrahmen, Luftansicht, Detail Dachfenster.
Port warehouse, Willemstad, Curaçao, 1950, three-pin frame, aerial view, detail of rooflight.

Vorige Seite **Ing./Ausf.: Nemaho; Hafenlagerhalle, Willemstad, Curaçao, 1950, Dreigelenkrahmen, Luftansicht, Innenansicht Bauzustand.**
Previous page Engineers/contractors: Nemaho; port warehouse, Willemstad, Curaçao, 1950, three-pin frame, internal view during construction.

Bogenbinderhallen großer Spannweite

Die bogenförmigen Binderhallen erreichten in den sechziger Jahren ihre größten Spannweiten mit bis zu 100 m. Sie wurden in der Regel als Zwei- oder Dreigelenkbögen ausgeführt, wobei die Anzahl der Stöße von den jeweiligen Transportbedingungen abhing. So wurde 1962 in Joinville in Frankreich eine 92 m weit spannende Halle und 1964 in Tours eine 98 m weit spannende Ausstellungshalle gebaut. Die im Abstand von 10 m stehenden parabelförmigen Binder wurden als Zweigelenkbögen mit zwei Montagestößen ausgebildet. Die Binder selbst sind zweiteilig mit je 14 x 150 cm Querschnittsabmessungen dimensioniert. Die Giebelbinder wurden noch höher (1,76 m) und zur Erhöhung der Querbiegesteifigkeit gespreizt ausgebildet. Damit waren auch die Extreme ästhetisch verträglicher Querschnittsabmessungen erreicht, wenn nicht gar überschritten.

Long-span glulam buildings

Arch-type glulam beams reached their maximum spans – up to 100 m – during the 1960s. Such spans were normally achieved with two- or three-pin arches, with the number of splices depending on the transport situation in each case. For example, a building with a span of 92 m was erected in 1962 in Joinville, France, and in 1964 a 98-m-span exhibition hall in Tours. The parabolic frames on a 10 m grid were designed as two-pin arches with two assembly joints. The arches themselves were made up of two parts each with a cross-section of 140 x 1500 mm. The gable frames were even deeper (1760 mm) and designed with a splayed form to improve transverse bending strength. These represent, if not exceed, the limits for aesthetically acceptable sections.

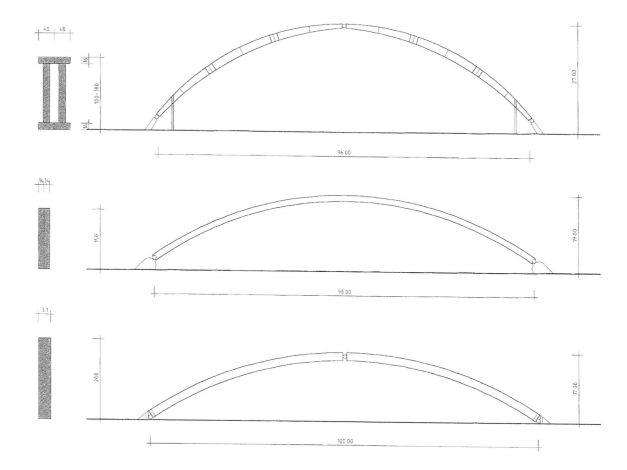

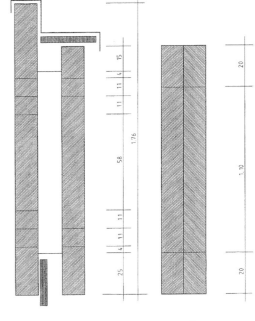

Der große Binderabstand verursacht für die Pfetten große Spannweiten, so daß sie in den steileren Dachbereichen mittig diagonal abgestützt werden müssen, um nur einachsig auf Biegung beansprucht zu werden. Gleichzeitig dienen sie im Bereich der Giebelpfetten als k-förmige Stabilisierungs- und Aussteifungsverbände.[73] Mit dem Erreichen dieser Spannweiten stieß die Entwicklung an ihre statischen und ästhetischen Grenzen und findet zur Zeit nur selten Anwendung. Die heutigen Gewerbe- und Sporthallen besitzen in der Regel Spannweiten zwischen 30 und 60 m.

Bei der Eislaufhalle in Bern wurden 1970 76-86 m weit spannende Bogenbinder verwendet, deren Auflager eine Höhendifferenz von über 10 m haben. Die schräg angebrachten Zugbänder sind konstruktiv zwar verständlich, führen aber zu einem stark einseitig betonten Raum, der durch diese sehr unruhig zerschnitten wird. Darüber hinaus wurden die Zugbänder aus starken Rechteck-Stahlprofilen ausgebildet, um so Beleuchtungskörper und andere Gegenstände befestigen zu können. Zur Stabilisierung der kastenförmigen 1,2 m hohen Binder dienten massive Querträger, die mittels Helikopter eingesetzt werden mußten. In den stärker geneigten Dachbereichen wurden die Koppelpfetten durch liegende Fachwerkträger vor Querbiegung bewahrt. Die Dachhaut besteht aus einer transluzenten Folie, welche tagsüber eine natürliche Belichtung der Halle ermöglicht.

The wide spacing of the frames means long spans for the purlins, which in turn have to be braced by diagonals at mid-span at the steeper areas of the roof to ensure that bending remains uniaxial. At the same time, they provide stability in the form of K-bracing in the region of the gable purlins.[73] These spans represent the limits to developments in both engineering and architectural terms and are hardly considered nowadays. Currently, spans of 30-60 m are customary for commercial and sports applications.

The ice rink in Bern (1970) employed arches spanning 76-86 m whose supports exhibit a height difference exceeding 10 m. The inclined ties seem logical in constructional terms but they dissect the interior and lead to a heavily one-sided appearance. Furthermore, the ties are made from large rectangular steel sections in order to carry the lights and other equipment. The box-shaped 1200-mm-deep arches are stabilized by massive transverse beams which had to be erected with the help of a helicopter. The continuous purlins had to be braced by horizontal girders at the steeper parts of the roof to prevent transverse bending. The roof covering comprises a translucent foil which, during the day, allows a maximum amount of daylight to illuminate the interior.

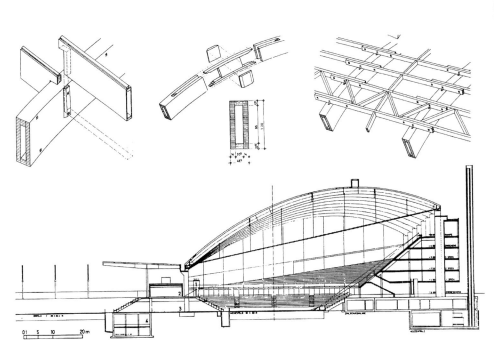

**Arch.: W. Schaar, F. Zulauf; Ing.: Emch & Berger;
Ausf.: ARGE des Zimmermeister-Verbandes von
Bern und Umgebung; Eislaufhalle, Bern, 1970,
Zweigelenkbogen mit abgehängtem Zugband.**
Oben links **Details: Pfettenstoß, Binderstoß, Teil-
isometrie, Schnitt.**
Oben rechts **Binder mit Koppelpfetten.**
Unten **Montage der Binder, Binderfußpunkt.**
Architects: W. Schaar, F. Zulauf; engineers: Emch &
Berger; contractor: ARGE des Zimmermeister-
Verbandes von Bern und Umgebung; ice rink, Bern,
1970, two-pin arch with suspended tie.
Left top Details: purlin splice, arch splice, part isometric
view, section.
Top right Arch with purlins.
Bottom Erecting the arches, springing.

Eislaufhalle Bern.
Vorige Doppelseite **Bauzustand, Montage der Binder.**
Linke Seite **Detail mit Stoß und Koppelpfetten mit Fachwerkträger.**
Rechts **Innenansicht, Außenansicht.**
Ice rink, Bern.
Previous double page Under construction, erecting the arches.
Left page Joint with continuous purlins and girders.
Right Internal view, external view.

In Berlin-Spandau wurde 1998 die Holzlagerhalle für die Firma Bauer errichtet, welche aus Dreigelenkbögen mit 25 m Spannweite besteht, die beidseitig 12,5 m auskragen. Die Ober- und Untergurte sind zweiteilig ausgebildet und mittig durch Diagonalen versteift. Ursprünglich sollten die Binder aus verdübelten Vollholzquerschnitten zusammengesetzt werden, wobei die ausführende Firma sich nicht in der Lage sah, diese zu biegen und letztendlich Brettschichtholz verwendet wurde. Die Deckenplatte wurde als Brettstapeldecke (hochkant stehende, zu Decken vernagelte oder verleimte Bretter) ausgebildet und dient damit gleichzeitig der Aussteifung. Jeweils zwei Binder sind gemeinsam rahmenartig ausgesteift. Diese Halle ist ein Beispiel, wie durch ein gut gestaltetes Tragwerk eine werbewirksame Selbstdarstellung eines Betriebes erreicht werden kann.[74]

A timber warehouse for the Bauer company was erected in Berlin-Spandau in 1998. This consists of three-pin arches with a span of 25 m and a 12.5 m cantilever on both sides. The upper and lower chords are each in two parts stiffened by diagonals fixed in between. Originally, the frames were intended to be fabricated from solid sections joined by dowels, but the contractor was not in a position to bend these and so glulam members were used in the end. The roof covering of boards laid on edge also serves to stabilize the construction. Each pair of arches is braced together. This building is one example of how a well-designed structure can itself act as an advertisement for the work of a company.[74]

**Arch.: Thomas Schindler, Waldkirch;
Ing.: Gerhard Pichler, Franz Stieglmeier, Berlin;
Ausf.: Meyer Holzbau GmbH; Holzlagerhalle
Bauer, Berlin-Spandau, 1998, Dreigelenkbogen
mit zwei Kragarmen, Querschnitt Hallenbinder.**
Architect: Thomas Schindler, Waldkirch;
engineers: Gerhard Pichler, Franz Stieglmeier, Berlin;
contractor: Meyer Holzbau GmbH; Bauer timber
warehouse, Berlin-Spandau, 1998, three-pin arch with
two cantilevers, section.

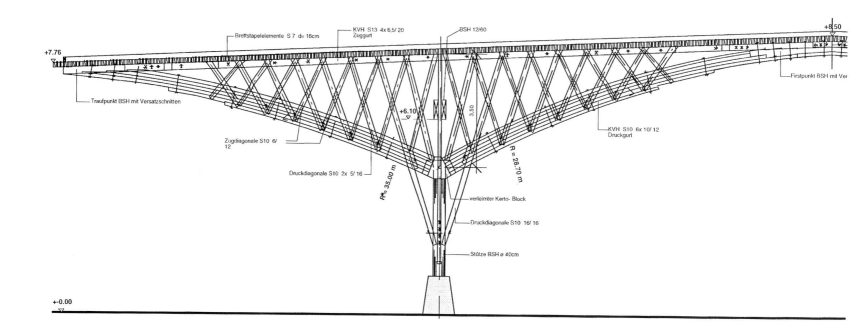

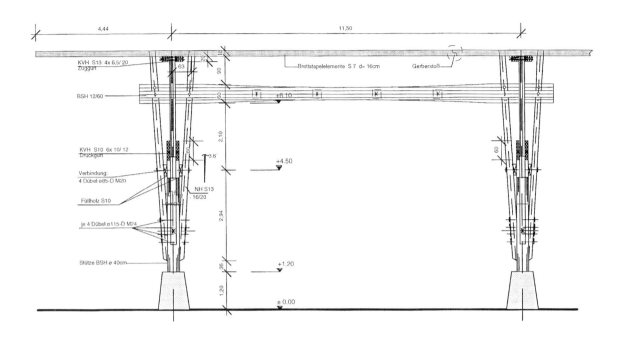

KVH S13 4x 6,5/ 20
Zuggurt

BSH 12/60

Brettstapelelemente S 7 d= 16cm

Gerberstoß

KVH S10 6x 10/ 12
Druckgurt

Verbindung:
4 Dübel ø85-D M20

Füllholz S10

NH S13
16/20

je 4 Dübel ø115-D M24

Stütze BSH ø 40cm

4,44

11,50

+6.10

+4.50

+1.20

± 0.00

Holzlagerhalle Bauer, Vertikalschnitt Hallenbinder, Ober- und Untergurt, Montage, Innenansicht, Außenansicht (nächste Doppelseite).
Bauer timber warehouse, section through top and bottom chords of main frame, erection, internal view, external view (next double page).

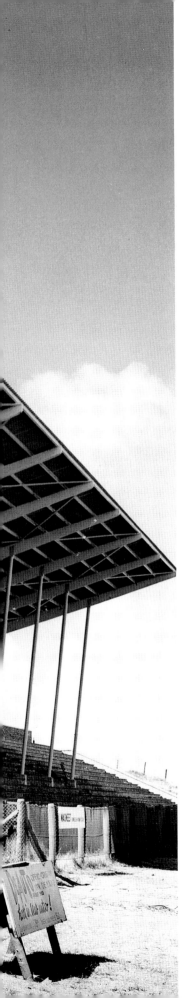

Kragdächer
Cantilever roofs

Kragdächer finden in der Regel dort Verwendung, wo mit einer großen gestalterischen Geste Aufmerksamkeit erregt werden soll oder Stützen zu Sicht- oder Nutzungseinschränkungen führen würden. Beim Bau der Tankstelle in Gladbeck zieht das 12 m weit auskragende Dach das Auge des Autofahrers auf sich.

Da der eingespannte Kragarm als statisches System große Verformungen mit sich bringt, sind große Querschnitte im Bereich der Einspannung erforderlich. Die beiden Kragbinder liegen daher leicht zurückgesetzt in der Dachhaut, so daß das Auge die gesamte Querschnittshöhe kaum wahrnimmt. Der dünne Dachrand unterstützt die Dynamik des Bauwerkes.

Bei der Tribünenüberdachung in Zandvoort kragt die Konstruktion 19 m weit aus, so daß eine alleinige Einspannung der Binder nicht mehr ausgereicht hätte. Daher wurden Pendelstützen notwendig, welche gezwungenermaßen das Sichtfeld beeinträchtigen.

Cantilever roofs are generally used in situations where a great design gesture is required to attract attention or where columns would impede sight-lines or restrict use. The 12 m cantilever roof of the petrol station in Walsum catches the eye of the motorist.

As the restrained cantilever is a structural system prone to large deflections, a large cross-section is necessary adjacent the support. Here, the two cantilever beams are partly above, partly below the roofline so that the full cross-section is not readily apparent. The slender edge to the roof reinforces the dynamic impression of the structure.

The roof over the grandstand at Zandvoort cantilevers 19 m. In this case the restrained (encastré) support is inadequate on its own. Therefore, pin-jointed columns were included, which of course interrupt spectators' sight-lines.

Um diese Sichtbeeinträchtigung zu reduzieren, sind abgehängte Dachkonstruktionen wie bei der Tribünenüberdachung des Steigerwaldstadions in Erfurt sinnvoll. Um zusätzlich den Binderabstand auf 10 m zu erhöhen, wurde hierbei eine textile Dachhaut gewählt, welche zweiachsig gegenläufig gekrümmt von Binder zu Binder spannt. Dadurch wird die nur auf Zugbeanspruchung tragende Membran vorgespannt und ausreichend stabilisiert.

Die zweiteiligen Holzleimbinder bestehen aus einer schrägen Stütze und einem abgehängten Kragträger, welcher von einem Pylon aus abgespannt wird. Der Pylon besteht aus gespreizten Stahlrohren. Zwischen den Bindern bilden Bögen aus Stahlrohren die Hochpunkte der Membran, welche zu den Bindern und dem rückwärtigen Fußpunkt der Pylone entwässert wird. Aufgrund der leichten Konstruktion wurde leider eine Abspannung von unten gegen Sog erforderlich, welche eine geringe Sichteinschränkung darstellt. Durch die leichte Krümmung der Tribüne erhält die Überdachung zusätzlichen Schwung und entwickelt mit ihren segelartigen Membranen eine hohe visuelle Kraft.

To overcome this problem, suspended roof constructions, like the one over the grandstand at the Steigerwald stadium in Erfurt, are a viable alternative. In this case, a two-way spanning textile roof covering was chosen in order to enable the spacing of the frames to be increased to 10 m. In this case, the purely tensile membrane is prestressed, ensuring adequate stability. The two-part glulam members each consist of one inclined column and one cantilever beam tied back to a pylon of splayed steel tubes. Between the frames, arches of steel tubes form the high points of the membrane, which drains to the frames and the rear base of each pylon. Owing to the lightweight construction, cable stays underneath to prevent uplift were unfortunately necessary, and these do impair the sight-lines slightly. The gentle curve of the grandstand gives the roof an additional dynamic and lends it a high visual impact through its sail-like membranes.

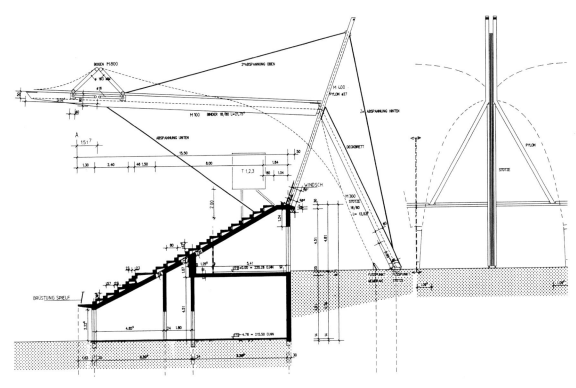

Tribünenüberdachung Steigerwaldstadion, Untersicht, Schnitt, Detail Knotenpunkt, Rückansicht.
Grandstand roof, Steigerwald stadium, underside of roof, section, detail of node, rear view.

Fachwerkträger und Trägerroste
Trusses, girders and beam grids

Obwohl die Notwendigkeit von Fachwerkträgern zur Überbrückung großer Spannweiten schon früh erkannt wurde, setzte die Verwendung von Fachwerkträgern im Holzleimbau erst in den fünfziger Jahren ein. Die bis dahin gebauten Hängesprengwerke, der Howe'sche Träger, die Bogenbinder in Stephan'scher Bauweise und alle sonstigen Fachwerkträger wurden fast ausschließlich in Vollholz ausgeführt.

Die Entwicklung der massiven Bogenbinder erreichte Mitte der sechziger Jahre mit über 100 m Spannweite ihren Höhepunkt, was hauptsächlich in den gestalterischen Grenzen begründet war. Die Binder hatten Querschnittsabmessungen von 1,5 m und mehr, was besonders im Auflagerbereich kaum als gut proportioniertes Anschlußdetail ausgebildet werden konnte. So lag es nahe, bei ähnlichen oder größeren Spannweiten Fachwerk-Bogenbinder einzusetzen. Eine verbesserte Verbindungstechnik mit Knotenblechen und Stabdübeln ermöglichte die Übertragung großer Kräfte – besonders Zugkräfte.

Die Anzahl der Fachwerkstäbe bildet häufig in seiner räumlichen Wirkung eine Vielzahl an Überschneidungen, welche den Raumeindruck unübersichtlich werden lassen. Dies läßt sich durch große Binderabstände vermeiden, wie am Beispiel der Olympiahallen in Lillehammer zu beobachten ist.

Although the need for trusses and girders for spanning large distances was recognized very early on, the first glulam versions did not appear until the 1950s. Prior to that the combined slung and arched framing, Howe trusses, Stephan-type arches and all the other forms of timber truss or girder were almost exclusively built using solid sections.

The development of the glulam arch of solid sections reached its peak in the mid-1960s with spans exceeding 100 m. This limit was primarily due to aesthetic reasons; for the members had reached depths of 1500 mm and more, and well-proportioned connections were hardly possible, especially at the supports. So the obvious move was to use open sections – trusses and girders – for similar or longer spans. Improved connection details employing gusset plates with pins rendered possible the transfer of larger forces, particularly tension.

The number of individual members in a truss or girder often gives the impression of a multitude of intersections, cluttering the overall appearance. This can be avoided by placing the frames further apart, like in the structures for the Winter Olympics in Lillehammer.

Arch.: Biong & Biong; Niels Torp;
Ing.: Sormorken & Hamre;
Ausf.: Moelven Limtre A.S.;
Olympiahalle, Lillehammer, 1994, Dreigelenk-
Fachwerk-Bogenbinder,
Querschnitt, Grundriß, Außenansichten.
Architects: Biong & Biong, Niels Torp;
engineers: Sormorken & Hamre;
contractor: Moelven Limtre A.S.;
Olympic Hall, Lillehammer, 1994, three-pin arched truss, section, plan, external views.

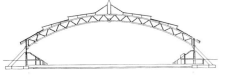

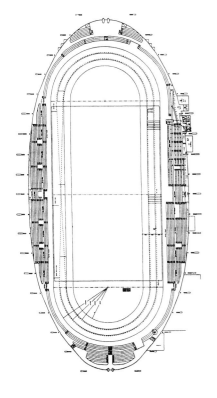

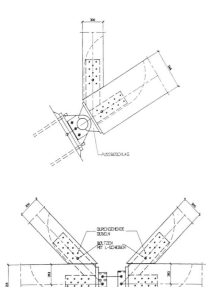

Olympiahalle, Lillehammer,
Aufbau von Knotenpunkten, Innenansicht.
Olympic Hall, Lillehammer,
detail of node, internal view.

Die größte der Hallen ist die „Hamar Olympiahall" für Eiskunstlauf, Eishockey und Eisschnellauf.[75] Die Zweigelenkbinder überspannen zwischen 48 m und 96,4 m. Trotz der großen Schneelast von 2,5KN/m² und dem hohen Binderabstand von 12 m erscheint der Fachwerkbinder mit 4 m vergleichsweise hoch. Hierbei waren die gestalterischen Belange maßgebend, um das richtige Verhältnis zwischen Querschnittsabmessungen und Gesamtbinderhöhe zu erzielen. Der Anschluß der Stäbe erfolgte durch 12 mm starke Stabdübel in Verbindung mit bis zu vier 8 mm starken Stahlblechen. Die Aussteifung in Längsrichtung erfolgt über den 250 m langen Gratbinder, der durch Aussteifungsdiagonalen mit den Querbindern verbunden ist. Die Halle ist die bisher größte in Holz ausgeführte Halle ihrer Art.[76]

Um die Klarheit der Tragwerke zu steigern, lassen sich auch die zugbeanspruchten Stäbe in Stahl ausführen. Besonders der unterspannte Träger ist hierfür ein gutes Beispiel, da hierbei in der Regel alle zugbeanspruchten Tragwerksteile in Stahl ausgeführt werden.

The largest of these is the Hamar Olympic Hall for figure skating, ice hockey and speed skating.[75] The two-pin arches span between 48 and 96.4 m. Although the snow load is heavy at 2.5 kN/m² and the spacing between the arches is 12 m, the 4000-mm-deep truss still seems comparatively deep. Architectural requirements took priority here, trying to achieve the right ratio of section size to overall truss depth. The members are connected using 12 mm dia. pins in conjunction with up to four steel plates 8 mm thick. Stability in the longitudinal direction is guaranteed by the crown truss 250 m long linked to the arches by means of diagonal bracing. This building is the largest of its kind built entirely of timber.[76]

To improve the clarity of loadbearing structures, tension members can also be made of steel. The beam with underslung framing is a good example of this because in this structural form the tension members are usually all made from steel.

Dieses Prinzip wurde bei der 1992 gebauten Produktionshalle der Firma Wilkhahn in Bad Münder angewendet. Der Architekt Thomas Herzog entwickelte eine dreiteilige Halle, zwischen deren vier Rahmen die 30 m langen unterspannten Träger hängen. Die Aussteifung in Längsrichtung und die Vorspannung in Höhe von 40 KN erfolgt über die diagonalen stählernen Zugstangen.

Die Rahmen stehen im Abstand von 6,6 m, die durch mit Rippen verstärkte Tafelelemente überspannt werden.[77] Die Dachfläche wurde trotz der großen Spannweite extensiv begrünt. Durch die klare Gliederung des Tragwerkes ist die Halle linear erweiterbar und kann so den notwendigen Veränderungen angepaßt werden.[78]

This principle was used for the Wilkhahn production plant in Bad Münder, completed in 1992. Architect Thomas Herzog designed a three-bay production building with 30-m-long trussed beams spanning between four frames. Diagonal steel ties with a 40 kN prestress ensure stability in the longitudinal direction. The frames are placed at 6.6 m centre to centre and are roofed over with ribbed panels.[77] Despite the long spans, the roof surface was able to be extensively planted. The structural system enables the facility to be easily extended and hence adapted to new requirements.[78]

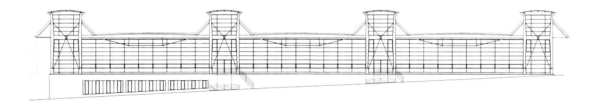

**Arch.: Thomas Herzog, München;
Ing.: Sailer + Stepan, München;
Produktionshalle Wilkhahn, Bad Münder-Einbeckhausen, 1992, an Rahmen aufgehängte unterspannte Träger, Seitenansicht, Entwurfsskizze, Außenansicht.**
Architect: Thomas Herzog, Munich;
engineers: Sailer + Stepan, Munich;
Wilkhahn production plant, Bad Münder-Einbeckhausen, 1992, trussed beams suspended from frames, side elevation, design sketches, external view.

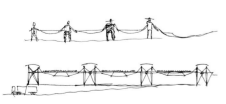

**Produktionshalle Wilkhahn, Außenansicht,
Innenansicht, Knotendetail der Zugstangen.**
Wilkhahn production plant, external view, internal
view, detail of node of steel ties.

Die Übertragung der einachsigen Spannrichtung der Fachwerkträger in eine zweiachsige erfolgt bei den Trägerrosten. Das enge Raster und die Richtungslosigkeit des Tragwerkes stellt ein Problem für die Wirkung der Räume dar, welche bei der Dachkonstruktion des Seeparksaales in Arbon gut beobachtet werden kann. Die Entwicklung der hölzernen Raumstabwerke wurde maßgebend von den stählernen Raumstabwerken beeinflußt. Aber erst die Verwendung eines stählernen Knotens, bestehend aus einer Stahlgußkugel, einem hochfesten Stahlbolzen und Blechen, welche durch Stabdübel mit den Hölzern verbunden waren, ermöglichten die geometrisch freie Verbindung mehrerer Stäbe. Aufgrund der aufwendigen Konstruktion des Knotens wird die erforderliche Stückzahl zu einem wichtigen wirtschaftlichen Entwurfskriterium.

Bei dem Seeparksaal in Arbon, Schweiz, überspannt das Tragwerk eine Fläche von 45 x 27 m mit Stabdicken von maximal 17 x 17 cm, wobei besonders belastete Stäbe in Buche ausgeführt wurden. Alle anderen Stäbe wurden aus Föhrenholz erstellt.[79]

The one-way-spanning truss or girder can be turned into the two-way-spanning beam grid. However, the dense grid and lack of a conclusive loadbearing direction can present an aesthetic problem for an interior, as can be readily seen in the roof over the Seeparksaal in Arbon, Switzerland. The development of timber space frames was essentially influenced by their equivalents in steel. However, it was only the invention of the node consisting of a cast steel sphere with high-strength steel bolts and plates joined to the timber members with pins that rendered possible the unconstrained connection of several members. The complicated construction of the node makes the total number of nodes in a structure a significant economic design criterion.

At the Seeparksaal in Arbon, the structure covers an area measuring 45 x 27 m using members of max. 170 x 170 mm. Particularly heavily loaded members are made from beech, while all other members are made from pine.[79]

Arch.: Adorni + Giesel, Plinio Haas, Schuster/De Lazzer/Fischer, Keller + Kappeler; Ing.: Wälli AG; Seeparksaal, Arbon, 1984-1985, Raumstabwerk, Innenansicht, Blick auf das Raumtragwerk im Bauzustand, Eindeckung des Raumtragwerks, Knotenpunkt.
Architects: Adorni + Giesel, Plinio Haas, Schuster/De Lazzer/Fischer, Keller + Kappeler; engineers: Wälli AG; Seeparksaal, Arbon, Switzerland, 1984-1985, space frame, internal view, view of space frame during construction, covering to space frame, node.

Seeparksaal, Arbon, Blick auf das Raumtragwerk im Bauzustand, Schnitt.
Seeparksaal, Arbon, Switzerland, view of space frame during construction, section.

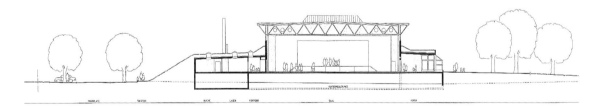

Arch.: Jourda Architectes, Paris;
**Hegger, Hegger und Schleiff, Kassel;
Ing.: Schlaich, Bergermann und Partner,
Stuttgart; Ausf.: Kaufmann, Reuthe;
Fortbildungsakademie, Herne, 1999,
Fachwerkträger, unterspannte Träger.**
Vorige Doppelseite **Eingangsansicht.**
Links **Rundholzstützen im Innen- und
Vordachbereich.**
Mitte **Stützen.**
Rechts **Stützendetail.**
Architects: Jourda Architectes, Paris,
Hegger, Hegger & Schleiff, Kassel;
engineers: Schlaich, Bergermann & Partner,
Stuttgart; contractor: Kaufmann, Reuthe;
vocational training academy, Herne, 1999,
girder, trussed beam.
Previous double page Entrance elevation.
Left Circular timber columns to interior
and canopy.
Centre Columns.
Right Detail of column.

Die Überdachung der Fortbildungsakademie in Herne stellt eine Kombination aus Fachwerkträgern und unterspannten Trägern dar. Die Halle besitzt eine Grundfläche von 72 x 168 m, welche durch 2,4 m hohe Fachwerkträger bis zu 24 m überspannt wird. Die Fachwerkträger sind als unterspannte Träger im Abstand von 3 m angeordnet.

Die gesamte Dachfläche wurde als eine Scheibe ausgebildet und wird über die in der Fassade enthaltenen Verbände gehalten. Dadurch können die runden Vollholzstützen gelenkig über gußeiserne Auflager und Stabdübel angeschlossen werden. Die Fassade besteht ebenfalls aus Fachwerkstützen. Ober- und Untergurte sind zweiteilig ausgebildet und umschließen die Diagonalstäbe.[80] Aus Gründen der Energiegewinnung wurden die Dachfläche und die Südfassade mit mehr als 10.000 m² Photovoltaikmodulen ausgestattet. In welchem Verhältnis der bauliche Aufwand zu den thermischen oder ökologischen Vorteilen steht, ist bisher umstritten.

The roof to the vocational training academy in Herne is a combination of girders and underslung framing. The building measures 72 x 168 m and the roof is formed by 2400-mm-deep trusses spanning up to 24 m. The girders are arranged with underslung framing at a spacing of 3 m. The whole of the roof has been designed as a plate restrained by the bracing in the facade. This enabled the solid circular timber columns to be pin-jointed in cast iron supports with steel pins. The facade also comprises trusses in the form of laced columns. Top and bottom chords are in two parts and enclose the diagonal members.[80] Over 10 000 m² of photovoltaic panels were attached to the roof and south facade to generate electricity. The merits of the thermal and ecological aspects compared to the cost of construction remain a matter for dispute.

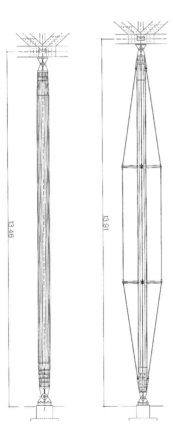

**Fortbildungsakademie, Herne,
Fußpunkt Außenstütze, Fußpunkt
Fassadenstütze, Dach im Bau, Anschlußpunkt
Fachwerkträger, Fassade.**
Vocational training academy, Herne,
base of outer column, base of facade column,
roof under construction, girder connection,
facade.

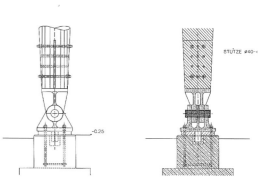

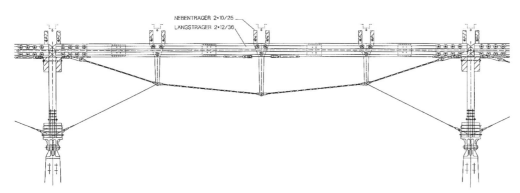

Fortbildungsakademie, Herne, unterspannter Längsträger mit Verspannung der Stützenköpfe, Kopf- und Fußdetails: Rundholzstütze, Gußteile, links Ansicht, rechts Schnitt, Fensterdetail, unterspannter Träger.
Vocational training academy, Herne, trussed longitudinal beam with cable-stayed column heads, head and base details of circular timber columns, cast parts; left: elevation; right: section, detail of window, trussed beam.

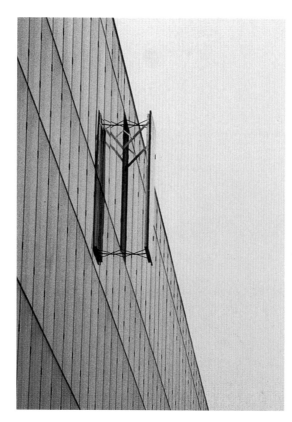

Als einachsig spannender Trägerrost auf einer Grundfläche von 76 x 100 m entstand der Französische Ausstellungspavillon (DECATHLON Store) für die Expo 2000 in Hannover. Die Deckenplatte wird gebildet von Hauptträgern im Abstand von 12 m und Querträgern im Abstand von 4 m. Diese Deckenplatte liegt auf um 4,7° geneigten Rundstützen, die sich in fünf Ästen verzweigen und Haupt- und Nebenträger abstützen. Die Knotenpunkte sind in Stahl ausgebildet. Die Äste und Träger sind in Brettschichtholz ausgeführt. Die Aussteifung erfolgt durch Verbände und Wandscheiben in den Giebelwänden.

A one-way-spanning beam grid covering an area of 76 x 100 m is to be used for the French exhibition pavilion (DECATHLON Store) for EXPO 2000 in Hannover. The roof structure is formed by main beams at 12 m centres and transverse beams at 4 m centres. This is supported on circular columns placed at an angle of 4.7° which diverge into five "branches" and carry primary and secondary beams. The nodes are fabricated from steel, the branches and beams are glued laminated timber. Stability is provided by bracing and shear walls at the gables.

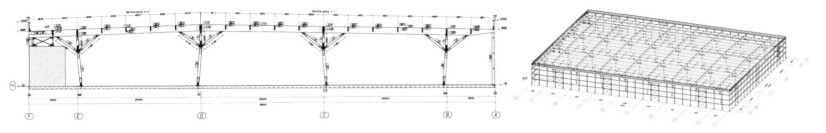

Arch.: Jourda, Paris; Ing.: Merz und Kaufmann, Hüttemann; Ausf.: Hüttemann Holz; Französischer Pavillon, EXPO 2000, Hannover, einachsig spannender Trägerrost, Seitenansicht, Isometrie, Innenansicht.
Architects: Jourda, Paris; engineers: Merz und Kaufmann, Hüttemann; contractors: Hüttemann Holz; French Pavilion, EXPO 2000, Hannover, one-way-spanning beam grid, side elevation, isometric view, internal view.

Rippenschalen und Kuppeln
Lattice shells and domes

hölzernes Netzwerk aus tlamellen 4,8 / 30

First

Firstlänge=Traufenlänge=81,25m

22 mm Schalung

8,135

Stahlbetonrähm mit Schwellholz

36,36

Stahlbetonkonstruktion

Hallenquerschnitt

Hallenlängsrichtung   Bogenspannrichtung

27÷27⁵ 2÷2³

A

ca. 2,39

1,02   1,02

Dachdetail in der Draufsicht

Brettlamelle

24   2 M18

Knotenpunkt A

Eine räumliche Weiterentwicklung der Binder-Pfetten-Bauweise stellt die bereits erwähnte Zollinger-Bauweise dar. Beim Bau der Halle Münsterland wurde 1947 eine Dachkonstruktion mit einer Spannweite von 36 m gebaut. Die einzelnen 2,39 m langen Lamellen wurden bereits mit zwei Bolzen verbunden, um eine höhere Biegesteifigkeit der Schale für unsymmetrische Belastungen zu erreichen. Trotz dieser Art der Ausführung war die Biegesteifigkeit nicht ausreichend und führte zu einer Torsionsbeanspruchung der Lamellen, die große Verformungen verursachte.[81] Es kam zu einem Absenken des Daches um mehr als 80 cm, was etwa 10% der Stichhöhe entsprach. Die Sanierung erfolgte durch die Überbauung mit einem Raumstabwerk, so daß nur noch der Innenraumeindruck erhalten blieb, die Tragwirkung aber aufgehoben wurde.

Diese Erfahrungen flossen 1989 in die Ausbildung der Dachkonstruktion der doppelstöckigen Sporthalle in Berlin-Charlottenburg ein. Aus der senkrecht stehenden Brettlamellenbauweise Zollingers entwickelten die Architekten Baller und das Ingenieurbüro Pichler in Zusammenarbeit mit der TU Berlin eine rautenförmige Rippenschale mit 23 m Spannweite. Durch die kraftschlüssige Verbindung der Rippen mit einer diagonalen Schalung werden die rautenförmigen Rippen ausgesteift. Der Abstand der einzelnen Rippen wurde auf 2 m erhöht und in zweiachsig gekrümmter Brettschichtholzbauweise hergestellt. Die in der Anzahl reduzierten Verbindungspunkte wurden durch Bleche

One three-dimensional further development of the frame-and-purlin form of construction was the Zollinger system mentioned earlier. The Münsterland Hall (1947) employed a roof structure with a span of 36 m. The individual members, each 2.39 m long, were already connected with two bolts in order to improve the bending strength of the shell for asymmetric loads. Despite this improvement, the bending strength remained inadequate and led to the members being subjected to torsion, which caused major deformations.[81] The roof deflected by more than 800 mm, corresponding to approx. 10% of the rise of the shell. Remedial measures involved the construction of a space frame over the top of the existing shell so that although the shell no longer performed any loadbearing function, the internal appearance remained intact.

This experience had repercussions for the roof over the two-storey sports hall in Berlin-Charlottenburg (1989). Starting with Zollinger's vertical boards, Baller architectural practice and Pichler consulting engineers collaborated with Berlin Technical University to develop a diamond-shaped lattice shell spanning 23 m. The shell is stiffened by the interlock between ribs and diagonal sheathing. The spacing of the individual ribs was increased to 2 m and the shell fabricated using glulam members curved in two directions. The connections, now fewer in number, were made rigid by using steel plates and pins. Notwith-

mit Stabdübeln biegesteif ausgebildet. Trotz dieser verstärkten Bauweise wurden vier stählerne Aussteifungsträger zusätzlich eingebaut, was angesichts der vorhandenen, wenn auch gekrümmten Dachscheibe in Zusammenwirkung mit den aussteifenden Giebelwänden viel erscheint. Die horizontalen Auflagerkräfte der Schale werden an den stählernen Kastenprofilen durch angehobene Zugbänder aufgenommen.[82]

standing this reinforced construction, four steel stiffening beams were added, which, in view of the existing – albeit – curved roof in conjunction with the stiff gable walls, seems excessive. The horizontal support reactions of the shell are resisted by raised ties at the steel box sections.[82]

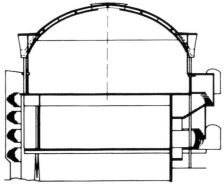

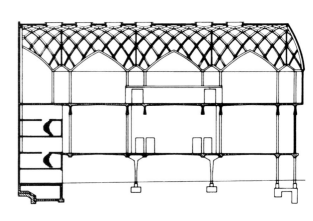

Sporthalle, Berlin-Charlottenburg, Querschnitt, Längsschnitt, Bauzustand, Knotendetail.
Charlottenburg sports hall, sections, under construction, detail of node.

**Sporthalle Berlin-Charlottenburg, Knotendetail,
Deckenausschnitt mit Oberlicht.**
Berlin-Charlottenburg sports hall,
detail of node, roof opening with rooflight.

Kuppeln

Seitdem der Mensch sich Behausungen baut, finden wir die Form des Rundbaus, welcher mit einer Kuppel überdeckt ist. Neben der Überdachung einfacher Wohnhäuser dienen diese Kuppeln ebenso zur Überdachung großer sakraler Räume wie zum Beispiel dem Pantheon in Rom (120–125 n. Chr.).

Kuppeln gehören zur Gruppe der Schalentragwerke, welche ihre Lasten hauptsächlich über Membrankräfte abtragen. Dieser sehr effiziente Lastabtrag erfolgt über Zug-, Druck- und Schubkräfte in der Schalenebene, welche den Querschnitt gleichmäßig belasten und damit dünnwandige Konstruktionen ermöglichen. Diese Schlankheit der Konstruktion muß daher in Hinsicht auf seine Beulproblematik (Ausweichen aus der Schalenebene unter Druckbeanspruchung) ausreichend untersucht werden.

Kuppeln besitzen darüber hinaus auf ihrem kreisförmigen Grundriß einen günstigen zweiachsigen rotationssymmetrischen Lastabtrag. In Holz gibt es bisher aufgrund seiner Anisotropie keine reinen Schalentragwerke, sondern räumlich aufgelöste Stabwerke.

Domes

The circular building covered by a dome has been found since the first inhabitants of this planet built shelters for themselves. Besides forming roofs to simple houses, domes are also used for the roofs of large sacred buildings, e.g. the Pantheon in Rome (120–25 AD).

Domes belong to the group of loadbearing shell structures which carry their loads mainly by way of membrane forces. This very efficient way of carrying loads is achieved by way of tension, compression and shear forces in the plane of the shell, which means that the stresses are evenly distributed throughout the cross-section and hence thin-walled constructions are possible. Therefore, this slender type of construction must be properly investigated with regard to the local buckling problem (compression loads causing a deviation from the plane of the shell).

Furthermore, domes on a circular base exhibit a beneficial two-way rotationally symmetric load-carrying behaviour. However, the anisotropy of wood means that no true loadbearing shell structures have been realized up to now but instead three-dimensional open frameworks.

Unterschiedliche Stabkuppel-Typen mit Grundriß und räumlicher Darstellung.
Oben links **Radiale Kuppel,**
Mitte **Trianguläre Kuppel,**
Unten **Hexagonale Kuppel;**
Oben rechts **Ensphere Kuppel,**
Mitte **Geodätische Kuppel,**
Unten **Geodätische Ableitung.**
Various lattice dome forms in plan and volumetric drawing.
Top left Radial rib dome;
Centre Triangular dome;
Bottom Hexagonal dome;
Top right Ensphere dome;
Centre Geodesic dome;
Bottom Geodesic derivation.

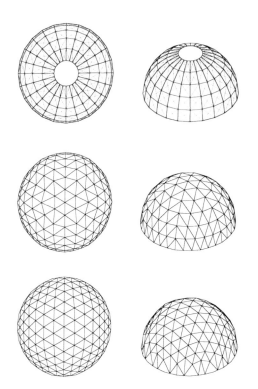

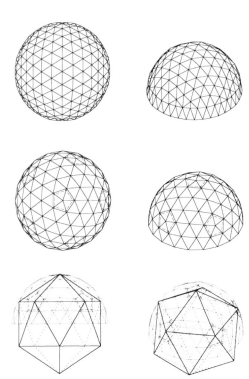

Arch.: A.P. Smits; Ing./Ausf.: Nemaho;
Synagoge, Enschede, 1928,
Dreigelenkbinder mit Druckring
Architect: A.P. Smits;
engineers/contractors: Nemaho;
Synagogue, Enschede, 1928,
three-pin ribs with compression ring.

Die Rippenkuppel

Eine der ersten verwendeten Tragwerksformen stellt die radiale Kuppel oder Rippenkuppel dar. Hierbei dienen radial angeordnete Dreigelenkbinder als Haupttragglieder, welche durch Ringpfetten miteinander verbunden werden. Aufgrund der Abmessungen der Binder wird in der Regel am Scheitel ein Druckring ausgebildet, um die Anschlußgeometrie zu bewältigen oder ein zentrales Oberlicht einzufügen. Bei großen Druckringen müssen die Binder biegesteif angeschlossen werden, um ein Kippen des Ringes zu verhindern. Als Torsionsaussteifung der Binder und zur Aufnahme von Schubkräften dienen diagonale Aussteifungsverbände.[83]

Die Überdachung der Hal au blé (1783) in Paris war als hölzerne Rippenkuppel konstruiert und besaß ohne radial angeordnete Ringpfetten kein Schalentragverhalten. Eine der ersten Rippenkuppeln aus Holzleimbindern baute die Firma Nemaho 1928 für die Synagoge in Enschede mit 18 m Spannweite.

Eine Rippenkuppel mit 105 m Spannweite entstand Anfang der achtziger Jahre in Žilina, Slowakien. Die zwi-

The radial rib dome

One of the earliest structural forms was the radial rib dome. In this case three-pin ribs arranged in a radial layout serve as the primary members; these are linked together by ring purlins. The dimensions of the ribs usually lead to a compression ring being necessary at the crown in order to accommodate the connections or act as the frame for a central rooflight. Rigid rib connections are necessary with large compression rings in order to preserve the stability of the ring. Diagonal bracing to the ribs accommodates torsion and shear.[83]

The roof to the Halle au blé (1783) in Paris was designed as a timber radial rib dome. However, it did not exhibit any shell behaviour because there were no ring purlins. One of the first glulam radial rib domes was one spanning 18 m built by the Nemaho company in 1928 for the synagogue in Enschede.

A radial rib dome with a span of 105 m was erected in the early 1980s in Žilina, now Slovak Republic. The ribs (800-1900 mm deep x 230 mm wide) are stabilized by deep transverse members. These sections

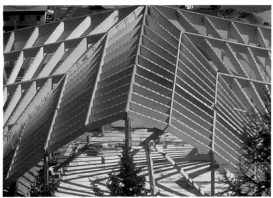

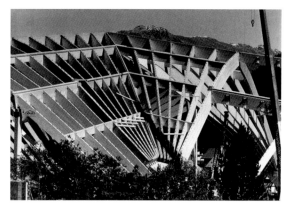

Arch.: Krähenbühl; Ing.: Walter Bieler, Chur; Ausf.: W. Zöllig AG, Arbon; Eissporthalle, Davos, 1979-1980, räumlicher Dreigelenkbinder, Außenansicht, Bauzustand.
Architect: Krähenbühl; engineer: Walter Bieler, Chur; contractor: W. Zöllig AG, Arbon; ice rink, Davos, Switzerland, 1979-1980, three-dimensional three-pin frame, external view, under construction.

schen 80 und 190 cm hohen Binder (b =23 cm) wurden durch hohe Querträger stabilisiert. Diese Querschnittsabmessungen erscheinen außerordentlich hoch, was sich durch die hohen Schneelasten begründen läßt.[84]

Die Eislaufhalle in Davos entstand als kreuzgewölbeartige Rippenkuppel aus Dreigelenkbindern. Aufgrund der hohen Schneelasten von 800 kg/m² und der großen Spannweite sind die Binder ausgesprochen stark dimensioniert. Die Haupt- und Nebenträger besitzen eine Höhe zwischen 1,68 m und 1,95 m Höhe. Das Tragwerk wirkt sehr wuchtig in seiner Erscheinung.[85]

Durch die Geometrie der Rippenkuppeln sind die Spannweiten der Pfetten sehr unterschiedlich, und auch die Befestigung der Schalung bringt geometrische Probleme im Scheitelbereich mit sich. Daraus leitete sich die Suche nach einer gleichmäßigen Struktur ab, die in der Entwicklung von Stabwerkskuppeln mündete.

seem enormous but are required to carry the high snow loads.[84]

The ice rink in Davos, Switzerland, is a cross vault of three-pin ribs. A high snow load (800 kg/m²) and large span resulted in correspondingly massive ribs; primary and secondary members have depths ranging from 1680 to 1950 mm. This structure has a very heavyweight appearance.[85]

The geometry of the radial rib domes means that the spans of the purlins vary considerably, and the fixing of the sheathing also causes geometric problems near the crown. This instigated the search for a structural form with identical members, leading eventually to the development of the geodesic dome.

Eissporthalle, Davos, Untersicht.
Ice rink, Davos, underside of roof.

Nächste Doppelseite **Innenansicht**
Next double page Internal view

Die Stabwerkskuppel

Stabwerkskuppeln sind sowohl vom Tragverhalten als auch vom Montageablauf her wirtschaftlicher als Rippenkuppeln. Die maßgebende Entwicklung erfolgte durch die Erforschung geodätischer Kuppeln, für die Richard Buckminster Fuller (1895–1983) 1954 das Patent erhielt.[86]

Geodätische Kuppeln werden erzeugt durch die Projektion eines Ikosaeders (aus gleichseitigen Dreiecken zusammengesetzter Zwanzigflächner) auf die einschließende Kugeloberfläche. In dem entstehenden Netz stoßen jeweils fünf Dreiecke in einem Punkt zusammen. Bei Ausfüllung der Struktur mit Dreiecken entsteht insgesamt eine Struktur, welche sich aus Sechsecken bildet, die in den Netz-Knotenpunkten durch Fünfecke miteinander verbunden sind. Die Unregelmäßigkeit der Länge der Randstäbe stellt beim Bau geodätischer Kuppeln ein gestalterisches Problem dar, wenn von der Halbkugel abgewichen wird.

Bereits 1953–1954 baute der Architekt G. Peterson ein „geodätisches Restaurant" in Woods Hole, Massachusetts. Diese Kuppel bestand aus Holzstäben und einer Klarsichtverkleidung aus Mylar-Kunststoffscheiben. Bei der Großraumkuppel der Union Car Company in Baton Rouge, Louisiana, wurde schon 1958 eine Spannweite von 117 m erreicht. Die bekannteste Kuppel ihrer Art entstand als Ausstellungshalle auf der Weltausstellung 1967 in Montreal.[87]

Bei großen Spannweiten in Holz spielte die Knotenproblematik eine wichtige Rolle, da einfache Schweiß- oder Steckverbindungen wie im Stahlbau nicht möglich waren. Um sowohl die Anzahl als auch die Kosten zu verringern, wurde die Stabanzahl reduziert und die Geometrie vereinfacht. Eine geodätische Kuppel dieser Bauweise entstand bereits 1958–1959 in Cuyahoga Falls, Ohio, mit einer Spannweite von etwa 67 m (220ft). Die Haupttragrippen hatten nur eine Abmessung von etwa 8 x 24,8 cm (3 1/4 x 9 3/4 inch), was beängstigend gering erscheint.

Schon 1959 veröffentlichte Verne Ketchum seinen Artikel „Timber domes – design and construction". Seine hexagonalen Kuppeln[88] besitzen ihre Rippen in drei Richtungen, so daß sich die gleichseitigen Dreiecke nur zu Sechsecken zusammensetzen. In ihrer Tragwirkung besaßen diese hexagonalen Kuppeln keine Stäbe in Ringrichtung, welche die Ringzug- und Druckkräfte aufnehmen konnten. Um diesen Nachteil zu beheben, entwickelte man eine trianguläre Kuppel unter Beibehal-

The geodesic dome

Research into the so-called geodesic dome, for which Richard Buckminster Fuller (1895–1983) was granted the patent in 1954,[86] was the main impetus in this search. Geodesic domes are more economic than radial rib domes, both in terms of loadbearing behaviour and erection procedure.

Geodesic domes are generated by projecting an icosahedron (20-sided three-dimensional figure composed of equilateral triangles) onto the enclosing spherical surface. In the ensuing network, five triangles meet at each node, so by filling the structure with triangles the overall effect is a net composed of hexagons connected by pentagons at the nodes. The irregular lengths of the edge members leads to a design problem when building geodesic domes which are not hemispherical.

As long ago as 1953–1954 the architect G. Peterson was responsible for a "geodesic restaurant" in Woods Hole, Massachusetts. This dome consisted of timber members and a transparent covering of Mylar plastic panels. A span of 117 m was reached as early as 1958 with the large dome of the Union Car Company in Baton Rouge, Louisiana. But the best-known dome of this kind is the exhibition hall at the 1967 World Exposition in Montreal.[87]

Nodes played an important role in large spans because the simple welded or "plug-in" connections of structural steelwork were not possible with timber. In order to reduce the number of nodes as well as the costs, fewer members were used and the geometry simplified. A geodesic dome employing this method and with a span of 220 ft (approx. 67 m) was then completed in 1959 in Cuyahoga Falls, Ohio. The primary loadbearing ribs were all of one size (3 1/4 x 9 3/4 inch – approx. 80 x 248 mm) and looked rather worryingly small!

An article entitled "Timber domes – design and construction" by Verne Ketchum was published already in 1959. As described there, his hexagonal domes[88] had ribs in three directions, so the equilateral triangles formed merely hexagons. These hexagonal domes had no members in the ring direction to accommodate the hoop tension and compression forces. To remedy this disadvantage, a triangular pattern dome was developed which maintained the arrangement of triangles but dispensed with their equilateral form. Only in this way was it possible to

tung der Dreieck-Struktur, aber unter Aufgabe der Gleichseitigkeit. Nur dadurch konnte wieder eine polygonale Ringrippe erzielt werden. Eine Kuppel in dieser Bauweise entstand in Beaverton, Oregon, mit 23 m Spannweite (75ft).[89]

obtain a polygonal ring rib. One dome employing this method (span 75 ft – approx. 23 m) was built in Beaverton, Oregon.[89]

Arch.: McGranahan, Messenger Associates, Tacoma; Wendel Rossman von Rossman, Schneider & Gadberry (Konzept Kuppel); Ing.: Hine, Wessel & Associates, Tacoma; Ausf.: Merit Construction, Jim Zarrelli, Tacoma; Western Wood Structures Inc., Marshall R. Turner, Tualatin; Tacoma Dome, Tacoma, Washington, 1982, Ensphere-System: Kombination aus triangulärer und hexagonaler Kuppel, Innenansicht.
Architects: McGranahan, Messenger Associates, Tacoma, Wendel Rossman with Rossman, Schneider & Gadberry (dome concept); engineers: Hine, Wessel & Associates, Tacoma; contractors: Merit Construction, Jim Zarrelli, Tacoma, Western Wood Structures, Inc., Marshall R. Turner, Tualatin; Tacoma Dome, Tacoma, Washington, 1982, ensphere system, combination of triangular and hexagonal domes, internal view.

Die Ensphere-Kuppel

Der Tacoma Dome entstand 1982 in Tacoma, Washington, als eine Stabwerkskuppel mit einer Spannweite von 160 m. Diese Kuppel wurde nach dem Ensphere-System errichtet, welches von dem Architekten W. E. Rossmann entwickelt wurde. Das Ensphere-System stellt eine Kombination aus hexagonaler und triangulärer Kuppel dar. Um den ungleichmäßigen Rand der hexagonalen Kuppel zu vermeiden, wurde der äußerste Ring der triangulären Kuppel verwendet. Alle weiteren Innenringe wurden als hexagonale Kuppel mit Rippen ausgebildet, welche zu drei Achsen parallel sind.

Die Hauptträger aus verleimter Douglasie haben eine Abmessung von 17–22 cm Breite und 75 cm Höhe. Die etwa 15 m langen Hauptträger wurden am Boden mit den Nebenträgern zu Dreiecken verbunden, welche als Ganzes dann durch Krane eingebaut wurden.[90] Die Verbindung erfolgte über hexagonale Stahlnaben, die mit Laschen und Bolzen verbunden wurden.[90] Die Schalung besteht aus 5 cm dicken Douglasienplanken mit Nut und Feder. Als Auflager dient ein vorgespannter Stahlbetonzugring. Die Montage des Daches erfolgte in nur zwei Monaten.

Die Halle faßt maximal 25.000 Sitzplätze, wobei nur 10.000 Sitzplätze fest eingebaut sind. So läßt sich entsprechend der Anforderung der jeweiligen Veranstaltung die Bestuhlung verändern. Neben Sportveranstaltungen wie Fußball, Rodeo, Eishockey, Basketball, Tennis und Moto-Cross können auch Konzerte abgehalten werden. Die klare Innenansicht der Dachkonstruktion wird durch die großen unregelmäßigen Tribüneneinbauten teils verstellt und durch die nachträglich benötigten Abhängungen beeinträchtigt.

In gleicher Bauweise wurde 1991 der Superior Dome als Sport- und Veranstaltungshalle der Northern Michigan University in Marquette errichtet. Die mit 161 m etwas größere Halle wurde auf einem etwa 2 m hohen Sockel gelagert und erscheint daher flacher in der Außenansicht. Im Innern geben zwei symmetrische Haupttribünen ein ruhiges, einheitliches Bild. Die beiden Tribünen besitzen eine Kapazität von 8000 Sitzplätzen und können maximal auf 16.000 erweitert wer-

The ensphere dome

The Tacoma Dome was built in 1982 in Tacoma, Washington, as a geodesic dome with a span of 160 m. This dome employed the ensphere system developed by the architect W. E. Rossmann. The ensphere system represents a combination of the hexagonal and triangular domes. The outermost ring of the triangular dome is used to avoid the irregular edge of the hexagonal dome. All other inner rings are formed as hexagonal domes with ribs, which are parallel in three axes. The primary members of glued Douglas fir measure 170-220 mm wide x 750 mm deep. These approx. 15-m-long primary members were joined to the secondary members on the ground to create triangles which were then erected by crane as complete units. The connections utilize hexagonal steel hubs connected with plates and bolts.[90] The sheathing is Douglas fir tongue-and-groove planks 50 mm thick. A prestressed concrete ring beam acts as the support. Two months were all that was needed to erect the roof.

The building can accommodate max. 25 000 seated spectators, although only 10 000 of these seats are permanent fixtures. Therefore, the seating can be adapted to suit the respective event. Besides sports events such as American football, rodeo, ice hockey, basketball, tennis and moto-cross, concerts are also a regular feature. The clear view of the underside of the roof construction is partly obstructed by the huge, irregular grandstands and spoiled by the necessary suspended elements added subsequently.

The same system was used in 1991 for the Superior Dome, the sports arena of Northern Michigan University in Marquette. The 161-m-span is supported on a 2-m-high plinth and therefore appears shallower from outside. Inside, the two symmetrical main grandstands, which can seat up to 16 000 spectators, create a calm, uniform appearance. Part of the timber roof covering was able to be left exposed and so help convey the impression of a completely wooden construction reaching right down to the supports. The other bays had to be clad for reasons of acoustics.

Tacoma Dome, Innenansicht Detail, Bauzustand.
Tacoma Dome, underside of dome, under construction.

Tacoma Dome, Knotendetail, Außenansicht.
Tacoma Dome, detail of node, external view.

**Ausf.: Western Wood Structures, Inc.;
Superior Dome, Marquette, Michigan, 1991,
Ensphere-Kuppel, Außenansicht, Fußpunkte
Binder, Innenansicht**
Contractor: Western Wood Structures, Inc.;
Superior Dome, Marquette, Michigan, 1991,
ensphere dome, external view, base of frame,
internal view.

  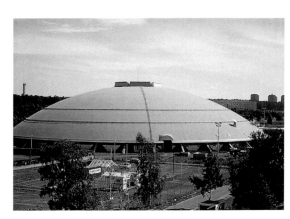

Arch.: Risto Harju, Oulu; Ing.: Pekka Heikkilä, Oulu; Ausf.: Mätsälliiton Teollisuus, Lohja; Sporthalle, Oulu, 1985, hexagonale Kuppel, Knoten-Detail, Bauzustand, Außenansicht, Schnitt.
Architect: Risto Harju, Oulu; engineer: Pekka Heikkilä, Oulu; contractor: Mätsälliiton Teollisuus, Lohja; sports hall, Oulu, Finland, 1985, hexagonal dome, detail of node, under construction, external view, section.

den. Ein Teil der hölzernen Dachschalung konnte sichtbar gelassen werden und vermittelt so den Eindruck einer klaren Holzkonstruktion, welche bis zu den Auflagern zu verfolgen ist. Die Verkleidung der restlichen Felder erfolgte aus akustischen Gründen.

Die 1985 in Oulu in Nordfinnland erstellte Kuppel ist zwar mit 115 m Spannweite nicht so groß, führte aber durch die Verwendung von Kerto-Schichtholz zu Querschnittsabmessungen von 14,8–20,4 x 70 cm bei einer Schneelast von 180 kg/m². Da das Kerto-Schichtholz eine produktionsbedingte Plattenstärke von 75 mm hat, wurden die einzelnen Träger aus zwei bis drei Teilen zusammengesetzt. Die Stahlnaben wurden durch anschließende Ausbetonierung feuergeschützt, was aber eine eher ungewöhnliche Vorgehensweise darstellt, zumal der Arbeitsaufwand beträchtlich und die Verbindungen nun nicht mehr zugänglich sind.[91]

The dome built in 1985 in Oulu, northern Finland, although smaller (span 115 m), made use of Kerto laminated veneer lumber (LVL) with sizes of 1480-2040 x 700 mm for a snow load of 180 kg/m². As the thickness of Kerto LVL is restricted to 75 mm for production reasons, the individual members were made up of two or three pieces. Fire protection to the steel hubs was achieved by filling them with concrete, a rather unconventional and labour-intensive approach which renders the connections inaccessible.[91]

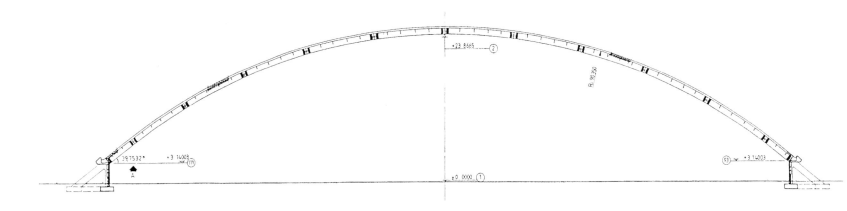

Arch.: Ollertz + Ollertz, Fulda;
Ing.: Trabert + Partner, Geisa;
Ausf.: Burgbacher Holzwerke, Trossingen;
Thermalbad, Bad Sulza, 1999,
Kuppelschale auf freiem Grundriß,
Montage.
Architects: Ollertz + Ollertz, Fulda;
engineers: Trabert + Partner, Geisa;
contractor: Burgbacher Holzwerke, Trossingen;
Bad Sulza thermal baths, 1999,
lattice dome over irregular plan, erection.

Als Rippenschale auf freiem Grundriß ist die Dachkonstruktion des Thermalbades in Bad Sulza ausgebildet. Sie besteht aus zwei ineinander übergehenden Kuppelbereichen, die auf Betonwiderlagern liegen. Zwischen den Widerlagern sind doppelt gekrümmte und verdrillte Randbögen angeordnet, an denen die Fassadenstützen angeschlossen sind. Die Form der Kuppel wurde aus der Umkehrung eines hängenden Seilnetzes ermittelt, bei dem die Auflagerhöhen und der Durchhang der Randseile als Randbedingungen vorgegeben werden.

Aufgrund der ausschließlichen Zugbeanspruchung des Seilnetzes ergibt dessen Umkehrung bei einer reinen Rippenkonstruktion nur Druckbeanspruchungen. Die ausgeführte Schalenkonstruktion trägt die Lasten zusätzlich über Schubkräfte ab, so daß auch unter Eigenlast Bereiche mit geringen Zugbeanspruchungen auftreten können. Im zweiten Schritt der Formfindung wurden deshalb diese Bereiche iterativ begrenzt.

Eine Biegebeanspruchung der Schale tritt im Bereich der Randbögen und bei stark ungleichförmiger Belastung zum Beispiel aus lokalen Schneeansammlungen oder Wind auf. Diese Biegebeanspruchung wird durch das Zusammenwirken der Brettschale und der Holzrippen aufgenommen. Die Rippenstäbe sind wie bei der Zollingerbauweise jeweils über zwei Felder durchlaufend und mit Hartholzdollen zusammengesteckt. Eine oberseitige Stahllasche dient als Sicherung für den Montagezustand.

Aufgrund der freien Form der Schale besitzen alle Holzrippenstäbe unterschiedliche Abmessungen und Krümmungen sowie einen unterschiedlichen Zuschnitt an den Stoßstellen. Die Bearbeitung erfolgte mit einer numerisch gesteuerten Abbundanlage. Die Anforderungen an die Genauigkeit sind sehr hoch, da sich die Schalenform bei der Herstellung im Freivorbau ausschließlich über die Geometrie der Rippen ergibt. Im Endzustand wird die Schalenwirkung durch das Zusammenspiel der Rippen mit den zwei diagonal angeordneten – vernagelten und verleimten – Brettlagen bewirkt.

Mit dieser Bauweise konnte erreicht werden, daß außer den Auflagerpunkten keine weiteren stählernen Verbindungen erforderlich sind und somit die Gefahr von Schäden an solebeanspruchten Stahlteilen vermieden ist.

The roof over the thermal baths in Bad Sulza was designed as a lattice shell on an irregular plan. It consists of two intersecting domes supported on concrete columns. Twisted perimeter arches curved in two directions, to which the facade posts are attached, are positioned between these columns. The form of the dome was determined by reversing a suspended cable net in which the heights of the supports and sag of the edge cables were predefined as boundary conditions. The exclusively tensile loads of the cable net results in purely compressive loads when reversed to form a true lattice construction. The shell actually built also carries the loads by way of shear, meaning that zones of low tension can occur under dead loads. Therefore, in the second stage of the form-finding process, these zones were limited by an iterative process.

Bending stresses in the shell occur in the region of the perimeter arches and with severely asymmetric loads caused by, for example, wind or local snowdrifts. These bending stresses are resisted by the interaction of the roof covering and the ribs. Like with the Zollinger system, each rib is continuous over two bays and is connected by way of hardwood dowels. A steel plate on the top of the joint serves to secure the construction during erection.

The irregular form of the shell means that all timber members have different dimensions and degrees of curvature as well as different shapes at the connections. Fabrication was carried out on a CNC assembly plant. The requirements regarding accuracy were very high because the shape of the shell during preassembly was determined exclusively by the geometry of the ribs. In the final state the shell effect is achieved through the interaction of the ribs with the two diagonally arranged – nailed and glued – layers of boards. This form of construction meant that, apart from the supports, no further steel connections were necessary and, consequently, the risk of damage to steel parts caused by the salt water could be avoided.

Thermalbad Bad Sulza.
Linke Seite **Deckendetail.**
Rechts **Innenansicht, Schnitt.**
Bad Sulza thermal baths.
Facing page Underside the roof.
Right Internal view, section.

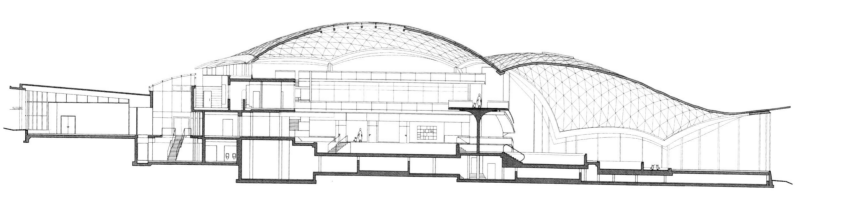

Thermalbad Bad Sulza, Außenansicht, Stabwerksstruktur, Stützenauflager, radiale Kuppel.
Bad Sulza thermal baths, external view, timber members, supports, radial dome.

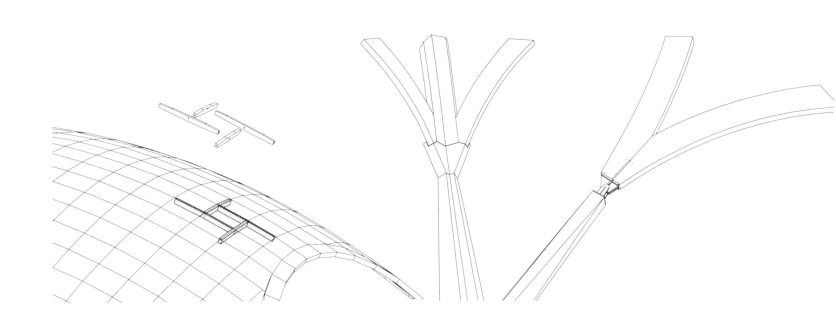

Hängeschalen
Suspended shells

Arch.: A. Lozeron, M. Moser, C. Châtelain, F. Martin; Ing.: R. Perreten, P. Milleret;
Festhalle der Schweizerischen Landesausstellung EXPO 1964, Lausanne, unterspannter Dreigelenkbogen mit hängenden, vorgespannten Sperrholzlamellen, Modell.
Architects: A. Lozeron, M. Moser, C. Châtelain, F. Martin; engineers: R. Perreten, P. Milleret; Festival Hall for Swiss National Exhibition EXPO 1964, Lausanne, trussed three-pin arch with suspended, prestressed plywood laminations, model.

Hängeschalen stellen einen Sonderfall der vorwiegend auf Zugkräfte beanspruchten Schalen dar. Zu ihrer Formstabilisierung bei Sog und für die notwendige Vorspannung müssen diese gegenläufig gekrümmt sein. In Holz werden diese als Rippenschalen ausgebildet.

Bereits 1932 entstanden in Amerika in Albany, New York, die ersten hängenden Dächer in Metall. Die Verbreitung dieser Konstruktionen in Deutschland wurde maßgeblich vorangetrieben durch die Veröffentlichung von Frei Ottos *Das hängende Dach*.[92] Dort berichtet er von einer tragenden Holzschale des Konstrukteurs Hans Osterwald, welche aus einem Druckring und einer mehrlagigen, aus Brettlamellen zusammengesetzten Holzschale bestand.[93]

Anläßlich der Deutschen Industrieausstellung in Berlin 1952 baute man für den Schweizer Pavillon ein hängendes Dach, welches aus einem Brettschichtholz-Druckring bestand, der auf den Fassadenstützen auflag. Die Dachhaut wurde von einem Seilnetz aus Trag- und Spannseilen getragen.[94]

The suspended shell represents a special variation of the shell primarily loaded in tension. To stabilize the form against wind suction and to achieve the necessary prestress, these shells must be curved in two directions. In timber these are realized as lattice shells.

The first suspended roofs – in Albany, New York, in 1932 – were of metal. This form of construction was made popular in Germany mainly through the publication of Frei Otto's book *Das hängende Dach*.[92] In this book he wrote about a loadbearing timber shell designed by Hans Osterwald which consisted of a compression ring and layers of boards.[93]

The Swiss pavilion erected for the 1952 German Industry Exhibition in Berlin featured a suspended roof consisting of a glulam compression ring supported on facade columns. The roof covering was carried by a cable net of loadbearing and tensioning cables.[94]

In 1953 the roof to the Raleigh Arena in Raleigh, North Carolina, aroused great interest. This cable net curving in two directions spanned between two in-

Besonders große Aufmerksamkeit erregte die Überdachung der Raleigh Arena 1953 in Raleigh, North Carolina. Diese gegenläufig gekrümmten Seilnetze spannten zwischen zwei schräg liegenden Stahlbetonbögen, welche auf den Außenstützen auflagen. Die Tragseile wurden durch gegenläufige Spannseile vorgespannt und ermöglichten damit die Aufnahme abhebender Kräfte.[95]

Im Jahre 1964 entstand die große Festhalle für die EXPO in Lausanne, welche ein hängendes Dach hatte. Dieses Dach bestand aus über 52 m langen, 1 m breiten und 13 mm dicken Sperrholzlamellen, welche an einem 87 m weit spannenden Dreigelenkbogen hingen, der zusätzlich unterspannt war. Am Fußpunkt wurden sie durch einen Druckring gehalten. Der Dreigelenkbogen und der Druckring wurden als zweiteiliger Querschnitt aus Brettschichtholz ausgeführt. Auf den Lamellen war eine Kunststoffhaut befestigt, die transluzent war und dadurch die Dachhaut streifenweise erhellte. Zur Aufnahme abhebender Kräfte wurden über die Sperrholzbänder Stahlkabel gespannt. Das Besondere der Lamellen bestand in den mit Araldit verleimten stählernen Anschlüssen, welche sich nicht als dauerhaft erwiesen. Die Halle mußte daher später wieder abgebaut werden.[96]

clined reinforced concrete arches supported on the outer columns. The loadbearing cables were prestressed by the opposing tensioning cables and hence countered uplift forces.[95]

The Lausanne EXPO of 1964 included a large festival hall with a suspended roof. This roof consisted of plywood laminations 1000 mm wide x 13 mm thick and over 52 m long which were suspended from a trussed three-pin arch spanning 87 m. The laminations were supported at the base on a compression ring. Both three-pin arch and compression ring were fabricated as two-part glulam sections. A translucent plastic skin was attached to the laminations to introduce illuminated bands into the roof covering. Steel cables were draped over the plywood to resist uplift forces. The special feature of the laminations was their steel connections glued with Araldite adhesive, which unfortunately did not stand the test of time – the hall later had to be demolished.[96]

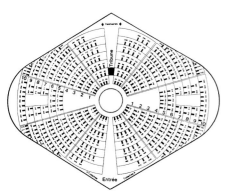

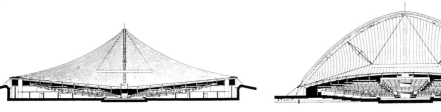

Festhalle der Schweizerischen Landesausstellung EXPO 1964, Grundriß, Querschnitt, Längsschnitt.
Festival Hall for Swiss National Exhibition EXPO 1964, Lausanne, sections, plan.

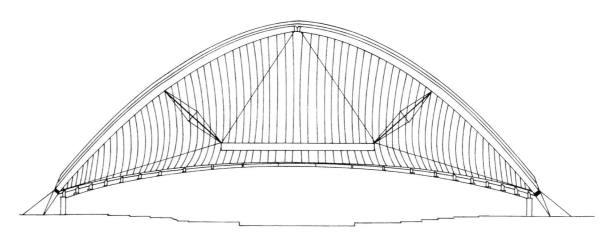

Linke Seite **Arch.: Frei Otto, Warmbronn; Planungsgruppe Gestering, Bremen; Ing.: Speich und Hinkes, Hannover; Produktionshalle Wilkhahn, Bad Münder-Einbeckhausen, 1987, Rahmen mit Zeltdach, Außenansicht.**
Facing page Architects: Frei Otto, Warmbronn, Planungsgruppe Gestering, Bremen; engineers: Speich & Hinkes, Hannover; Wilkhahn production plant, Bad Münder-Einbeckhausen, 1987, frame with membrane roof, external view.

Eine ähnliche Konstruktion im Bereich des Industriebaus wurde 1987 für die Produktionsgebäude der Firma Wilkhahn in Bad Münder verwendet. Prof. Frei Otto plante vier Pavillons, die jeweils eine Grundfläche von 22 x 22 m zeltartig überspannen. Die Dachform wird durch einen mittig aufgestellten gespreizten Dreigelenkrahmen gebildet, der gleichzeitig das Oberlicht aufnimmt. Die vorgekrümmten, sehr schlanken Rippen (6 x 8 cm) spannen vom Binder zum Druckring, der als Achteck ausgebildet auf der Fassade aufliegt. Die Hängerippen sind mit Schalung und textiler Dachbespannung versehen.[97]

Der entstehende Raum ist beeindruckend in seiner Qualität hinsichtlich Belichtung, Belüftung und Akustik. In einer der Hallen, welche als Schneiderei genutzt werden, arbeiten über 30 Mitarbeiter. Aufgrund der Raumqualität sind die Hallen ausgesprochen beliebt.

A similar design was used – albeit for an industrial building – in 1987 for the Wilkhahn company's production plant in Bad Münder. Prof. Frei Otto planned four tent-like pavilions each covering an area of 22 x 22 m. The shape of the roof was determined by a central splayed three-pin frame which at the same time accommodated the rooflight. The precambered, very slender ribs (60 x 80 mm) spanned from the frame to the octagonal compression ring supported on the facade. The suspended ribs are provided with sheathing and a textile roof covering.[97]

The quality of the interior is impressive in terms of its lighting, ventilation and acoustics. Over 30 employees work in one of the pavilions, which houses the cutting shop. The quality of the working environment has made the buildings highly popular.

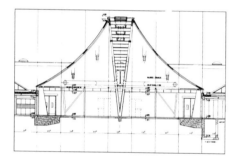

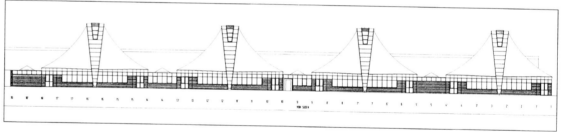

Produktionshalle Wilkhahn, Schnitt, Seitenansicht, Nachtansicht.
Wilkhahn production plant, section, side elevation, view at night.

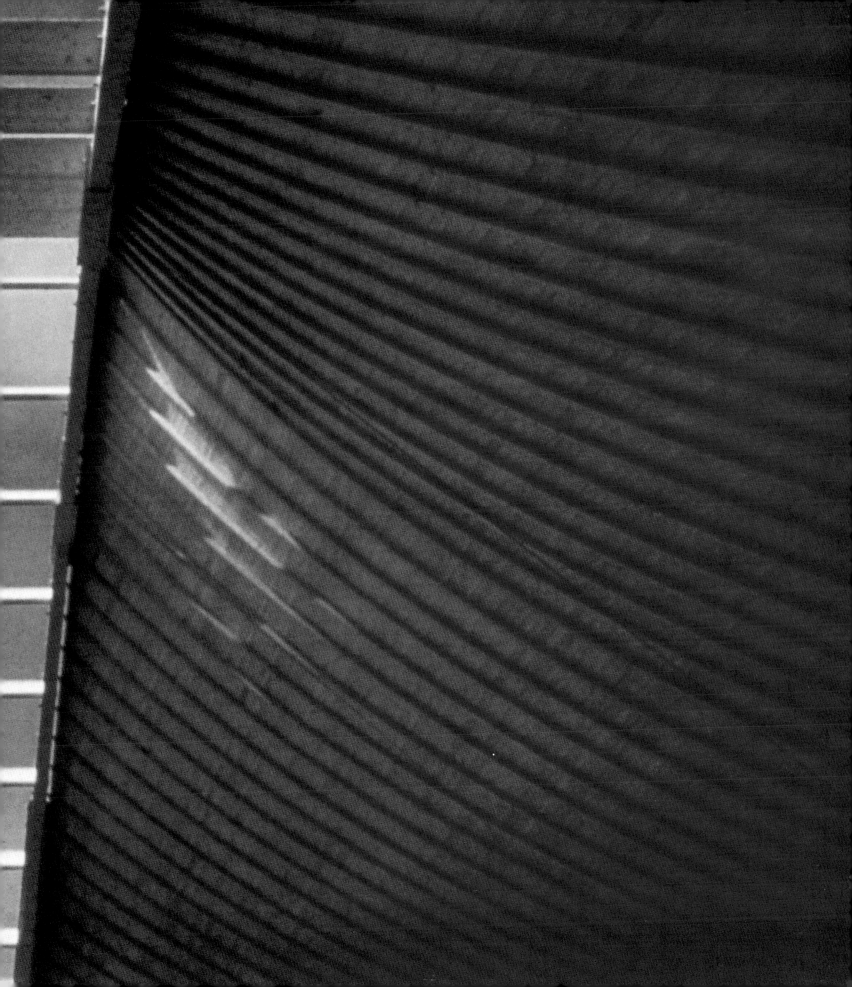

Produktionshalle Wilkhahn, Bauzustand, Außenansicht, Decke mit Oberlicht.
Vorige Doppelseite **Innenansicht**
Wilkhahn production plant, under construction, external view, rooflight.
Previous double page Internal view.

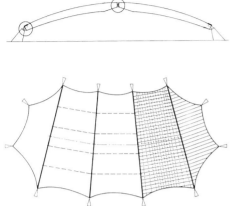

Für das Dach der Ausstellungshalle des Autohauses Deffur in Hückelhoven-Brachelen wurden vier Dreigelenkbögen errichtet, welche die Hängerippen tragen. Die Verbindung erfolgt über Flachstahllaschen und Stabdübel. Die 34 mm starke Holzschalung wurde zusätzlich durch Stahlspannbänder vorgespannt, um sowohl die aussteifende Wirkung für die Binder als auch die verschiedenen Beanspruchungen aus Windsog abzutragen. An den Schmalseiten werden die Hängerippen durch Ringzuganker gehalten. Diese sind zweiachsig gekrümmt und wurden in zwei Arbeitsschritten lagenweise auf einer Rüstung hergestellt.[98]

The roof over the Deffur car showroom in Hückelhoven-Brachelen uses four three-pin arches to carry the suspended ribs. Flat steel plates and pins form the connections. The 34-mm-thick timber sheathing was also prestressed by means of steel straining straps in order to brace the arches and resist uplift due to wind. The suspended ribs are held on the narrow sides by means of ring tension beams. These curve in two directions and were produced in two stages in layers on a scaffold.[98]

Arch.: Bernd Baier + Leo Graff;
Ing.: Führer–Kosch–Stein;
Ausf.: PHB Prümer Holzbau;
Autohaus Deffur, Hückelhoven-Brachelen, 1991,
Rippenschale mit vier Dreigelenkbögen,
Schnitt, Grundriß, Bauzustand, Außenansicht,
Innenansicht.
Architects: Bernd Baier + Leo Graff;
engineers: Führer–Kosch–Stein;
contractor: PHB Prümer Holzbau;
Deffur car showroom, Hückelhoven-Brachelen, 1991, lattice shell with four three-pin arches, section, plan, under construction, external view, internal view.

Autohaus Deffur, Bauzustand.
Deffur car showroom, under construction.

**Arch.: Lukas M. Lang, Wien;
Ing.: Natterer und Dittrich, München;
Ausf.: Moll, Arge Pfisterer und Kaufmann,
Loharens; Recyclinghalle, Wien, 1982,
Rippenschale mit Pylon, Montage.**
Architect: Lukas M. Lang, Vienna; engineers: Natterer
& Dittrich, Munich; contractor: Moll, Arge Pfisterer &
Kaufmann, Loharens; recycling plant, Vienna, 1982,
lattice shell with pylon, erection.

Die bisher am weitesten gespannte hängende Rippenschale entstand 1982 zur Überdachung der Abfallrecyclinganlage in Wien. Von einem 67,35 m hohen Stahlbetonturm spannen 48 radial angeordnete Hängerippen, die einen Querschnitt von 20 cm auf 80–110 cm haben. Der Gesamtdurchmesser des Daches beträgt 170,6 m, so daß die einzelnen Rippen eine Länge von 102 m erreichen. Sie sind durch elf Ringpfetten zug- und druckfest miteinander verbunden. Zur Erreichung einer Schalenwirkung wurde die doppelte Bohlenlage kreuzweise vernagelt und im Bereich des Ringankers noch zusätzlich durch Diagonalen ausgesteift.

Die Schalenwirkung wird hauptsächlich zur Abtragung unsymmetrischer Wind- und Schneelasten benötigt.[99] Je zwei Rippen wurden am Boden miteinander durch Pfetten verbunden und mit der Schalung versehen, bevor sie durch Kräne eingehoben wurden.[100]

The largest suspended lattice shell built to date is the roof over the waste recycling plant in Vienna. Completed in 1982, the 48 radial ribs (200 x 800-1100 mm) are suspended from a reinforced concrete tower 67.35 m high. The overall diameter of the roof is 170.6 m with the individual ribs reaching a length of 102 m. Connections capable of resisting tension and compression join the ribs to the 11 ring purlins. The shell effect is achieved by nailing the double layer of boards crosswise and extra stability ensured by adding cross-bracing adjacent the ring beam. This shell effect is mainly required to carry asymmetric wind and snow loads.[99] Pairs of ribs were joined together by purlins on the ground and provided with the boarding before being hoisted into position by crane.[100]

**Recyclinghalle, Details: Anschluß Pfetten an
Hängerippe mit Bohlenlage und
Verstärkungsblechen, Rippenaufhängung am
Pylon an umlaufendem Stahlring, Anschluß
Holzkonstruktion an Stahlbetonscheibe.**
Recycling plant, details: Connection between purlins and suspended rib with Layer of boards and strengthening plates, rib suspension point at pylon on perimeter steel ring, connection between timber construction and reinforced concrete support.

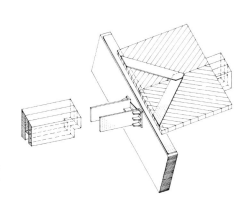 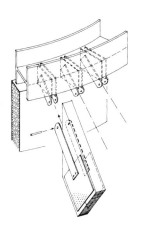 

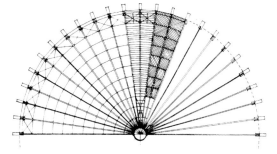

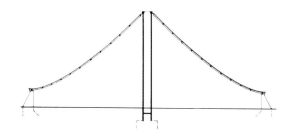

Recyclinghalle, Bauzustand, Montageablauf, Grundriß, Schnitt, Außenansicht.
Recycling plant, under construction, erection procedure, plan, section, external view.

Recyclinghalle, Innenansicht.
Recycling plant, intenal view.

Die freieste Weiterentwicklung stellt die Überdachung des Solebades in Bad Dürrheim dar, die durch die Architekten Geier und Geier in Zusammenarbeit mit den Ingenieuren Wenzel, Frese und Barthel 1987 entstand.[101] Hier wurde die Übertragung der für die Bauten der Olympiade in München entwickelten Zeltkonstruktionen auf den Baustoff Holz erreicht, der aufgrund seiner bauphysikalischen Eigenschaften besonders gut zur Überdachung von Schwimm- und Solebädern geeignet ist.[102] Verbindungsmittel in Stahl sollten wegen der korrosiven Dämpfe vermieden oder geschützt ausgebildet werden.[103]

Über einem sehr freien Grundriß entstanden fünf 9,1-11,5 m hohe Baumstützen, welche um einen kleinen Innenhof stehen. Sie tragen an ihren 6 bzw. 8 m großen Zugringen die Rippenschale, welche aus hängenden Meridianrippen und Ringrippen bestehen, die durch eine zweilagige, diagonal versetzte Schalung schubsteif miteinander verbunden wird. Die Meridianrippen hängen der Kettenlinie angepaßt von Ring zu Ring oder von Ring zum Randbogen. Die Lage der Rippen wurde den Hauptspannungstrajektorien angepaßt, wodurch sie hauptsächlich auf Zug belastet werden und nur einen Querschnitt von 20 x 20,5 cm haben. Die Ringrippen sind in einem Abstand von 80 cm in die Meridianrippen eingelassen und haben Querschnitte von 8 x 8 cm bzw. 12 x 14 cm. Die teilweise zweifach gekrümmten und verwundenen Rippen wurden aus 10 bis 20, einige Bauteile sogar aus 98 Querschnitten verleimt, was mit einem Zwischenschritt des Auftrennens und erneuten Verleimens erreicht wurde.

Die Baumringe und Randbögen sind als Kastenprofile so konstruiert, daß die Meridianrippen mittig einlaufen und durch Stabdübel angeschlossen werden.

One very liberal interpretation of this idea can be seen in the roof to the brine baths at Bad Dürrheim, which was designed by the architects Geier and Geier in collaboration with the engineers Wenzel, Frese and Barthel in 1987.[101] This project transfers the tent structures developed for the Munich Olympics to timber, whose building science properties make it ideal for roofing over swimming pools and brine baths.[102] Owing to the corrosive atmosphere, steel fasteners should be avoided or at least well protected.[103]

Five "tree" columns, between 9.1 and 11.5 m high, were placed around a small inner court in a very irregular layout. These support the lattice shell on their 6 or 8 m tension rings. The shell consists of suspended meridian and annular ribs with shear-resistant connections linking them by way of two layers of diagonally offset sheathing. The meridian ribs are suspended, following the catenary line, from ring to ring or from ring to perimeter arch. These follow the primary stress trajectories, are mainly loaded in tension and measure just 200 x 205 mm. The 80 x 80 mm or 120 x 140 mm annular ribs at 800 mm centre to centre are let into the meridian ribs. The glulam ribs, some in double curvature and twisted, were made up of 10-20, some components of as many as 98 sections, a feat accomplished by separating and regluing during production.

The tension rings and perimeter arches are designed as box sections in such a way that the meridian ribs can be fixed by pins in the centre. The two box-section parts were joined together with hexagon-head screws and hardwood dowels. Cast steel bearings are integrated in the beech plywood panels in the corners of the perimeter arches in order to, above

Arch.: Geier und Geier; Ing.: Prof. Wenzel (Frese, Pörtner, Haller) + T. Barthel, Karlsruhe; Ausf.: Burgbacher Holzwerke, Trossingen; Solebad, Bad Dürrheim, 1987, Rippenschale auf fünf Baumstützen, Ringrippen, Randbögen.
Architects: Geier & Geier; engineers: Prof. Wenzel (Frese, Pörtner, Haller) + T. Barthel, Karlsruhe; contractor: Burgbacher Holzwerke, Trossingen; brine baths, Bad Dürrheim, 1987, lattice shell on five "tree" columns, annular ribs, perimeter arches.

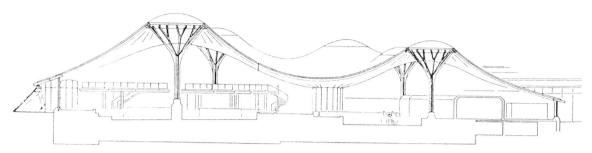

**Solebad Bad Dürrheim, Schnitt, Nachtansicht,
Eckpunkt, Tiefpunkt, Lager.**
Brine baths, Bad Dürrheim, section, view at night,
corner, low point, bearing.

Die beiden Kastenquerschnittsteile wurden dann mit Schlüsselschrauben und Zwischenhölzern miteinander verbunden. In den Ecken der Randbögen befinden sich in Buchensperrholzplatten eingelassene Gußstahllager, die vor allem die horizontalen Auflagerkräfte aufnehmen. Das Gewicht der Randbögen wird über die Fassaden abgetragen.

Die Baumstützen setzen sich aus neun Segmenten zusammen, welche sich gleichsam abgewickelt aufspreizen, wobei der Ring mittels Zapfen und Hartholzdollen korrosionsfrei auf den Ästen fixiert ist. Zur Kontrolle der Stützenkräfte sind kleine justierbare Zwischenfundamente unter den Baumstützen vorhanden, so daß auf eine Spannbarkeit der Rippenschale verzichtet werden konnte.

Abschließend muß festgestellt werden, daß der absolut minimierte Materialeinsatz bei diesem Tragwerk durch einen erheblichen Aufwand in der Vorfertigung und vor Ort bei der Erstellung einer mittels Rillennägel erzielten schubsteifen Schale erkauft wurde. Doch die architektonischen Ergebnisse und die bauphysikalischen Anforderungen lassen diesen Aufwand mehr als gerechtfertigt erscheinen. Dieser erhöhte Planungsaufwand führt dazu, daß diese Bauweise vor allem bei Solitärbauten mit hohem Gestaltungsanspruch zum Einsatz kommen wird.

all, accommodate the horizontal support reactions. The weight of the perimeter arches is carried by the facades. The tree columns comprise nine identical segments which splay out at the top, with the ring being fixed, to avoid corrosion, by means of tenons and hardwood dowels on the "branches". Small, adjustable intermediate pads were incorporated beneath the tree columns to control the forces so that the lattice shell did not need to be tensioned.

It was subsequently realized that the price to be paid for reducing the amount of material to an absolute minimum in this structure was considerable extra work during preassembly and on site when fixing the shear-resistant shell by means of helical-threaded shank nails. However, the architectural outcome and the building science specification more than justify this extra expense. The extra planning effort necessary with this form of construction will be favoured for, principally, one-off structures with high aesthetic demands.

Solebad Bad Dürrheim, Details der Baumstütze, Dachaufsicht der Hängerippenschale, Dachuntersicht.
Brine baths, Bad Dürrheim, details of "tree" column, plan on suspended lattice shell roof, underside of roof.

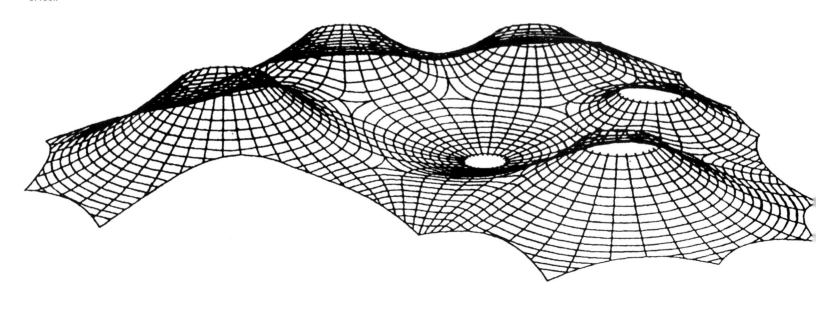

Solebad Bad Dürrheim, Innenansicht.
Brine baths, Bad Dürrheim, internal view.

Arch.: Herzog und Partner;
Ing.: Natterer und Burger;
Ausf.: Poppensieker & Derix;
Expodach 2000, Hannover, 2000,
Rippenschale auf Baumstützen, Grundriß, räumliche Darstellung.
Architects: Herzog & Partner;
engineers: Natterer & Burger;
contractor: Poppensieker & Derix;
Expodach 2000, Hannover, 2000, lattice shells on
"tree" columns, plan, perspective view.

Für die Expo 2000 in Hannover entstand eine Überdachung aus zehn freistehenden einzelnen Schirmen, welche jeweils eine Fläche von 39 x 39 m überspannen. Dieses Dach stellt eine Mischung aus einem Kragdach und einer eingehängten Rippenschale dar und steht damit am Ende dieses Kapitels.

Die mittige, 18 m hohe Turmkonstruktion trägt so als im Fundament eingespannte Stütze mit einem allseitig 18 m weit auskragenden Dach. Durch diese Vorgabe ist die Konstruktion hohen Beanspruchungen an der Einspannstelle des Daches und am Fußpunkt ausgesetzt. So sind verschiedene Winddruck- und Sogbelastungen, einseitige Schneelasten und mittige Schneeansammlungen zu berücksichtigen. Um eine dynamische Erregung der Schirme mit gegenläufigen Verformungen zu verhindern, wurden die Schirme über Kopplungselemente aus Stahl miteinander verbunden.

Die aus vier konischen Einzelstäben bestehenden Türme weiten sich daher zum Fußpunkt auf und sind durch dreieckige Furnierschichtholzplatten (FSH) miteinander verbunden. Im Knotenpunkt zwischen Dach und Stütze wird das Dach in die Stütze eingespannt. Aufgrund der hohen Beanspruchung wurde dieser Punkt als pyramidenförmige Stahlkonstruktion ausgebildet. An dem Stützenkopf sind vier Kragarme befestigt, welche als Kastenträger aus Brettschichtholz und FSH-Stegen bestehen. Durch die elastische Einspannung der Kragträger in die Stütze führen die Verdrehungen des Stützenkopfes zu linearen Senkungen der Kragträger, die sich mit den Verformungen des Kragarms überlagern. Dies führt dazu, daß die Steifigkeit der Stütze besonders groß sein muß und begründet damit die gespreizte Ausbildung.

Ten enormous free-standing canopies each covering an area of 39 x 39 m have been built for EXPO 2000 in Hannover. Each of these roofs represents a combination of cantilever roof and suspended lattice shell and hence marks the conclusion of this chapter.

The central 18-m-high tower, restrained at the foundation, supports a roof cantilevering 18 m to all sides. This design places great demands on the tower base and the roof-tower junction. Therefore, various wind pressure and suction loads, asymmetric snow loads and a build-up of snow in the middle all have to be considered. In order to prevent the dynamic excitation of the canopies with opposing deformations, steel coupling elements were used to link them together.

The towers, fabricated from four separate conical members, widen out towards the base and are interconnected by way of triangular laminated veneer lumber (LVL) panels. The roof gains restraint by being built into the tower. The high stresses at this point meant that a pyramid-type steel solution was necessary. Four cantilever arms are fixed to the head of the tower; these consist of box sections made from glulam with LVL webs. The elastic restraint of the cantilever arms at the head of the tower means that twisting of the tower head leads to yielding of the arm supports superimposed on the deflection of the cantilever arms themselves. This in turn means that the tower must be sufficiently stiff – hence the need for a splayed arrangement.

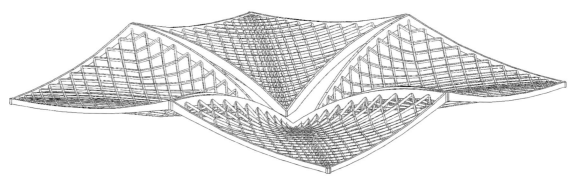

Das Dach selbst trägt als an den Kragarmen gestützte und doppelt gekrümmte Gitterschale, welche aus gestapelten Brettlamellen zusammengesetzt ist. Die netzförmig angeordneten Brettrippen bestehen aus 8 bis 10 Brettlamellen, welche abwechselnd durchlaufen und miteinander kontinuierlich verschraubt und in Teilbereichen verleimt sind. Der Rippenabstand ist dem Kräfteverlauf angepaßt und liegt zwischen ca. 0,36 m im zentralen Bereich und 1,5 m in den Randbereichen.

Als Aussteifung der Rippenschale ist eine diagonal zu den Rippen verlaufende Schalungslage angeordnet. Sie besteht aus zwei orthogonal verlaufenden Brettlagen (24 x 100 mm). Die Bretter sind im lichten Abstand von 10 cm verlegt, so daß für eine gewisse Lichtdurchlässigkeit und eine vollständige Umlüftung der tragenden Bauteile gesorgt ist. Die Befestigung erfolgt über Schlitzbleche und Stabdübel. Die Schalungslage ist an den Rippen mit Schrauben angeschlossen.

Die Dachabdichtung erfolgt mit einer Dachhaut aus Kunststoff, die aus Gründen des konstruktiven Holzschutzes im Abstand von 5 cm die Gitterschale überspannt. Dadurch wird Umlüftung der Bauteile ermöglicht und Schäden durch Staunässe vermieden. Die Schirme wurden in vier Elementen vorgefertigt und dann auf der Baustelle in die Kragarme eingehängt.

The roof itself acts as a double-curvature lattice shell – fabricated from boards laid on edge – supported on the cantilever arms. The net-like arrangement of ribs consists of 8-10 alternately continuous laminations screwed together at regular intervals and also glued in some places. The spacing of the ribs depends on the flow of forces and lies between approx. 0.36 m in the centre and 1.5 m near the edges. Bracing to the lattice shell is provided by attaching the boards at an angle to the direction of the ribs. This sheathing consists of two layers of boards (24 x 100 mm) at right-angles. The boards are laid at a clear spacing of 100 mm so that a certain degree of transparency and good all-round ventilation of the loadbearing components is assured. Fixing is by means of slotted plates and steel pins. The layer of boards is screwed to the ribs. The roof is sealed with a synthetic roof covering attached 50 mm clear of the lattice shell in order to protect the timber. This ensures that the elements are ventilated to prevent damage caused by a build-up of trapped moisture. Each canopy was prefabricated in four pieces and then lifted onto the cantilever arms by crane on site.

Expodach 2000, Bauzustand.
Expodach 2000, under construction.

Expodach 2000, Bauzustand, Detail der Dachkonstruktion, Dachuntersicht mit Stützen.
Expodach 2000, detail of roof construction, underside of roof with columns.

**Expodach 2000, Untersicht, Stützenfußpunkt,
Stahlknoten der Stütze von unten, Stützendetail.**
Expodach 2000, underside of roof, base of columns,
steel node of column from below, detail of column.

Expodach 2000, Ausschnitt mit Kopplungspunkt der Kragträger.
Expodach 2000, roof detail with joint of cantilever arms.

Brücken
Bridges

Linke Seite **Ing.: Setzpfand und Partner; Ausf.: Paul Stephan, Gaildorf; Fußgängerbrücke, Jena-Niederwöllnitz, 1994, schräg abgehängte Trogbrücke, Ansicht.**
Facing page Engineers: Setzpfand & Partner; contractor: Paul Stephan, Gaildorf; footbridge, Jena-Niederwöllnitz, 1994, skew, suspended trough bridge, view.

Seit dem Beginn des Brückenbaus entwickelten sich Stein- und Holzbrücken parallel abhängig von den jeweiligen Rahmenbedingungen des Ortes. Steinbrücken fanden fast ausschließlich als Bogenbrücken Verwendung und benötigten so eine gewisse Mindesthöhe für die Steinbögen unterhalb der Fahrbahn. Diese Bauweise ermöglichte in bergigem Gelände große Spannweiten, beschränkte aber in flachem Gelände ihre Spannweite durch die begrenzten möglichen Steigungsverhältnisse. Die geringe Spannweite der Brücken führte zu einer größeren Anzahl von Flußpfeilern, welche immer eine Behinderung der Schiffahrt darstellten und bei Eisgang zu Schaden kommen konnten.

Holzbrücken besaßen in der Regel ihre Tragwerke oberhalb der Fahrbahn, so daß sie in geringer Höhe den Flußlauf überspannen konnten. Meist wurden sie als Hängewerke kastenförmig ausgebildet. Bei großen Spannweiten wurden diese Hängewerke durch lamellierte Bögen verstärkt und erreichten wie die Brücke von Grubenmann bei Wettingen eine Spannweite von 60 m.

Das Vertrauen in die neue Hetzer'sche Bauweise war von Anfang an so groß, daß bereits im Jahr 1910 das Büro Terner und Chopard zwei Brücken in Basel und Lausanne errichtete. In Beaulieu bei Lausanne entstand für die Eidgenössische Landwirtschaftliche Ausstellung eine 20,5 m weit spannende Fußgängerbrücke aus zwei parabelförmigen Dreigelenkbindern. Der aufgeständerte Fußweg lagerte auf zwei Doppelbindern (2 x 12/50 cm), welche mit einem diagonalen Aussteifungsverband (14 x 16 cm) versehen waren. Die Brücke war für Verkehrslasten von 350 kg/m² bemessen und wurde später wieder abgebaut.[104]

Since the very dawn of bridge-building, stone and timber bridges evolved alongside each other depending on the respective conditions of each site. Stone bridges were almost invariably of the arch variety and so required a certain minimum height for the stone arch beneath the deck. This form of construction permitted long spans in undulating or mountainous regions but was rather more restricted in other areas owing to the span/height ratio necessary. This meant short spans and hence a larger number of piers, which obstructed navigation and could be damaged in icy conditions.

Timber bridges generally positioned their load-carrying structure above the deck, so they could cross rivers at a lower height. Most were constructed as arched frames in box form. For long spans these arched frames were strengthened by laminated members and thus achieved spans of 60 m, like the Grubenmann specimen near Wettingen.

Confidence in the new Hetzer system was initially so high that the Terner/Chopard practice erected two bridges in Basel and Lausanne as early as 1910. In Beaulieu near Lausanne a temporary footbridge consisting of two parabolic three-pin arches spanning 20.5 m was built for the Swiss Agriculture Exhibition. The raised deck rested on two pairs of arches (each member 120 x 500 mm) provided with diagonal bracing (140 x 160 mm). The bridge was designed for imposed loads of 350 kg/m² and was later demolished.[104]

Ing.: Terner und Chopard, Temporärer Fußgängersteg, Lausanne, 1910, Details am Fußpunkt (oben) und Firstpunkt (unten), Seitenansicht, Grundriß, Ansicht.
Engineers: Terner & Chopard, temporary footbridge, Lausanne, 1910, details of springing (top) and crown (bottom), side elevation, plan, view.

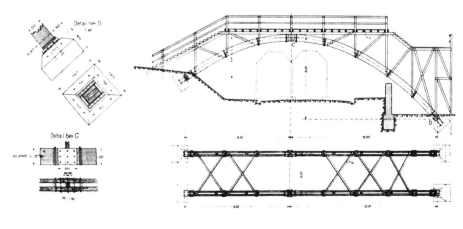

**Ing.: Terner und Chopard,
Ausf.: Zimmergeschäft Riesterer-Asmus,
Brücke über die Wiese bei Basel, 1910,
parabelförmiger Zweigelenkbogen, Seitenansicht, Horizontalschnitt, Draufsicht, Ansicht.**
Engineers: Terner & Chopard; contractor:
Zimmergeschäft Riesterer-Asmus;
bridge over the River Wiese near Basel, 1910,
parabolic two-pin arch, side elevation, horizontal
section, plan, view.

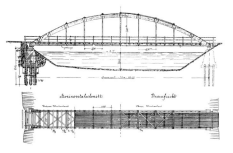

Im Gegensatz dazu war die Brücke über die Wiese bei Basel von Beginn an für eine Nutzungszeit von 15–20 Jahren ausgelegt. Sie spannte mit ihrem oben liegenden parabelförmigen Bogen über 33 m bei einer Stichhöhe von 5 m, wobei die Horizontalkräfte am Auflager durch ein Zugband aus Flußeisen aufgenommen wurden. Der Fußweg wurde alle 3,3 m an den Doppelbindern (2 x 14/60cm) abgehängt. Der Achsabstand der Doppelbinder betrug 2,8 m. Oberhalb der Durchgangshöhe waren sie durch einen Aussteifungsverband gehalten. Die maximale Spannung infolge einseitiger Verkehrslast wurde im Binder mit 66 kg/cm² (0,66 KN/cm²) angenommen.[105] Als Witterungsschutz des Binders dienten ein Anstrich mit Carbolineum und Abdeckbleche.

Trotz der relativ geringen vorhergesagten Nutzungsdauer konnte sich diese Holzkonstruktion aus Kostengründen durchsetzen. Eine Stahlbetonkonstruktion wäre wesentlich teurer gewesen (17.000 gegenüber 9300 SFr.), wobei die späteren Unterhaltungs- und Reparaturkosten den Kostenvorteil verschlechterten. Die Verstärkungen an den Auflagern und deren besserer Schutz im Jahr 1919 kosteten bereits 3500 SFr. Schon 1922 wurden Reparaturmaßnahmen am Windverband, am Belag und an den Querträgern erforderlich, welche

In contrast, the bridge over the River Wiese near Basel was intended to last for 15-20 years. Its parabolic arches above the deck spanned more than 33 m for a rise of 5 m, with the horizontal reaction forces being resisted by a cast iron tie. The deck was suspended from the two-piece arches (2 No. 140 x 160 mm) every 3.3 m. The pairs of beams were spaced 2.8 m apart and braced by diagonals above head height. The maximum stress in the arches caused by an asymmetric imposed load was assumed to be 66 kg/cm² (0.66 kN/cm²).[105] Cover plates and a coating of carbolineum served to protect the members from the elements.

Despite the relatively low prediction for the use expectancy, this form of timber construction was favoured on grounds of cost. Reinforced concrete would have been considerably more expensive (SFr 17 000 compared to just SFr 9300), although the later maintenance and repair costs eradicated some of this cost advantage. Strengthening of and better protection to the abutments in 1919 alone cost SFr 3500. And repairs to the wind girder, deck surfacing and transverse beams as soon as 1922 cost another SFr 2900. But even these measures only managed to prolong the life of the bridge for a few years,

nochmals 2900 SFr. kosteten. Aber auch diese Maßnahmen hielten nur wenige Jahre vor, so daß die Brücke im Jahr 1928 abgebrochen und durch eine Stahlbrücke ersetzt wurde.[106]

Aufgrund dieses eher unbefriedigenden Witterungsverhaltens kam es kaum zum Bau von weiteren ungeschützten, permanenten Brücken in Holzleimbauweise. Bei temporären Brücken oder Schalungsgerüsten wurden verleimte Bogenbinder häufiger eingesetzt, so auch für die Mauerwerksbrücke über die Schöllenen bei Göschenen im Jahr 1915, deren Stützweite 27 m betrug.[107]

Die Entwicklung des Brückenbaus hatte wie bereits geschildert besonders in Amerika seit Beginn des 19. Jahrhunderts eine beachtliche Entwicklung genommen, da in dieser Zeit die Straßen- und Eisenbahnbrücken fast ausschließlich in Holz ausgeführt wurden. Die damit verbundene ingenieurtechnische Entwicklung wies bereits weit in die Zukunft. Schon 1851 berichtete Karl Culmann nach seiner Reise durch Nordamerika von den Ideen Remmingtons, der versteifte Spannbandkonstruktionen zur Überbrückung grosser Spannweiten bis zu 200 m vorschlug.

Die Spannbandkonstruktionen stellen im Grunde flache Hängeseilbrücken dar, wobei durch den geringen Durchhang entsprechend hohe Zugkräfte entstehen. Und obwohl anscheinend niemand diese Idee sonderlich ernst nahm, erkannte Culmann den richtigen ingenieurmäßigen Ansatz dieser Idee: „So gebührt ihm [Remmington] doch jedenfalls das Verdienst, der

and in 1928 it had to be demolished and replaced by a steel construction.[106]

Therefore, owing to this rather unsatisfactory weathering resistance, hardly any other unprotected, permanent glulam bridges were built. However, glulam arches did find favour for temporary bridges or as formwork for reinforced concrete bridges, and also as centering for the masonry arch over the River Schöllenen near Göschenen in 1915, whose span was 27 m.[107]

As already mentioned, the development of timber bridge-building had proceeded apace in America in particular since the beginning of the 19th century because during this period road and railway bridges were constructed almost exclusively in this material. The associated engineering developments were already way ahead of their time. As early as 1851 Karl Culmann, following a journey across North America, reported on the ideas of Remmington, who proposed stiffened tension ribbon bridges for spanning great distances of up to 200 m.

Tension ribbon bridges are basically shallow suspension bridges in which the low sag creates correspondingly high tensile forces. Although nobody seemed to take these ideas particularly seriously, Culmann recognized the correctness of the engineering approach behind this idea: "So he [Remmington] certainly deserves to be recognized for having given timber construction a direction (timber in tension), which means that at least three to five times more

Lehrgerüst für eine Mauerwerksbrücke über die Schöllenen bei Göschenen, 1915.
Centering for a masonry arch over the River Schöllenen near Göschenen, 1915.

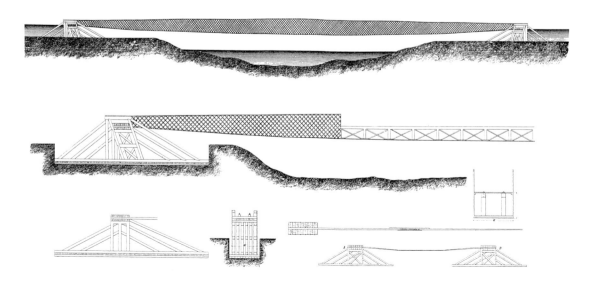

Remmington, Entwurf für eine Spannbandbrücke, 1848.
Remmington, design for a tension ribbon bridge, 1848.

Holzkonstruktionsweise eine Richtung gegeben zu haben (Zugbeanspruchung von Holz), auf der wenigstens 3 bis 5mal mehr geleistet werden kann als auf dem bisher verfolgten Wege, und darauf aufmerksam gemacht zu haben, daß dünne Verteilung die Dauerhaftigkeit des Holzes erhöht und durch Leime und andere chemische Mittel manchmal viel bessere Verbindungen hergestellt werden können als durch Verzahnungen und Keile, die immer Quellen der Fäulnis für alle Holzkonstruktionen sind."[108]

Das hauptsächlich zugbeanspruchte Bauteil ist aufgrund seiner gleichmäßigen Spannungsverteilung im Querschnitt und der nicht vorhandenen Stabilitätsproblematik jedem druck- und biegebeanspruchten Bauteil überlegen. Über 100 Jahre dauerte die Entwicklung des Holzleimbaus, bis zuverlässige, keilverzinkte Vollstöße hergestellt werden konnten, die so lange Bauteile erst ermöglichten. Auch die Entwicklung hoch beanspruchter Montagestöße vor Ort und entsprechender Lagerdetails bedurfte dieser Zeit.

Der Architekt Richard J. Dietrich entwickelte 1986 in Zusammenarbeit mit den Ingenieuren Brünninghoff und Rampf eine Spannbandbrücke als Fußgängerbrücke über den Main-Donau-Kanal bei Essing. Neun 190 m lange Brettschichtholzträger spannen über vier Felder von 30, 32, 73 und 35 m. Der Durchhang der einzelnen Felder wurde entsprechend der Spannweite so gewählt, daß möglichst gleiche Zugkräfte in allen Feldern entstehen.[109]

can be achieved than with the methods employed hitherto, and for having brought to our attention that thin lamination increases the durability of timber, and that adhesives and other chemical means can sometimes produce much better connections than scarfing and keying, which always prove to be a source of rot for all timber constructions."[108]

A component stressed primarily in tension is, owing to the uniform stress distribution within the cross-section and the absence of stability problems, superior to a component subjected to compression or bending. It took over 100 years of development in glulam construction before reliable finger joints could be produced which rendered possible long components. Highly stressed in-situ assembly joints and corresponding bearing details also required a similar, lengthy period of development.

In 1986 architect Richard J. Dietrich, in conjunction with engineers Brünninghoff and Rampf, designed a tension ribbon bridge for pedestrians over the Main-Danube canal near Essing. Nine 190-m-long glulam beams are laid across four spans of 30, 32, 73 and 35 m. The sag of each span was chosen such that the tensile forces in all spans would be as uniform as possible.[109]

The nine beams of 220 x 650 mm are utilized to only 40% by the tensile forces of 4000 kN which occur. The dimensions of the beams, however, are determined by dynamic loads caused by wind. The

Arch.(Entwurf und Planung): Richard J. Dietrich; Ing.: H. Brünninghoff, Rampf, Grundmann; Ausf.: Huber und Sohn Holzbau, Bachmehring, Grossmann, Rosenheim; Spannbandbrücke bei Essing, 1986, Luftbild, Seitenansicht.
Architects: Richard J. Dietrich; engineers: H. Brünninghoff, Rampf, Grundmann; contractor: Huber & Sohn Holzbau, Bachmehring, Grossmann, Rosenheim; tension ribbon bridge near Essing, 1986, aerial view, side view.

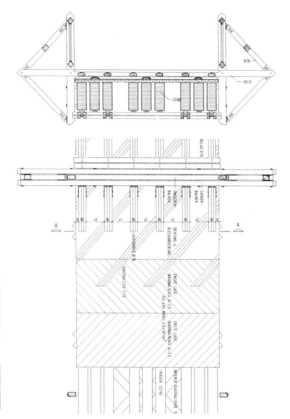

Spannbandbrücke bei Essing, Keilzinkenstoß, Details: Querschnitt, Lagen des Gehbahnbelags, Bauzustand.
Tension ribbon bridge near Essing, finger joint, details: section, deck surfacing, under construction.

Die neun Träger mit Querschnitten von 22 x 65 cm werden durch die auftretenden Zugkräfte in Höhe von 4000 KN nur zu 40% ausgenutzt. Die erforderlichen Querschnittsmaße leiten sich aber aus den dynamischen Belastungen infolge Wind ab. Durch die Wahl geringer Querschnittshöhen wurde die Biegebeanspruchung infolge Längsdehnung reduziert, die damit nur 10 % der Gesamtbeanspruchung entspricht.

Der durch diese geringe Biegesteifigkeit erhöhten Schwingungsanfälligkeit wurde durch die torsionssteife Verbindung aller neun Träger entgegengewirkt. An der Oberseite befinden sich zwei Diagonalschalungen und auf der Unterseite doppelte diagonale Aussteifungsverbände. Als konstruktiver Holzschutz wurde unter dem Gehbelag eine Blechabdeckung eingebaut. Die durch den Transport längenbegrenzten Bauteile wurden vor Ort mit einem Keilzinkenvollstoß verbunden, der bis dahin so noch nie ausgeführt worden war.

Im Bereich der Hängewerke und Fachwerke war der Anschluß von Druckkräften durch Ausbildung von Versätzen und Zapfen recht einfach zu erzielen.

choice of lower depths reduced the bending stresses as a result of longitudinal expansion, which therefore corresponds to just 10% of the total stress. The increased vulnerability to vibration caused by this low bending strength was counteracted by joining all nine beams via torsion-resistant connections. On top there are two layers of boards laid diagonally and on the bottom twin diagonal wind girders. Metal sheeting was attached below the deck surfacing to protect the wood. The length of the components was restricted by transportation requirements and so they were joined on site with finger joints, a feat which had never before been carried out in situ in this way.

Transferring compressive forces in arched frames and trusses was easily achieved by forming various tenon and bridle joints. Tension forces, on the other hand, were often accommodated by way of metal straps and pins and were normally not suitable for transferring large forces. The invention of the Howe truss in 1840 with its vertical steel tie rods now enabled all timber diagonals to be loaded in compres-

**Spannbandbrücke bei Essing, Sattelpunkt,
Aufsicht, Untersicht.**
Tension ribbon bridge near Essing, saddle point,
deck, underside.

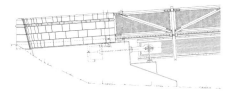

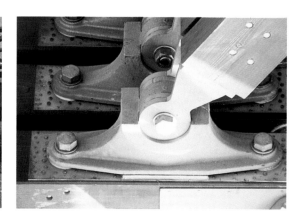

Spannbandbrücke bei Essing, Endauflager, Seitenansicht Widerlager, Stützenfußpunkt, Seitenansicht, Grundriß.
Tension ribbon bridge near Essing, end bearing, side elevation of abutment, support wind girder, side elevation, plan.

Zugkräfte dagegen wurden oft über Eisenlaschen und Bolzen angeschlossen und waren in der Regel nicht geeignet zur Übertragung großer Kräfte.

Seit 1840 ermöglichte die Erfindung des Howe'schen Trägers durch die Ausbildung der Zugvertikalen aus Rundstahl sämtliche Holzdiagonalen auf Druck zu beanspruchen. Um dies auch bei wechselnden Lastfällen zu gewährleisten, wurden die Zugstäbe vorgespannt und bildeten so ein vielfach statisch unbestimmtes vorgespanntes Fachwerk. Heute finden in der Regel hauptsächlich Knotenbleche in Verbindung mit Stabdübeln und Paßbolzen Verwendung, welche eine Übertragung großer Kräfte ermöglichen.

Bei allen Brücken spielt die Unterhaltung eine wichtige Rolle für die Lebensdauer, wobei Holzbrücken besondere Anforderungen stellen. Überall dort, wo die Feuchtigkeit nicht schnell wieder abtrocknen kann, kommt es auf Dauer zu Staunässe und Schäden. Die einfachste Art des konstruktiven Holzschutzes stellt die Einhausung dar, wie sie von vielen Beispielen bekannt ist.

sion. In order to guarantee this condition even upon load reversal, the ties were prestressed and so formed a frame with several degrees of indeterminacy. Today, gusset plates in conjunction with pins and close-tolerance bolts are generally used, thus enabling large forces to be transferred.

Maintenance plays a vital role for all bridges, with wooden bridges in particular calling for special treatment. If water cannot quickly run off or evaporate, then over time the build-up of moisture leads to damage. The simplest form of physical protection is to

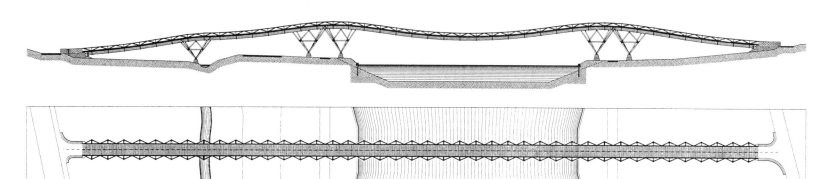

Eine moderne Variante mit einer Einhausung aus Glas ist die Fußgängerbrücke in Remseck. Diese Brücke überspannt mit 80 m frei den Neckar. Sie ist als Dreigurtfachwerkträger ausgebildet, der in Brückenmitte eine Höhe von 6,55 m besitzt. Aus statischen und gestalterischen Gründen weitet sich die Querschnittshöhe und -breite zur Flußmitte um 1,0 m. Durch die Ausbildung als Dreigurtbinder ist der Obergurt ausreichend stabilisiert und ein ansonsten notwendiger Portalrahmen wird überflüssig. Die Brücke wurde an Land montiert und in zwei Arbeitsschritten eingeschwommen.

Die Knotenpunkte sind als eingelassene Stahlbleche ausgebildet, die mit Bolzen und Stabdübeln gehalten werden. Als konstruktiver Holzschutz wurde die Brücke mit einer geschuppten Sicherheitsverglasung verkleidet, welche überlappend mit Lüftungsschlitzen ausgebildet ist.[110]

enclose the timber, as is evident in many examples.

One modern variation with an enclosure of glass is the new footbridge in Remseck. This bridge crosses the River Neckar in one span of 80 m. It is designed as a three-chord truss and rises to a height of 6.55 m in the centre. For structural and aesthetic reasons the depth and width of the cross-section increases by 1000 mm above the middle of the river. The use of three chords means that the upper chord is sufficiently stable and the portal frame otherwise necessary becomes superfluous. The bridge was assembled on the bank and floated into position in two stages. The joints are formed by steel plates set into the timber and fixed with bolts and pins. To provide protection for the wood the bridge is clad in overlapping "tiles" of laminated glass, but with gaps to allow the air to circulate.[110]

Ing.: Milbrandt und Sengler, Stuttgart; Ausf.: Paul Stephan, Gaildorf; Fußgängerbrücke, Remseck, 1988, Dreigurtbinder, Detailaufriß des Auflagers und des Strebenanschlusses an die Hauptträger-Untergurte, Seitenansicht.
Engineers: Milbrandt & Sengler, Stuttgart; contractor: Paul Stephan, Gaildorf; footbridge, Remseck, 1988, three-chord girder, details of support and strut connection to bottom chord of main girder, side elevation.

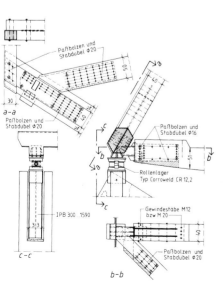

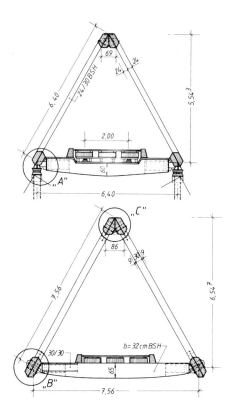

Fußgängerbrücke, Remseck, Schnitt am Auflager (oben) und in Brückenmitte (unten), Endauflager, Ansicht der Überdachung.
Footbridge, Remseck, sections through support (top) and centre of bridge (bottom), end of truss, view through truss.

Ing.: Setzpfand und Partner; Ausf.: Hellmich Baugesellschaft; Loharens Ingenieurbau; Fußgängerbrücke, Magdeburg-Cracau, 1997, Schrägseilbrücke, Ansichten, Seitenansicht und Grundriß, Schnitt durch Pylon.
Engineers: Setzpfand & Partner; contractor: Hellmich Baugesellschaft; Loharens Ingenieurbau; footbridge, Magdeburg-Cracau, 1997, cable-stayed bridge, views, side elevations and plan, pylon, section.

Bei der Überbrückung der alten Elbe bei Magdeburg wurde 1997 eine Schrägseilbrücke mit trogförmigem Brückenträger verwendet. Die Spannweite beträgt 36,9, 72, 27, 27 und 24 m. Aufgrund der unterschiedlichen Spannweiten wurde der 50 m hohe stählerne A-förmige Pylon leicht geneigt und am ersten Widerlager rückverankert. Die Unterbauten und Vorlandbrücken sind als Stahlbetonkonstruktion ausgeführt. Die 2 m hohen Brettschichtholzträger sind in der Höhe so angeordnet, daß Rollstuhlfahrer eine Sicht über die Brüstung des Geländers haben. Zum Witterungsschutz wurden die Träger mit einer Kiefernschalung verkleidet. Zur Stabilisierung der Träger und der Auflagerung des Belages werden die Träger mit einer rahmenartigen Stahlkonstruktion miteinander verbunden. Zur Erhöhung der Rutschsicherheit wurde der Belag aus Douglasie mit einer gesandeten Epoxidharzbeschichtung versehen.

Eine kastenförmige Fachwerkbrücke spannt mit 60 m Spannweite über die Dahme bei Niederlehme. Die zwei parallelen Träger besitzen nur Diagonalstäbe, welche ihre Neigung gemäß ihrer Belastung zum Auflager hin von 30° auf 40° verändern. Dadurch wer-

A cable-stayed bridge with trough beams was chosen for the River Alte Elbe near Magdeburg in 1997. The spans are 36.9, 72, 27, 27 and 24 m. To accommodate the varying spans, the 50 m steel A-frame pylon is positioned at an angle and tied back to the first abutment. The substructure and approach spans are in reinforced concrete. The 2000-mm-deep glulam beams are arranged such that even wheelchair users can see over the balustrading. Pine cladding provides protection against the weather. A frame-like steel construction links and hence stabilizes the beams and also provides a support for the deck. To improve the anti-slip characteristics, the deck of Douglas fir was given a coating of sanded epoxy resin.

A box-section truss bridge spans 60 m over the River Dahme near Niederlehme. The two parallel frames only have diagonal members, the angle of which changes from 30° to 40° towards the supports according to the loading. This means that the members in compression are shorter and hence less susceptible to buckling. The long, slender diagonals and the rise of the upper chord lend the bridge a light-

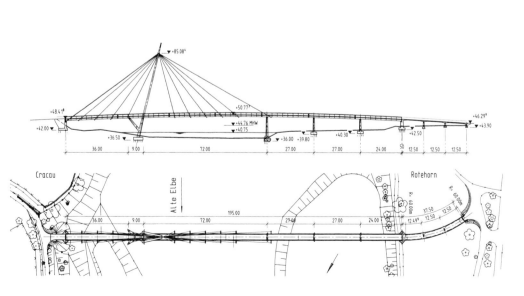

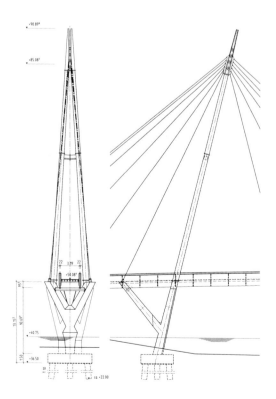

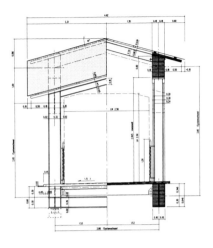

Ing.: Leonhardt, Andrä und Partner, Stuttgart; Ausf.: Holzbau Amann, Weilheim-Bannholz, Fußgängerbrücke über die Dahme, Niederlehme, 1999, zwei ebene Fachwerkträger, Schnitt, Montage des Gehbahnbelags, Bauzustand beim Einschwimmen.
Engineers: Leonhardt, Andrä & Partner, Stuttgart; contractor: Holzbau Amann, Weilheim-Bannholz, footbridge over the River Dahme, Niederlehme, 1999, two plane frames, section, installing the deck surfacing, floating bridge into position.

den die druckbeanspruchten Stäbe kürzer und geringer auf Knicken beansprucht. Die langen schlanken Diagonalen und der Stich des Obergurtes verleihen der Brücke eine große Leichtigkeit. Die Aussteifung der Fachwerkträger erfolgt durch eine 6,3 cm starke Kertoplatte in Decken- und Untergurtebene in Zusammenhang mit dem stählernen Portalrahmen am Anfang und Ende, welcher für eine Holzbrücke gestalterisch nicht ganz befriedigend ist.

Die Fußgängerbrücke in Niederwöllnitz bei Jena spannt als schräg abgehängte Trogbrücke mit einem einseitigen Pylon über die Bundesstraße. Der Brückenträger ist so ausgebildet, daß die Brettschichtholzträger sogleich als Geländer dienen. Trotz oberen Abdeckblechs ist die seitliche freie Bewitterung oft so stark, daß es zu Schädigungen kommt. Eine Verblendung durch eine hinterlüftete Schalung kann hierbei ein sinnvoller Schutz sein.

weight appearance. The trusses are braced by a 63-mm-thick Kerto plate at deck and bottom chord level in conjunction with the steel portal frames at the ends – in aesthetic terms not a totally satisfactory solution for a timber bridge.

The footbridge in Niederwöllnitz near Jena crosses the main road as a skew, suspended trough bridge with a pylon on one side. The bridge is designed in such a way that the glulam beams also serve as the balustrades. Cover plates to the top do not, however, protect the sides, which are often exposed to such severe weather that damage occurs. A ventilated cladding arrangement can be a sensible answer in such situations.

Fußgängerbrücke über die Dahme, Seitenansichten.
Footbridge over the River Dahme, Side elevations.

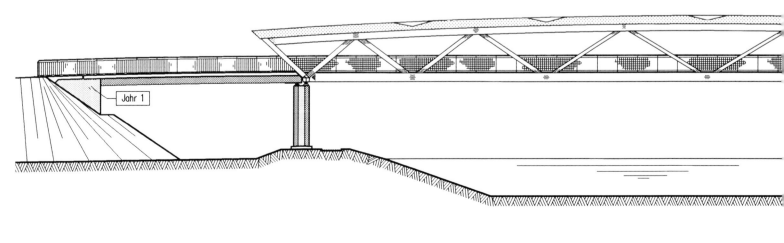

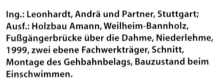

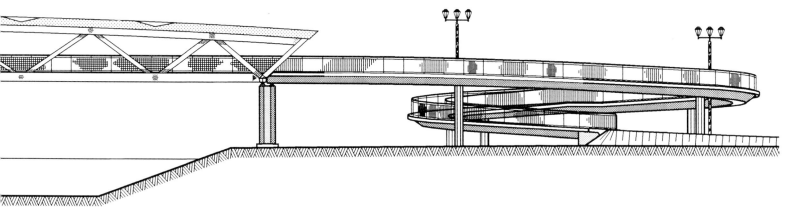

**Ing.: Setzpfand und Partner; Ausf.: Paul Stephan,
Gaildorf; Fußgängerbrücke, Jena-Niederwöllnitz,
1994, schräg abgehängte Trogbrücke,
Querschnitt, Detailansicht und -grundriß,
Seitenansicht, Grundriß, Blick auf die Brücke.**
Engineers: Setzpfand & Partner; contractor: Paul
Stephan, Gaildorf; footbridge, Jena-Niederwöllnitz,
1994, skew, suspended trough bridge, section, detail
elevation and plan, view.

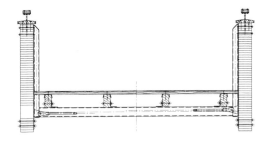

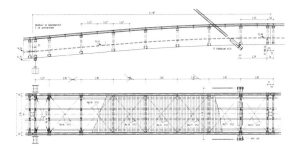

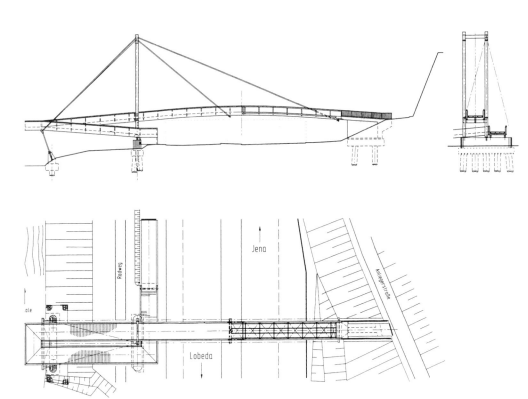

Bei Tragwerken unterhalb der Fahrbahn reicht in der Regel diese Abdeckung als Witterungsschutz aus, wie bei der Brücke in Essing und bei der Thalkirchener Brücke zu sehen ist. Bereits seit 1903 bestand bei München-Thalkirchen eine hölzerne Straßenbrücke über die Isar und den Isarkanal. Der Neubau dieser Bücke wurde als einachsig gerichtetes Raumstabwerk ausgebildet, da die bestehenden Brückenpfeiler im Abstand von 13 m erhalten blieben. Das Raumstabwerk spannt sich als Durchlaufträger bogenförmig von Pfeiler zu Pfeiler.

Der erste Entwurf war als frei bewitterte Bauweise in Bongossiholz geplant. Durch den Tropenholzboykott wurde einheimische Fichte verwendet, welche kesseldruckimprägniert werden mußte. Da bisher keine Zulassung für die dynamisch beanspruchten Knoten vorlag, mußte ein Gußknoten entwickelt werden, welcher durch die Vorspannung der Schrauben eine Bewegung der Verbindung ausschließt. Die Stabköpfe wurden mit einem Gußkopf versehen, welcher mit Stabdübeln angeschlossen ist. Diese Art der Verbindung ist so ausgelegt, daß auch einzelne Stäbe nachträglich ausgetauscht werden können. Aus verkehrspolitischen Gründen wurde die Nutzlast der Brücke auf 3 to Verkehrslast beschränkt, obwohl die Brücke für Einzelfahrzeuge bis 12 to ausgelegt ist und bereits bedeutend schwerere Fahrzeuge die Brücke benutzten.[111]

So selten Straßenbrücken zur Zeit in Holz hergestellt werden, um so wichtiger sind diese Bauwerke, um Erfahrungen zu sammeln und um nicht zuletzt aus ökologischen Gründen die Verwendung von Holz im Brückenbau wieder selbstverständlich werden zu lassen.

Structures below the road deck frequently require no additional protection, like the bridges in Essing and Thalkirchen. A wooden road bridge crossing the River Isar and the Isar Canal at Munich-Thalkirchen was erected as early as 1903. This was rebuilt in the form of a one-way-spanning space frame because the existing bridge piers at 13 m centres were still in good condition. The space frame spans as a continuous arch from pier to pier.

The original design called for an exposed construction in bongossi wood. However, the boycott of tropical timbers led to indigenous spruce being employed, which had to be pressure-impregnated. As the dynamically loaded nodes did not have any approval certificate, a cast node had to be developed which ruled out movement in the connection by prestressing the screws. The ends of the members were provided with castings attached with pins. This type of connection allows even individual members to be subsequently replaced. Local traffic policy limits the load on the bridge to 3 tonnes, although it is designed to carry individual vehicles weighing up to 12 tonnes and has already been used by considerably heavier vehicles.[111]

New road bridges in timber are so rare that this fact alone makes them vital as sources of experience. The growing awareness of ecological issues should make the use of timber for bridges once again an everyday occurrence.

**Arch. (Entwurf und Planung): Richard J. Dietrich;
Ing.: Suess und Staller, Thalkirchener Brücke,
München, 1993, räumliches Stabwerk, Schnitte,
Ansichten.**
Vorige Doppelseite **Ansicht von unten, Seitenansicht.**
Architect (design and planning): Richard J. Dietrich;
engineers: Suess & Staller; Thalkirchen bridge,
Munich, 1993, space frame, sections, elevations.
Previous double page View from below, side elevation.

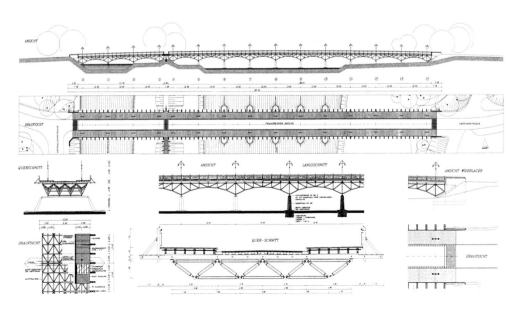

Thalkirchener Brücke, Knoten-Detail, Untersicht.
Thalkirchen bridge, detail of node, underside.

Glossar
Glossary

Abbund Das Aufrichten einer vorgefertigten Holzkonstruktion, z.B. eines Dachstuhles.

Adhäsion Anziehungskraft zweier verschiedener Stoffe (hier: Holz und Leim), welche häufig stärker als die Kohäsion ist. Bei der Verleimung von Holz ist es wichtig, daß die Leimfuge tragfähiger als das umgebende Holz ist, da dann die Leimfuge als Schwachpunkt nicht statisch nachgewiesen werden muß.

Anisotropie Ungleiches Materialverhalten in verschiedenen Richtungen. Da der Baum in der Natur besonders längs zur Faser durch Zug oder Druck beansprucht wird, ist die Tragfähigkeit von Holz längs wesentlich höher als quer zur Faser.

Balken Schnitthölzer meist rechteckigen Querschnitts, die als waagrechte Träger vertikale Lasten abtragen.

Biegedrillknicken Seitliches Ausweichen des Druckgurts (Obergurt) in Feldmitte, welcher nur auf Biegung beansprucht wird, wobei der Träger sich verdreht (tordiert oder verdrillt) – oft auch als Kippen bezeichnet.

Binder Hauptträger einer Halle oder eines Daches, auf dem die Pfetten oder Sparren liegen.

Bohle Schnittholz von mehr als 40 mm Dicke, mindestens dreimal so breit wie dick.

Bohlenbinder Aus Bohlen zusammengesetzter Träger.

Bolzen Runder Metallstift zur Verbindung von Teilen, hier: Hölzern.

Brettschichtholz (BSH) Mehrlagig aus Brettlamellen verleimtes Holz.

Dollen Verbindungsdorne aus Stahl oder Hartholz.

Dreigelenkbinder Statisch bestimmtes Tragwerk aus zwei Binderhälften, welches gelenkig gelagert und mit einem Gelenk verbunden ist.

Fachwerk Tragwerk, das aus Stäben besteht, die gelenkig miteinander verbunden sind.

Firstpfette Träger oder Pfette am First eines Gebäudes.

Flächentragwerk Tragwerk, welches über die Fläche trägt, mit hauptsächlicher Beanspruchung in der Ebene (z.B. ein Zelt).

Furnierschichtholz (FSH) Mehrlagig aus Furnieren, also dünnen Holzschichten (max. 10 mm), verleimtes Holz.

Gleichstreckenlast Über einen Träger gleichmäßig verteilte Last, konstante Lastverteilung.

Hängewerk Tragwerk, bei dem die Lasten über Zugstützen hochgehängt und dann über Streben zu den Auflagern abgetragen werden. (Tragwerk oberhalb der Belastungsebene, findet häufig bei Brücken und Dachstühlen Verwendung).

Hänge-Sprengwerk Mischform aus Hänge- und Sprengwerk.

adhesion The attractive force between two materials (in this case wood and glue), which is frequently stronger than the cohesion. When gluing wood it is important that the glue joint has a higher loadbearing capacity than the surrounding wood because then the glue joint is not the weak link and does not need to be analysed structurally.

anisotropy Describes material behaviour which varies depending on direction. As trees in their natural state are subjected to tensile and compressive forces along the grain in particular, the loadbearing capacity of wood is considerably higher along the grain than across it.

arched framing Structure in which the loads are suspended on ties which are in turn carried by struts back to the supports. Structure above the plane of the loads, often used for bridges and roof structures.

axial force (N) A force along the axis of a member, causing a constant distribution of stresses within the cross-section. We distinguish between tension and compression.

beam, joist Sawn timber member usually with a rectangular cross-section used horizontally to carry vertical loads.

board Sawn timber max. 47 mm thick x min. 100 mm wide.

buckling, torsional-flexural Lateral yielding in the centre of a member subjected to bending, characterized by the member twisting.

cantilever Member supported rigidly at one end, e.g. a canopy.

catenary curve To determine the line of pressure an inverted chain line is used for form-finding; this is only subjected to tension. Reversing the model changes all forces to compression. A constant linear load produces a parabola. The self-weight of the chain alone produces a catenary curve which is a little less steep than a parabola.

chord Topmost and bottommost longitudinal members of an open frame.

cohesion The attractive force between two materials or within one material. With water, for example, the cohesion is less than the adhesion between water and glass, which is why water rises at the edge of a glass.

column, pinned Vertical member hinged at both ends and only subjected to axial loads.

composite member Member made up of planks or boards fixed together by mechanical means.

dowel Hardwood or steel fastener of circular cross-section.

equilibrium diagram See "pressure, line of"

finger joint Adhesive joint formed by cutting a series of V-shaped notches in the pieces of wood to be joined, which are then pressed together.

flange Topmost and bottommost longitudinal parts of a (mainly) solid cross-section.

Hängepfosten Pfosten, der auf Zug belastet wird.

Keilzinkung Zur Ausbildung eines Stoßes werden keilförmige Vertiefungen eingeschnitten, die zur Verleimung ineinandergepreßt werden.

Kernholz Kern eines Stammes. Die inneren, breiteren Jahresringe sind von geringerer Festigkeit als die späteren, äußeren Jahresringe.

Kettenlinie Zur Ermittlung einer Stützlinie wird in Umkehrung eine Kette zur Formfindung benutzt, welche bei Belastung nur auf Zug beansprucht trägt. Bei Spiegelung zur Horizontalen trägt sie entsprechend auf Druck. Unter konstanter Streckenlast entsteht eine Parabelform. Unter Eigengewicht der Kette entsteht die Kettenlinie, welche etwas weniger steil als die Parabel verläuft.

Kohäsion Anziehungskraft zweier gleicher Stoffe bzw. binnen einer Materie. Bei Wasser ist zum Beispiel die Kohäsionskraft geringer als die Adhäsionskraft zwischen Wasser und Glas, so daß sich das Wasser am Glasrand hochzieht.

Kragträger Auskragender Träger, der eingespannt wird, um seine Last abzutragen; wird zum Beispiel bei Vordächern häufig verwendet.

Moment M Durch eine Biegebeanspruchung entsteht eine lineare Spannungsverteilung im Querschnitt, deren resultierende Wirkung als Moment bezeichnet wird. Bei reiner Biegung sind die Randspannungen maximal.

Normalkraft N Kraft in Richtung des Trägers, welche eine konstante Spannungsverteilung im Querschnitt bewirkt. Sie wird in Druck- und Zugkräfte unterschieden.

Ober- und Untergurt Oberer und unterer Teil eines Doppel-T-Profils, auch Flansche genannt.

Pfetten Träger quer zu den Bindern.

Querkraft Q Kraft quer zum Träger. Wirkt als Schubspannung im Träger.

Pendelstütze Beidseitig gelenkig gelagerte Stütze, welche nur in Stabachse beansprucht wird.

Pfosten Vertikales Rund- oder Kantholz, das in Längsrichtung auf Druck beansprucht wird.

Querkraft Q Kraft quer zum Träger. Wirkt als Schubspannung im Träger.

Rahmen Abgewinkeltes Tragwerk mit biegesteifen Ecken.

Rippenschale Schalentragwerk, welches aus Rippen und Schalung besteht.

Schäftung Bauteilstoß mit zwei abgeschrägten Verleimungsflächen.

Schalung Hölzerne Decken- oder Wandverkleidung aus Brettern.

Scherkraft Kraft parallel zur Faser, die zum Abscheren eines Bauteils führt. Abscheren tritt zum Beispiel am Endauflager bei Versätzen auf.

Schnittkräfte Durch eine äußere Belastung eines Tragwerkes entstehen im inneren Querschnitt Spannungen, die als resultierende Kraft in Schnittkräften zusammengefaßt werden (N,Q,M).

frame Structure consisting of straight members interconnected by way of rigid joints.

glued laminated timber Member made up by gluing together at least four laminations (max. 50 mm thick) with their grain essentially parallel.

glulam Abbreviation for glued laminated timber.

hanger Post subjected to tension.

heartwood Wood from the centre of a tree trunk, characterized by wider annual rings and lower strength.

internal forces External loads applied to a structure cause stresses within the cross-section which combine to form a resultant force.

laminated veneer lumber (LVL) Member made up by gluing together thin timber veneers (max. 10 mm thick).

load, uniformly distributed A load spread evenly and constantly along a member.

moment (M) The action of bending gives rise to a linear distribution of stresses within the cross-section, the effect of which is designated as (bending) moment. Pure bending leads to maximum stresses at the edges of the member.

pin Metal fastener of circular cross-section.

plank Sawn timber 47-100 mm thick x min. 275 mm wide.

plate Structure which carries loads such that it is principally stressed in the plane of the structure (e.g. a tent).

post Vertical member subjected to axial compression.

pressure, line of The shape of a structure which, for a given loading, carries the loads in compression only, without any moments.

purlin Member transverse to roof frame.

radial rib shell Shell structure consisting of ribs and sheathing.

rafter Member transverse to purlins.

ridge beam/purlin Beam or purlin at the apex of a roof.

sapwood Outer part of a tree trunk, characterized by high moisture content and risk of shrinkage, softer than heartwood.

scarf joint Adhesive joint between two members, characterized by two sloping faces.

shear force (Q) A vertical force transverse to the axis of a member, causing a shear(ing) stress parallel to the grain within the cross-section.

sheathing Roof covering of wooden boards.

Schwinden Austrocknen und Schrumpfen des Holzes (oder anderer Materialien), kann zum Lockern von Verbindungen und unplanmäßigen Verformungen führen.

Spannungstrajektorien Kurven der Hauptdruck- und Hauptzugspannungen in einem belasteten Bauteil.

Sparren Träger der Dachschalung quer zu den Pfetten.

Splintholz Äußerer Teil des Stammes mit hoher Feuchtigkeit und Schwindgefahr; Splintholz ist weicher als Kernholz.

Sprengwerk Tragwerk, bei dem die Lasten über Druckstreben zum Auflager abgetragen werden. Tragwerk unterhalb der Belastungsebene (z.B. Fahrbahn oder Geschoßdecke), horizontale Auflagerkräfte sind am Auflager abzutragen.

Stäbe Lineare Tragwerksteile; ein Stabwerk- oder Fachwerkträger besteht aus Stäben.

Stabwerk Aus Stäben bestehendes Tragwerk.

Statisch bestimmt Ein Tragwerk wird als statisch bestimmt bezeichnet, wenn seine Schnittkräfte allein durch die Gleichgewichtsbedingungen bestimmbar sind. Das statisch bestimmte Tragwerk ist unempfindlich gegen Setzungen (Beipiel Dreigelenkbinder).

Statisch unbestimmt Die Schnittkräfte statisch unbestimmter Tragwerke können nur durch die Gleichgewichts- und Verträglichkeitsbedingungen bestimmt werden.

Steg Mittlerer vertikaler Teil eines Doppel-T-Profils.

Stoß Verbindungsstelle zweier Bauteile.

Streben Stäbe, die im Regelfall der Aussteifung dienen.

Stützlinie Form eines Tragwerkes, die bei einer vorgegebenen Belastung momentenfrei nur druckbeansprucht trägt.

Zangen Zweiteilige Hölzer, die zum Beispiel eine Stütze oder einen Binder umschließen.

Zapfen Zimmermannsmäßige Holzverbindungsmittel.

Zugbänder Bauteile zur Aufnahme von horizontalen Auflagerkräften.

Zweigelenkbinder Einfach statisch unbestimmtes Tragwerk aus einem Binder, das gelenkig gelagert ist. Ein Zweigelenkbinder ist empfindlich für Lagerverschiebungen, welche die Schnittkräfte im Tragwerk verändern.

shrinkage Drying-out and contraction of the wood (or other materials). Can lead to loosening of connections and unexpected deformations.

strutted frame Structure in which the loads are transferred to the supports via compression members (struts). Structure below the plane of the loads, e.g. road deck or building floor. Horizontal support reactions must be resisted at the supports.

splice A joint between two parts of the same member.

statically determinate A structure is statically determinate when the magnitude and direction of the forces acting in its members can be determined by the direct application of the laws of static equilibrium. A statically determinate structure is not adversely affected by settlement (e.g. three-pin arch).

statically indeterminate A structure is statically indeterminate when the number of unknown quantities exceeds the number of quantities which can be determined by using the laws of static equilibrium.

stress trajectory Line of main tensile or compressive stresses in a loaded member.

strut Linear compression member.

tenon Projecting piece of wood used in purely wooden joints.

three-pin arch Statically determinate structure consisting of two half-arches with hinged supports and joined at the crown via a third hinge.

tie, collar Linear tension member.

truss Structure consisting of straight members interconnected by way of (nominally) hinged joints.

two-pin arch Simple, statically indeterminate structure on two hinged supports. A two-pin arch is vulnerable to displacement at the supports, which changes the internal forces in the structure.

web The (mainly) solid part between two flanges.

Anmerkungen und Literaturverzeichnis
Notes and references

1 Steifigkeit des zusammengesetzten Querschnittes:
I = b x (2 x h)3 /12 = 4 x I° >> I° = b x 2 x h3 / 12 = Steifigkeit der einzelnen Querschnitte.
Stiffness of composite section:
I = b x (2 x h)3/12 = 4 x I° >> I° = b x 2 x h3/12 = stiffness of individual sections

2 Leupold, Jacob: Theatrum Pontificale oder Schauplatz der Brücken und des Brückenbaues, Leipzig 1726

3 Palladio, Andrea: Quattro libri dell'architettura, Venedig, 1570. Deutsch: Die vier Bücher zur Architektur, Übers. Andreas Beyer und Ulrich Schütte, Zürich 1983
English edition: The Four Books of Architecture, trans. Isaac Ware, London, 1738; reprint, New York 1965

4 Palladio, Andrea: Die vier Bücher zur Architektur, Zürich 1983

5 Straub, Hans: Die Geschichte der Bauingenieurkunst, Basel 1949

6 De l'Orme, Philibert: Nouvelles Inventions, Paris 1561

7 Graefe, Rainer: Holzleimbau-Vorgänger, Die Bogendächer von Philibert de l'Orme, in: Zur Geschichte des Konstruierens, Stuttgart 1989

8 Rüsch, Eckart: Baukonstruktion zwischen Innovation und Scheitern, Michael Imhof Verlag 1997

9 Gilly, David: Handbuch der Landbaukunst, mit einem Anhang über Erfindungen, Braunschweig 1797

10 Doebber, A.: Lauchstädt und Weimar, eine Theaterbaugeschichtliche Studie, Berlin 1908

11 Doebber, A.: Lauchstädt und Weimar, Zentralblatt der Bauverwaltung, 1908, S. 596

12 Wagner: Das Goethetheater in Lauchstädt, Zentralblatt der Bauverwaltung, 1908/H.80, S. 533-535

13 Graefe, Rainer: Holzleimbau-Vorgänger, Die Bogendächer von Philibert de l'Orme, in: Zur Geschichte des Konstruierens, Stuttgart 1989

14 Warth, Otto: Die Konstruktionen in Holz, I.M.Gebhardt´s Verlag, Leipzig 1900, Tafel 66

15 Gesteschi, Theodor: Das Zollbau-Lamellendach, Die Bautechnik, 1928/H.10

16 Krabbe, E. und Niemann, H.-J.: Tragverhalten eines hölzernen Zollbau-Lamellendaches am Beispiel der Halle Münsterland, Bauingenieur 2/83, S.277-284

17 Killer, Joseph: Die Werke der Baumeister Grubenmann, 2.Aufl., Zürich 1959

18 Culmann, Karl : Der Bau der hölzernen Brücken in den Vereinigten Staaten von Nordamerika, Allgemeine Bauzeitung mit Abbildungen, hrsg. v. L. Förster, Wien 1851, S.69-129

19 Emy, A.. R.: Traité de l'art de charpenterie, Paris 1841

20 Ardant, Paul Joseph.: Theoretisch-praktische Abhandlung über Anordnung und Construktion der Sprengwerke von großer Spannweite, Dt. hrsg.v. August v. Kaven, Hannover 1847

21 Kersten, Christian: Freitragende Holzbauten, 2. Aufl., Berlin 1926

22 Ardant, Paul Joseph.: Theoretisch-praktische Abhandlung über Anordnung und Construktion der Sprengwerke von großer Spannweite, Dt. hrsg.v. August v. Kaven, Hannover 1847

23 Graefe, Rainer: Holzleimbau-Vorgänger, Die Bogendächer von Philibert de l'Orme, in: Zur Geschichte des Konstruierens, Stuttgart 1989

24 Hoeltje, Georg: Georg Ludwig Friedrich Laves, Steinbock Verlag

25 Gehri, Ernst: Entwicklungen des ingenieurmäßigen Holzbaues seit Grubenmann, Schweizer Ingenieur und Architekt, 1983/ H33+34, S. 808-815

26 Wiebeking, Carl Friedrich: Beyträge zur Brückenbaukunde, München 1809

27 Informationszentrum Holz: Brettschichtkonstruktionen

28 Gem. Bauakte: Schneidemühle, Kesselhaus und Schmiede 1898, Parkettfabrik, Trockenkammer, Pferdestall, Niederlage für fertige Ware und Wohnhaus 1899, Neubau der abgebrannten Niederlage 1904, Leimerei und Abbindehalle 1915, Erweiterungsbau der Schneidemühle 1919
Taken from building documentation: sawmill, boiler house and forge 1898, parquet flooring works, drying chamber, stables, store for finished goods and house 1899, replacement for store destroyed by fire 1904, glue shop and assembly shop 1915, extension to sawmill 1919

29 Hetzer, Otto: Otto Hetzers Holzpflege- und Parkett-Fabrik, 1900

30 Bauakte, Bauarchiv Weimar

31 Hetzer, Otto jun.: Lebenlauf 1927

32 Hengeveld, D.J.: Het Gelamineerde Hout In Nederland, Delftse, Universitaire Pers, 1979

33 Haarmann, A.: Fußböden aus Rotbuchenholz, Centralblatt der Bauverwaltung, 1894/H.7 S.69

34 Hetzer, Otto sen.: Otto Hetzer, Weimar - Neue Holzbauweisen, Weimar 1908

35 Bis heute sind auch in Privatarchiven keine Unterlagen auffindbar, die eine Auskunft darüber geben, womit das Holz getränkt wurde und zum anderen belegen könnte, warum es zu einer Härtung kam.
No documents have yet to come to light which provide information on the substances used for impregnating the wood, nor on why this led to a hardening.

36 Adams: Neuere Holzbauweisen, Zentralblatt der Bauverwaltung, 1907/H.21 S.147-148

37 Huebner, Fritz: Versuche mit Holzbalken nach Bauweise Hetzer, Schweizerische Bauzeitung, 1924/ H.5, S.51-55 und H.6, S.65-67

38 Urban, K. A.: Denkschrift über Hetzer's neue Holzbauweisen, 1913

39 Zusammenstellung der Patente:

Land	Nr.	Datum	Inhaber	Inhalt
Deutschland	60156	15.4.1892	Piek	Kaseinleim
	63018	5.7.1892	Hetzer	Fußboden
	125895	6.7.1900	Hetzer	zusammengesetzter Holzbalken
	163144	10.5.1903	Hetzer	zusammengesetzter Holzbalken
	197773	22.6.1906	Hetzer	gebogene Holzkonstruktion
	225687	21.9.1907	Hetzer	Fachwerkträger aus Holz
	307196	3.5.1916	Schütte-Lanz	Verf. Für Kaseinleim
	309423	24.12.1916	Schütte-Lanz	Verf. Für Kaseinleim
	550647	25.7.1929	I.G.Farben	Kauritleim
	736618	13.12.1936	Klemm	Kaurit-Leim WHK
Schweiz	24405	28.6.1901	Hetzer	zusammengesetzter Holzbalken
	33871	2.6.1905	Hetzer	zusammengesetzter Holzbalken
	40409	13.6.1907	Hetzer	gebogene Holzkonstruktion
	50660	10.3.1910	Hetzer	Holzbinder mit Diagonalstäben
Schweden	28715	21.06.1906	Hetzer	gebogene Holzkonstruktion
	34156	29.08.1910	Hetzer	Fachwerkbalken

List of patents:

Country	No.	Date	Owner	Content
Germany	60156	15 Apr 1892	Piek	Casein glue
	63018	5 Jul 1892	Hetzer	Floor
	125895	6 Jul 1900	Hetzer	Composite timber beam
	163144	10 May 1903	Hetzer	Composite timber beam
	197773	22 Jun 1906	hetzer	Curved timber construction
	225687	21 Sept 1907	Hetzer	Timber truss
	307196	3 May 1916	Schütte-Lanz	Casein glue
	309423	24 Dec 1916	Schütte-Lanz	Casein glue
	550647	25 Jul 1929	I.G.Farben	Beetle cement
	736618	13 Dec 1936	Klemm	Beetle cement WHK
Switzerland	24405	28 Jun 1901	Hetzer	Composite timber beam
	33871	2 Jun 1905	Hetzer	Composite timber beam
	40409	13 Jun 1907	Hetzer	Curved timber construction
	50660	10 Mar 1910	Hetzer	Timber beam with diagonal members
Sweden	28715	21 Jun 1906	Hetzer	Curved timber construction
	34156	29 Aug 1910	Hetzer	Timber girder

40 Friebe: Neue Holzbauweisen, Zentralblatt der Bauverwaltung, 1910/ H.86, S.561-563

41 Lizenznehmer und Verbreitung durch Holzleimbaubetriebe:

Schweiz	1909	Ingenieurbüro Terner und Chopard, Zürich, Schweizerische Aktiengesellschaft für Hetzersche Holzbauweisen
Belgien	1913	Oscar Rayon, Arch., Charleroi
Schweden	1919	Töreboda Limtrae
Holland	1921	Eerste Nederlandsche Maatschappij voor Houtconstructies (Nemaho), Doetinchem
Dänemark		Kornerup und Koch
		N. Jürgens, Hadersleben
Österreich		Johann Lerchbauer, Klagenfurt
Österreich		Other und Sohn, Graz
Italien		E. Burkhard, Lugano
		Bonfiglio & Co., Mailand
Spanien		Domingo, Barcelona
Tschechien		Müller und Kapsa, Pilsen
USA	seit 1933	Unit Structures, Peshtigo, Wisconsin

Licenses and locations of glulam operations:

Switzerland	1909	Terner & Chopard, consulting engineers, Zürich, Schweizerische Aktiengesellschaft für Hetzersche Holzbauweisen
Belgium	1913	Oscar Rayon, architect, Charleroi
Sweden	1919	Töreboda Limtrae
Netherlands	1921	Eerste Nederlandsche Maatschappij voor Houtconstructies (Nemaho), Doetinchem
Denmark		Kornerup & Koch
		N. Jürgens, Hadersleben

Austria		Johann Lerchbauer, Klagenfurt
		Other & Sohn, Graz
Italy		E. Burkhard, Lugano
		Bonfiglio & Co., Mailand
Spain		Domingo, Barcelona
Czech Republic		Müller & Kapsa, Pilsen
USA	since 1933	Unit Structures, Peshtigo, Wisconsin

42 Schweiz. Bauzeitung, 72. Jhrg. Heft 50, S. 734

43 Schweiz. Bauzeitung, 78. Jhrg. Heft 48, 1.Dezember1960 S. 786

44 Wilson, T.R.C.: The glued laminated wooden arch, Technical Bulletin No. 691, 10/1939

45 Rhude, Andreas Jordahl: Structural glued laminated timber: history of its origins and development

46 Tenning, Kurt: Fran "Hetzer Binder", Till Limträ Konstruktioner, Töreboda, 1987, unveröffentlicht

47 Hengeveld, D.J.: Het Gelamineerde Hout In Nederland, Delftse, Universitaire Pers, 1979

48 Rhude, Andreas Jordahl: Structural glued laminated timber: history of its origins and development

49 Präsident: Peter Thompson, Vizepräsident: Max Hanisch, sen. (1882-), Sekretär: Max Hanisch, jun. (1910-1992), Kaufmänn. Leiter: Christ J. Thompson, Direktor: Herbert Hanisch (1911-1936), Direktor:Theodore Thompson
President: Peter Thompson, Vice-President: Max Hanisch, sen. (*1882), Secretary: Max Hanisch, jun. (1910-92), Commercial Director: Christ J. Thompson, Director: Herbert Hanisch (1911-1936), Director: Theodore Thompson

50 Wilson, T.R.C.: The glued laminated wooden arch, Technical Bulletin No. 691, 10/1939

51 Blömer, A.: Ein Beitrag zur Geschichte des Leimes und Leimbaues, Deutscher Zimmermeister, Berlin, 1958, H. 22, S. 533-535, H. 23, 24, S. 553-559

52 Bloss, E.: Das älteste deutsche Leimbüchlein, BASF, H. 5/6, 1957, S.188-190

53 Frech, P.: Sanierung von Brettschichtholz, Manuskript zum Lehrgang am 8. und 9. Juni 1995

54 Hetzer, Otto sen.: Otto Hetzer, Weimar - Neue Holzbauweisen, Weimar 1908

55 Baer, D. H.: Die Hetzersche Holzbauweise, Die Schweizerische Baukunst, 1910, H.10, S.133-142

56 Friebe: Neue Holzbauweisen, Zentralblatt der Bauverwaltung, 1910/H.86 S. 561-563

57 Schaechterle, K.: Ingenieurholzbauten bei der Reichsbahndirektion Stuttgart

58 Chopard, Charles: Die neue Lokomotive-Remise der S.B.B. auf dem Aebigut in Bern, Schweizer Bauzeitung, 1913/H.22 S.289-290

59 Schaechterle, K.: Ingenieurholzbauten bei der Reichsbahndirektion Stuttgart, S. 39

60 Chopard, Charles: Einstielige Perrondächer in Hetzer'scher Holzbauweise, Schweizer Bauzeitung, 1925/H.9, S.118.

61 J.Taylor Thompson: Cantilever Beams in laminated wood, Wood 10/1957, S. 402-403

62 Hetzer, Otto (Sen.):Otto Hetzer, Weimar - Neue Holzbauweisen, Weimar 1908

63 Kersten, Christian: Freitragende Holzbauten, 2.Aufl., Berlin 1926

64 Mannheimer, Franz: Eisenbahnhalle, Der Industriebau, 1910, H.8, S. 206-216

65 Ernst, Max: Flugzeughallen Bauart Hetzer Industriebau 1914, H.4, S. 88-92

66 Bestimmungen über die bei Hochbauten anzunehmenden Belastungen und die Beanspruchungen der Baustoffe: Preußische Ministerielle Bestimmungen vom 31.1.1910, Berlin 1912

67 Gesteschi, Theodor: Der neuzeitliche Holzbau im Eisenbahnwesen, Die Bautechnik, 1923, H.12, S. 89-98

68 Kersten, Christian: Freitragende Holzbauten, 2. Auflage, Berlin 1926, S. 216

69 Bautechnik, 1923, S.89

70 Chopard, Charles: Die neue Lokomotive-Remise der S.B.B. auf dem Aebigut in Bern, Schweizer Bauzeitung, 1913, H.22, S. 289-290

71 Schaechterle, K.: Ingenieurbauwerke bei der Reichsbahndirektion in Stuttgart, Schweizerische Bauzeitung, S. 214-219

72 Hengeveld, D.J.: Het Gelamineerde Hout In Nederland, Delftse, Universitaire Pers, 1979

73 Bauen mit Holz, 7/64, S. 309-310

74 Pichler, Gerhard, Stieglmeier, Franz: Ingenieurholzbau für ein Holzlagerhalle, Bautechnik, 1999, H. 11, S. 949-958.

75 Moelven Industrier A.S: Firmenprospekt,1994
Mai, Greiner: Meisterleistung im norwegischen Ingenieurholzbau, Bautechnik, 4/92, S. 12 ff.

76 Superlative: 96 m Spannweite, 250m Länge. Das geht auch in Holz, Bauen in Holz, 4/92, S. 270-271

77 Herzog, Thomas: Kulturlandschaft - Produktionshallen der Firma Wilkhahn in Bad Münder am Deister. Deutsche Bauzeitung, 2/94, S. 14-21

78 Arbeitsgemeinschaft Holz e.V., Informationsdienst Holz: Fertigungspavillons Fa. Wilkhahn,

Bad Münder, 12/93

79 von Büren, Charles: Funktion und Form, Basel 1985

80 Keil, Andreas: Umhüllte Stadt, Bauen mit Holz, 6/99, S. 7-13

81 Ewald, G.: Zur Ausbildung der Knotenpunkte bei Rautenlamellen Konstruktionen, Bauen mit Holz, 4/85, S. 222-223

82 Arbeitsgemeinschaft Holz e.V., Informationsdienst Holz: Sporthalle in Berlin Charlottenburg, 3/90

83 Ketchum, Verne: Timber domes/design and construction, wood, 10/59, S. 400-404 und 11/59, S. 440-443

84 Frais, J.: Kreiskuppel als Sporthallenüberdachung, Bauen in Holz, 6/85, S. 376-377

85 von Büren, Charles: Funktion und Form, Basel 1985

86 Buckminster Fuller, R.: Bedienungsanleitung für das Raumschiff Erde...; Rowohlt Verlag 1973

87 Frei Otto, Das hängende Dach, 1954, Ullstein AG, Berlin

88 Verne Ketchum zeigt eine geodätische Kuppel, die nach hier nach Engel als hexagonale Kuppel bezeichnet wird, Engel, H.: Tragsysteme, Deutsche Verlagsanstalt, Stuttgart 4. Aufl. 1977

89 Ketchum, Verne: Timber domes and construction, wood, 10/59, S. 400-404 und 11/59, S. 440-443

90 von Büren, Charles: Funktion und Form, Basel 1985

91 Moser, Karl: Entwicklungstendenzen im modernen Holzbau

92 Frei Otto, Das hängende Dach, 1954, Ullstein AG, Berlin

93 Frei Otto, Das hängende Dach, 1954, Ullstein AG, Berlin, S. 35

94 Frei Otto, Das hängende Dach, 1954, Ullstein AG, Berlin, S. 102

95 Frei Otto, Das hängende Dach, 1954, Ullstein AG, Berlin, S. 89

96 Ende, W.F.: Holzbauten an der Expo 1964, Holz in Technik und Wirtschaft, Lignum, Zürich 1965

97 Arbeitsgemeinschaft Holz e.V., Informationsdienst Holz: Fertigungspavillons Fa. Wilkhahn, Bad Münder, 1988

98 Bogen- und Seillinien bilden das Dach, Bauen mit Holz, 3/91, S. 156-158

99 Möhler, K.: Ingenieurholzbau als Hauptthema des 11. Kongresses der IVBH, Bauen mit Holz, 10/80, S. 592-594

100 von Büren, Charles: Funktion und Form, Basel 1985;
Natterer J., Winter W.: Hängedach aus Holz für eine Recyling-Anlage, Bau, 8/81

101 Wenzel, Fritz, Frese, Bernd, Barthel, Rainer: Die Holzrippenschale in Bad Dürrheim, Bauen mit Holz, 5/87, S. 282-287

102 Geier, I. und R.: Solebad in Bad Dürrheim, Detail 6/87, S. 17-22

103 Geier, I. und R.: Solebad "Solemar" in Bad Dürrheim, Bauwelt, 30/88, S. 1255-1259

104 Chopard, Charles: Die Hetzersche Holzbauweise, Schweizer Bauzeitung, 1911, H. 16, S. 214-219

105 Chopard, Charles: Die Hetzersche Holzbauweise, Schweizer Bauzeitung, 1911, H. 16, S. 214-219

106 Akten des Baudepartements des Kantons Basel-Stadt, Tiefbauamt

107 Ros, M.: Der Bau von Gerüsten und Hochbauten aus Holz in der Schweiz, EMPA Zürich 1929

108 Culmann, Karl: Der Bau der hölzernen Brücken in den Vereinigten Staaten von Nordamerika, Allgemeine Bauzeitung mit Abbildungen, hrsg. v. L. Förster, Wien 1851, S. 69-129

109 Ein riesiges Spannband in Holzbauweise, Bauen mit Holz, 12/87, S. 796-800

110 Ein Dreiecksfachwerk als Haupttragsystem, Bauen mit Holz, 12/88

111 Dietrich, R.J. und Huber: Sie folgt der Momentenlinie und bildet dabei Bögen, Bauen mit Holz, 12/93, S. 1003-1009

Namensregister
Index of names

Bildnachweis
Illustration credits

Archiv Arge Holz: 91, 119, 129, 130, 141, 153, 154, 155, 156, 162, 163, 164, 165, 166, 167, 168, 169 188, 189,
Archiv Denkmalpflege Zürich: 44, 45
Archiv Hüttemann: 127
Archiv Andreas Keil, Büro Schlaich, Bergermann und Partner: 122, 123, 124, 125, 126
Archiv Kerto: 144
Archiv Büro Krone: 192
Archiv LAP: 192, 193
Archiv Lignum, Zürich: 19, 114, 115, 134, 135, 136, 137, 139, 140, 141, 150
Archiv Christian Müller: 32, 33, 39, 74, 76, 82, 97, 99, 132, 142, 143, 151
Archiv Nemaho: 50, 51, 53, 54, 76, 82, 83, 84, 86, 89, 90, 92, 93, 94, 95, 96, 108, 109, 133
Archiv Ohnesorge: 20, 21, 42, 60, 61, 63, 69, 75, 76
Archiv PHB: 158, 159, 160, 161
Archiv Rolf Schmidt: 81, 85
Archiv Setzpfand und Partner: 190, 191, 194, 195
Archiv Stephan: 178, 187, 188, 189, 195
Archiv Büro Trabert: 145, 147, 148
Archiv Unit Structures: 28, 29, 30, 87, 88
Archiv von Büren: 70
Badener Neujahrsblätter: 15
Baer, D. H.: Die Hetzersche Holzbauweise, Die Schweizerische Baukunst, 1910, H.10, S.133-142: 47, 48
Bauen mit Holz, 7/64, S. 309-310: 98
Breuer, Robert: Deutschland auf der Brüsseler Weltausstellung, Moderne Bauformen 1910. S.301-302: 58
Büro Bothe Richter Teherani: 66
Büro Kees Christiaanse: 78
Büro Richard Dietrich: 182, 183, 184, 185, 186, 197, 198, 199, 200, 201
Büro Thomas Herzog: 117, 171
Chopard, Charles: Die Hetzersche Holzbauweise, Schweizer Bauzeitung, 1911, H.16 S.214-219 67, 68, 71, 179
Culmann, Karl: Der Bau der hölzernen Brücken in den Vereinigten Staaten von Nordamerika, Allgemeine Bauzeitung mit Abbildungen, hrsg. v. L. Förster, Wien 1851, S.69-129: 15, 181
De l'Orme, Philibert: Les Nouvelles Inventions, Paris 1561, Herzogin Anna Amalia Bibliothek: 10, 11
Deming: 12
Doebber, A.: Lauchstädt und Weimar, Zentralblatt der Bauverwaltung, 1908 S.596, Taf. 1, S.129 ff.: 13
Emy, A.. R.: Traité de l'art de charpenterie, Paris 1841: 15, 16
Frahm, Klaus: 64, 65, 66
Friebe: Neue Holzbauweisen, Zentralblatt der Bauverwaltung, 1910/ H.86, S.561-563: 48
Fricke, Susann: 40, 41, 46, 47, 52, 57, 72, 73, 74, 77, 99, 102, 103, 117, 118, 128, 129, 130, 131, 146, 147, 148, 149, 153, 157, 169, 170, 173, 174
Gilly, David: Handbuch der Landbaukunst, mit einem Anhang über Erfindungen, Aufl. Braunschweig 1797, Herzogin Anna Amalia Bibliothek: 12, 13
Graefe, Rainer: Holzleimbau-Vorgänger, Die Bogendächer von Philibert de l'Orme, in: Zur Geschichte des Konstruierens, Stuttgart 1989: 14
Hetzer, Otto (Sen.):Otto Hetzer, Weimar - Neue Holzbauweisen, Weimar 1908: 31, 43
Janssen, TH.: Neue Holzbauweisen; Deutsche Bauzeitung: 1914, H4. Jg.48, S. 50 - 55: 69
Kersten, Christian: Freitragende Holzbauten, 2.Aufl., Berlin 1926: 9, 14, 15, 16, 19, 27, 56
Krabbe, E. und Niemann, H.-J.: Tragverhalten eines hölzernen Zollbau-Lamellendaches am Beispiel der Halle Münsterland. Bauingenieur 2/83, S.277-284: 129
Leenders, Peter: 172, 173, 174, 175, 176
Leistner, Dieter: 110, 111, 112, 113
Leupold, Jacob: Theatrum Pontificale oder Schauplatz der Brücken und des Brücken- baues, Leipzig 1726: 8
Mannheimer, Franz: Eisenbahnhalle, Der Industriebau, 1910, H.8, S. 206-216: 60
Messow, Christoph: 53, 63, 132
Moelven Industrier A.S.: Firmenprospekt,1994: 116
Palladio, Andrea: Die vier Bücher der Architektur, Vincenza 1786: 10
Patentamt München: 22, 23, 25
Schindler: 104, 105, 106, 107
S.I.A. Normen für Holzbauten, Ergebnisse der Festigkeitsuntersuchungen an der E.M.P.A.

mit Bauhölzern in den Jahren 1924/1925 als Grundlage für die Normen der S.I.A: 181
Stadtmuseum Weimar: 180
Die Hetzersche Hozbauweise: Schweizerische Bauzeitung, Bd. 58, Nr. 16, v. 14.10.1911: 47, 60, 68, 71, 179
Schaechterle, K.: Ingenieurbauwerke bei der Reichsbahndirektion in Stuttgart, Schweizerische Bauzeitung, S. 214-219: 72
Schuck, Maik: 62
Tenning, Kurt: Fran „Hetzer Binder", Till Limträ Konstruktioner, Töreboda, 1987, unveröffentlicht: 26
Urban, K. A.: Denkschrift über Hetzer's neue Holzbauweisen, 1913: 49, 61, 67, 69, 72, 74, 180
Van der Vlught: 78, 79
von Büren, Charles: Funktion und Form, Basel 1985: 99, 100, 101, 120, 121, 151
Zimmermann: 113